Mechanisms for Stability and Welfare:

Increasing Cooperation among

Self-interested Agents

Reshef Meir
School of Engineering and Applied Science
Harvard University

Published by

AI Access

AI Access is a not-for-profit publisher with a highly respected scientific board that publishes open access monographs and collected works. Our text are available electronically for free and in hard copy at close to cost. We welcome proposals for new texts.

ISBN 978-1-291-97962-6

AI Access
Managing editor: Toby Walsh
Monograph editor: Kristian Kersting
Collected works editor: Pascal Poupart
URL: aiaccess.org

Contents

II　Welfare   71

7　Mechanism Design without Money I   73

8　Mechanism Design without Money II   87

9　Parking Allocation and Online Matching   95

Acknowledgements

This monograph was submitted as the thesis for a PhD degree at the School of Computer Science and Engineering of The Hebrew University in Jerusalem, Israel, under the supervision of Prof. Jeffrey S. Rosenschein. The thesis won the Max Schlomiuk award from the Hebrew University of Jerusalem, and received an Honourable Mention for the IFAAMAS Victor Lesser Distinguished Dissertation Award.

I am grateful to my coauthors and to other people who enlightened me with their comments, read the drafts, found errors, or otherwise contributed: Omri Abend, Noga Alon, Yossi Azar, Shaull Almagor, Yoram Bachrach, Craig Boutilier, Niv Buchbinder, Yiling Chen, Vince Conitzer, Elad Dokow, Edith Elkind, Piotr Faliszewski, Uri Feige, Moran Feldman, Amos Fiat, Kobi Gal, Nick Jennings, Gil Kalai, Omer Lev, Kevin Leyton-Brown, Yoad Lewenberg, Tyler Lu, Zur Luria, Enrico Malizia, Assaf Michaely, Noam Nisan, Renato Paes-Leme, Maria Polukarov, Nir Potchter, Tim Roughgarden, Toumas Sandholm, Peter Stone, Lirong Xia, Yair Zick (who also made the great figures in Chapter 4), Aviv Zohar, Michael Zuckerman, and a long list of anonymous referees.

I thank Ofek Birnholtz for saving me precious hours by scaring me off Facebook.

Special thanks to Ariel Procaccia, Michal Feldman and Ilan Nehama for countless hours of discussions and numerous enlightening comments.

To Moshe Tennenholtz, *my boss*, who gave me the opportunity to spend my entire time on research, and saw to it that this time will always be filled with open problems to work on. Microsoft Research rocks!

To Jeff Rosenschein, my advisor, for being the perfect advisor for over 8 years, giving endless support and just the right amount of guidance. Jeff is the main reason that my PhD was both an important experience and fun (yes, grad school *can* be fun). Above all, I thank Jeff for opening the gates of academia and showing me the path from being a student into being a scholar.

Last but certainly not least, my PhD is dedicated to my loving wife Adi, who on top of being extremely supportive in high and low times, is a true companion to my intellectual and academic life. With her philosophy, unyielding logic, and merciless comments on my half-baked ideas and drafts, Adi makes me a better researcher. Adi, you earned this thesis.

Abstract

Too often an interaction among self-interested parties—be it human decision makers, firms, or automated agents—leads to an outcome that is not in the best interest of any of them. Examples include group decisions that are biased due to personal interests, collapse of public projects, congestion of roads and online networks, and so on.

In this thesis I look at such interactions as *games*, so that the loss of stability and welfare can be measured and studied using the standard concepts of game theory (such as *equilibrium* and *utility*). I then study and design *mechanisms* that alter these games in order to induce more cooperation, stable outcomes, and higher utility for the participants—who are still assumed to each pursue their best personal interests.

My research spans multiple domains, aiming for two primary goals. Part I of the thesis is about mechanisms that increase *stability*. This part covers subsidies in cooperative games, restricted cooperation with and without explicit social models, and iterative models of voting. New notions of individual and coalitional stability are introduced, in order to better understand the likely outcomes of studied interactions, and mechanisms are presented in order to achieve higher stability in corresponding games.

Part II of the thesis is dedicated to *welfare*. I look for mechanisms that are *truthful* on the one hand (i.e. where all participants are better off reporting their true preferences), and approximately optimal on the other hand. I start with mechanisms for public facility location, supervised learning and other domains, showing the best approximation ratio of the optimal outcome (for society) that a truthful mechanism can achieve. Finally, several approximately optimal pricing mechanisms for parking allocation are presented, that are practical and simple to implement.

In the closing chapter I discuss some of the global questions that arise throughout the work, and suggest some directions that could promote the design of mechanisms for stability and welfare.

Chapter 1

Introduction

In the well-known Prisoner's Dilemma, two people that behave in the only *rational* way end up in the worst possible outcome (see Example 2.1 for details). Unfortunately, this example is a useful analogy for many situations in real life, where *individually rational* behavior leads to problems for society.

Game theory is a branch of mathematics that seeks to model situations of conflict as *games*, which can in turn be formally analyzed. Even though important aspects of the actual interaction or conflict might be abstracted away in the modeling process, the analysis of the formal model may still help us to predict what players would or should do, as in the analogy of the Prisoner's Dilemma above. *Mechanisms* are games designed with a particular purpose, so that players interacting via the mechanism will end up in a particular outcome that the designer sees as desirable.

Why are mechanisms required? Adam Smith's [1776] "invisible hand" approach asserts that when multiple self-interested parties each pursue their individual goals without any central intervention, the parties will converge to a socially desirable state. In the language of game theory, such an outcome can be thought of as a good *equilibrium* (see below). However, while decentralized markets can sometimes lead to high welfare for the participants, Smith was overly optimistic. Numerous events—like projects that collapse due to disagreements, and groups who fail to reach a joint decision—show that interactions do not always converge, and an equilibrium may not be reached.

Moreover, even the simple example of the Prisoner's Dilemma vividly demonstrates that stability by itself is not a guaranty of a good outcome (in terms of welfare or in other terms). Some equilibria may be better than others, and sometimes all equilibria are bad. Thus, competition often quells cooperation, and outcomes may be undesirable and even disastrous for society.

This is where I see the main role of *mechanism design*, in injecting just the right amount of intervention required to induce cooperation among self-interested parties. My approach in this work is to analyze, to modify, and to develop new mechanisms for various problems, in order to promote stability and social welfare. This approach will be described in detail after providing some background on the origins and current state of mechanism design.

1.1 Background

Two if the most fundamental concepts to game theory are *utility* and *self-interest*—that is, the assumptions that there is a single number that reflects the value of an outcome to each player, and that every player acts strategically in order to maximize this value. A *non-cooperative game* is simply a description of the utilities that follow from any combination of players' actions [von Neumann and Morgenstern, 1944].

Utilities facilitate the natural definition of the next key concept of game theory, which is *equilibrium*. The most studied type of equilibrium in non-cooperative games—*Nash equilibrium* (NE)—is a state where no player can increase her utility by deviating from her current action, provided that all other players also keep their current actions. Since in every non-equilibrium state there is at least one player that can improve her utility, the common assumption is that players will end up in an equilibrium state, if one exists.

Cooperative games are also founded on the basic concepts of utility and self-interest, but provide a different abstraction level that focuses on the utilities that coalitions of players may gain by cooperating, and on how these gains should be shared. The prominent equilibrium notion in cooperative games is the *core*, where all possible subcoalitions are satisfied with their share of the gain.

Research in game theory focuses on characterizing and identifying equilibrium states in games, on defining new *solution concepts* (typically various equilibrium notions, see Chapter 2), and on studying the dynamics that lead the players to end up in one equilibrium state or another.

Mechanism design   Mechanism design is sometimes called "reverse game theory" [Papadimitriou, 2005; Rahwan and Larson, 2009], as its starting point is a desired outcome, and the goal is to design a game (or to modify an existing game) such that this outcome emerges as a prominent or unique equilibrium.

Modern work in mechanism design started with the modeling of situations where a central authority is trying to achieve some *goal* (typically maximizing the social welfare or its own revenue), relying on *information* gathered from self-interested agents. Such mechanisms—for voting procedures, resource allocation, auctions, etc.—induce *games* where players each report their information or preferences. As players may report false information in order to achieve a better outcome for themselves, the designer tries to incentivize the players to report truthfully (or in some other way that will support the designer's goal), by properly setting the rules of the game (see, e.g., [Varian, 1995; Nisan, 2007; Hartline, 2011]).

A more general approach to mechanism design is not restricted to mechanisms that aggregate information, but rather sees *any* game as a mechanism (see e.g., [Papadimitriou, 2001; Maskin, 2008]). Thus a game may be designed in order to elicit truthful information (as above), but also to incentivize all kinds of behavior that the designer cannot directly control. The tools at the disposal of the designer may include monetary payments (like taxes and bonuses), revealing or hiding information from players, restricting the actions available to players, etc. Indeed, the second, more general approach is the one I follow in this thesis.

Computational mechanism design   With the rapid delegation of decision making to automated agents, the role of game theory and mechanism design within artificial intelligence is becoming increasingly important. In particular, game-theoretic principles must be taken into account in the design of systems and environments in which agents operate (human and automated alike) [Roth, 2002; Dash et al., 2003]. For example, crafting a proper protocol for negotiation among automated agents can guarantee that they will reach a better agreement, and faster [Rosenschein and Zlotkin, 1994].

In the other direction, runtime considerations and other limitations of computerized and networked systems are crucial in the implementation of mechanisms that interact with a large number of agents. For example, algorithms for computing an equilibrium, for setting appropriate payments or allocations, or for learning players' behavior and preferences are an integral part of many mechanism design challenges. Furthermore, techniques from computer science (such as *approximation*) appear to be useful in answering economic and game-theoretic questions. See [Nisan et al., 2007] for detailed discussions.

1.1.1 Voting mechanisms

Voting procedures are perhaps the simplest and oldest form of mechanisms, with roots in the 18th century and even before [de Borda, 1781; de Condorcet, 1785] (see, e.g., [McLean and Urken, 1995]). A voting or *social choice* mechanism is a function that aggregates the declared preferences of all voters over a set of candidates or alternatives (e.g., referees of the Academy award voting on movies), and selects a winner. In the most common voting rule, known as Plurality, every voter reports her most preferred candidate, and the candidate with the highest number of votes wins.[1] For other voting rules and an overview of social choice theory from a computer science perspective, see [Brandt et al., 2012].

While the model of voting is simple, it was proved by Gibbard [1973] and Satterthwaite [1975] that in every reasonable voting rule there are situations where some voters are incentivized to misreport their preferences. Since then, there have been several studies applying game-theoretic solution concepts to existing voting rules, aimed at understanding the relationship between preferences of a population, their behavior, and the final outcome of elections.

Equilibrium analysis in voting   Typically, a single voter is powerless to affect the outcome regardless of her actions. As a result, almost every state is a Nash equilibrium, and therefore NE does not give any meaningful prediction. Some solutions have been suggested to overcome this problem, for example by taking into account uncertainty, or cooperation of several voters (see Section 5.6 for an overview).

1.1.2 Auctions

Auctions are perhaps the most widely used and profitable application of mechanism design today. Agents bid their value for the proposed item (or items), and the mechanism decides on an allocation and payments based on these bids. A mechanism that guarantees both truthfulness and optimal social welfare is the Vickrey-Clarke-Groves (VCG) mechanism (see, e.g., [Nisan, 2007]), which sets the payments in a way that perfectly aligns the incentives of each player with those of society. VCG payments can be applied to most auction settings, and in fact to most games. Quite expectantly, most research on auctions has focused on the *revenue* of the seller [Myerson, 1981; Riley, 1989; Likhodedov and Sandholm, 2005; Hart and Nisan, 2012]. However there has also been work on bidders' welfare, see e.g. [Mirrokni et al., 2008; Bhawalkar and Roughgarden, 2011].

Within auction theory, much attention has been given to *position auctions* (or *ad auctions*), where bidders compete over ad placements of different quality. The equilibrium outcomes of position auctions are well understood, especially when there is no uncertainty over bidders' valuations [Varian, 2007; Edelman et al., 2007; Lucier et al., 2012].

---

[1]Some political scientists oppose this assertion that Plurality is the most common rule, pointing to the fact that most countries use voting procedures with several rounds, partitions to regions and so on. However, political elections constitute just a tiny fraction of the occasions in which groups of agents (people, firms, programs, etc.) take a coordinated decision by voting.

1.1.3   Mechanisms without money

Consider a mechanism whose purpose is to place a public facility (e.g., a library) based on the reported locations of users. As explained above, when the designer's goal is social welfare and the mechanism can use payments, truthfulness and an optimal outcome can both be achieved. Indeed, most research on mechanisms with payments either deals with efficiently implementing good mechanisms (as VCG payments may be hard to compute), or concerns design goals other than welfare.

Unfortunately, in many settings where welfare is our goal, transferring payments (such as VCG payments) among the players is impractical, undesirable, unethical, or even illegal. Voting scenarios described above and polls on the preferred location of a library are examples of such settings. Despite the strong negative result of Gibbard and Satterthwaite on general voting rules, there are restricted settings where there exist truthful and optimal mechanisms [Schummer and Vohra, 2007].

Approximate mechanism design without money (AMDw/oM)   When optimal truthful mechanisms do not exist,[2] we resort to truthful mechanisms that are *approximately optimal*, just as approximation algorithms are used for optimization problems in computer science that are computationally hard.

The first formal analyses of approximation ratios of truthful mechanisms were in the domain of supervised machine learning with multiple strategic experts [Dekel et al., 2008; Meir et al., 2008]. The approximation agenda was later made more explicit and applied to public facility location problems by Procaccia and Tennenholtz [2009]. Problems in AMDw/oM have since been studied in multiple domains, including voting [Alon et al., 2011], resource allocation [Guo et al., 2009], matching problems [Ashlagi et al., 2010], scheduling [Koutsoupias, 2011], and even money-free auctions have been crafted [Harrenstein et al., 2009]. Typically the goal of the designer in these papers is to maximize social welfare, but other optimization criteria (such as *egalitarian welfare*) have also been considered.

1.1.4   Taxes and subsidies

The mechanisms described so far were required to deal with the designer's lack of information—information that only the agents held regarding their preferences. A different type of intervention is using payments to change the preferences of players over *actions*, and thereby the outcome of the game. For example, a high tax on asocial behavior in games like the Prisoner's Dilemma can assist in aligning the incentives of the individuals with those of society, and make them cooperate.

As mentioned above, VCG payments can always guarantee that players will each prefer the welfare-maximizing outcome. However, VCG payments do not prevent deviations by *coalitions*, may require large positive and negative payments, and may be hard to compute and/or to implement. Thus, designing a good mechanism becomes a non-trivial optimization problem with many factors and constraints.

Subsidies in non-cooperative games   Monderer and Tennenholtz [2004] investigated a very general setting where an interested party wishes to influence the behavior of agents in a game. They assume that the interested party can promise players non-negative bonuses if a particular outcome is realized, thereby changing the utilities of various actions in the game. The designer wishes to create an incentive for the players to follow some desired outcome in the new game, while minimizing

---

[2]Approximation is also used when complex optimal mechanisms do exist, but a simpler mechanism is preferred due to practical reasons. See [Hartline, 2011].

the actual amount being spent. The authors show that desired outcomes can often be implemented *without paying anything*. A similar approach was applied to a specific class of games (Boolean games) in [Wooldridge et al., 2012].

Subsidies have also been studied in the context of *cooperative games*, as a means of increasing the stability of large coalitions. For a detailed review see Section 3.6.

1.2   Thesis Outline and Main Results

My research is multi-disciplinary in nature, involving tools and ideas from economics, computer science, mathematics, artificial intelligence, and cognitive science. The work consists of several projects, ultimately aiming for a better understanding of games. Problems studied in the thesis range from voting theory and cooperative games to matching and facility location, and new equilibrium concepts are suggested along the way. Indeed, I believe that there is no one way to model cooperation, as this is an abstract concept whose realization strongly depends on the domain and the underlying assumptions.

The content of this thesis should be accessible to readers at the graduate level of computer science or mathematics, and little to no knowledge in game theory is assumed. In Chapter 2, I lay out the main concepts and definitions of cooperative and non-cooperative game theory, which are referred to throughout the thesis. The remaining chapters are mostly self-contained for readers with basic background in game theory.

Stability   Chapters 3 through 6 deal with *stability*. In Chapter 3, I study the minimal subsidy that is required in order to induce cooperation in games (known as the *cost of stability*). I show tight upper and lower bounds on the cost of stability for broad classes of cooperative games, and in particular study the relation between the cost of stability and a different measure of stability known as the *least core*. The culmination of this line of research is in Chapter 4, where I show a direct link between the minimal subsidy required to stabilize a game, and the structure of the society that determines which coalitions may arise. Myerson [1977] suggested to model this network of social connections between players as a graph. I prove that the cost of stability of *any game* is bounded by the *treewidth* of the underlying network (which was only known for trees), and that this bound is tight.

Voting games are studied in Chapter 5. There, I propose a new game-theoretic model for voting in an iterative setting. The main result is that if voters follow a natural best-response dynamics, they will always converge to a stable outcome. Since the introduction of the original model, several researchers have studied variations of it, and their results are also presented and compared to mine.

In Chapter 6, I introduce a new solution concept for non-cooperative games called *stability scores*, which takes into account the *number* of coalitions that may try to deviate from a particular outcome. The usefulness of stability scores is then demonstrated on various games, including congestion games, ad auctions, and voting games. In particular, stability scores can be used to analyze the most stable outcome under the Plurality voting rule. In the context of ad auctions, I analyze the scores of the two most common ad auction mechanisms (VCG and GSP), showing that the latter is much more stable.

Welfare   While stability is important in its own right, one often cares more about the *welfare* of the population in those stable outcomes, which is the focus of Chapters 7 through 9. In Chapter 7, I look at the popular problem of finding an optimal location for a public facility, using mechanisms that are truthful and do not use payments. The goal is to place the facility as close as possible to all agents, *on average*. The main positive result is a randomized mechanism that guarantees a $3 - \frac{2}{n}$ approximation ratio—where no truthful mechanism can do better. On the other hand, it is shown that no deterministic mechanism can guarantee a constant approximation ratio for locating a facility on a discrete cycle. This result has several interesting implications (it also has the most technically involved proof in the thesis).

Mechanisms without money for problems in the domains of binary classification and judgment aggregation are studied in Chapter 8. I show how a simple mapping between these domains and facility location allows us to handle all of them within a unified approach, thereby answering most of the remaining open questions regarding the approximation ratio of truthful mechanisms in these domains.

Prices become the focus once again in Chapter 9, where I study online matching mechanisms that maximize the welfare of participating agents by attaching posted prices to nodes. The model is inspired by parking systems in urban centers, with various assumptions on the information available to the designer. In particular, I show that when the preferences of drivers is known (but not their order of arrival), online prices that lead to optimal welfare can be found by simulating an offline position auction.

Appendices   In some cases the technical details of proofs are important to better understand the conceptual contribution and limitations. However, in order to allow continuous reading, most proofs have been omitted from the main text, sometimes replaced with a proof sketch or outline. All omitted proofs from each chapter can be found in the corresponding appendices.

1.3   Bibliographic Notes

The current thesis is based on a selection of my work in the years 2009 through 2013. As the central theme of my work is *cooperation*, I decided to include only the research and results that are directly related to a better understanding and promotion of cooperation in games. A second criterion for inclusion of a result in the thesis was the centrality of my role in it. The strict page limit imposed by the Hebrew University required further selection. Papers that were not included in the thesis but are still relevant are briefly discussed below.

It is important to note that the results described here have been accomplished via joint work with many other researchers. Their names are explicitly mentioned when discussing unpublished work (coauthors of published work are visible in the list of publications). I am the primary or sole contributor of every result that appears with its proof (in the text, or in the appendix). Results presented without a proof are not part of the original contribution of this thesis, and appear with a citation (see, e.g., Theorem 3.4).

The contents of Chapter 3 are based mainly on [Meir, Bachrach, and Rosenschein, 2010; Meir, Rosenschein, and Malizia, 2011]. Chapter 4 is based on [Meir, Zick, and Rosenschein, 2012; Meir, Zick, Elkind, and Rosenschein, 2013]. Chapter 5 is based on [Meir, Polukarov, Rosenschein, and Jennings, 2010]. Chapter 6 is based mainly on [Feldman, Meir, and Tennenholtz, 2012]. Chapters 7 and 8 are based on [Dokow, Feldman, Meir, and Nehama, 2012], and on results from [Meir, Procaccia, and Rosenschein, 2012] that were *not* included in my M.Sc. thesis [Meir, 2008]. Chapter 9 is based on [Meir, Chen, and Feldman, 2013].

1.3.1 Papers not included in the thesis

A paper that is aimed directly at improving social welfare is [Meir and Rosenschein, 2013], dealing with pricing costly resources, such as fuel for leased cars. We show the benefits of imposing the cost of a consumed resource on the users rather than on the supplying company. In short, we proved that under mild assumptions the unique equilibrium that emerges is preferred by both users and supplier, and suggested a simple mechanism that facilitates the transition to per-use payments.

Agent failures in games constitute another line of research that tackles both questions of stability and welfare. We showed how mild failure probabilities can increase stability in cooperative games [Bachrach, Meir, Feldman, and Tennenholtz, 2011], and can eliminate undesired equilibria in non-cooperative games, thereby increasing social welfare [Meir, Tennenholtz, Bachrach, and Key, 2012]. In a recent working paper with Noga Alon and Moshe Tennenholtz, we study how uncertainty regarding agent failures can be exploited by *signaling mechanisms* (which reveal selective information) to further improve welfare [Alon, Meir, and Tennenholtz, 2013; Alon, Falik, Meir, and Tennenholtz, 2013].

In two other papers I focused on the incentives of the *designer* rather than those of the society, showing how to increase the profit in ad auctions [Feldman, Meir, and Tennenholtz, 2011], and how one can pass a complex decision in a committee by clustering several issues together [Alon, Falik, Meir, and Tennenholtz, 2013].

Finally, when several firms each design their own mechanism in order to attract clients or workers, they induce a new game where firms compete with one another. I formulated and studied such models in the contexts of group discounts [Meir, Lu, Tennenholtz, and Boutilier, 2013], labor markets [Meir and Tennenholtz, 2013, (manuscript)], and online services in a network environment [Feldman, Meir, and Tennenholtz, 2013].

Chapter 2

Preliminaries

Throughout the document, we will mostly use bold characters to denote vectors, for example $\mathbf{a} = (a_1, a_2, a_3, \ldots)$. We use upper case letters from the beginning of the alphabet, $A, B, C, \ldots$, to denote sets, and letters from the end of the alphabet, X, Y, Z, to denote random variables. Other complex objects such as sets of sets are typically denoted either with calligraphic letters, $\mathcal{A}, \mathcal{B}, \mathcal{C}$, or with bold upper case letters, $\mathbf{A}, \mathbf{B}, \mathbf{C}$. Also, given a vector $\mathbf{x}$ and a set S, we write $x(S)$ to denote $\sum_{i \in S} x_i$. For a natural number n, we denote $[n] = \{1, 2, \ldots, n\}$. For an event E, $[\![E]\!]$ stands for the corresponding indicator random variable.

In the remainder of this chapter we introduce some notation and concepts of game theory, mechanism design, and voting. Readers that are familiar with game theory can skip most of this chapter. For more background on game theory, see [Peleg and Sudhölter, 2003; Maschler et al., 2013].

2.1 Non-cooperative Games

Game forms and games A *game form* $GF = \langle N, \mathbf{A}, C, g \rangle$ consists of a set of agents N, a set of *actions* (also called pure strategies) for each agent $\{A_i\}_{i \in N}$, where $\mathbf{A} = \times_{i \in N} A_i$ contains all combinations of agents' actions. C is the set of possible outcomes , and g is a mapping $g : \mathbf{A} \to C$. A joint selection of strategies for each agent $\mathbf{a} = (a_i \in A_i)_{i \in N}$ is called a *strategy profile*. A *partial profile* for a subset of agents $S \subseteq N$ is denoted by $a_S = (a_i \in A_i)_{i \in S}$. The profile of all agents *except i* is denoted by $a_{-i} = (a_j \in A_j)_{j \neq i}$.

The set of strategies A_i does not have to be discrete. For example, the strategy may be to decide on an amount of money to spend, where money is assumed to be continuous.

A *non-cooperative game* $G = \langle GF, \mathbf{u} \rangle$ consists of a game form GF, plus a *utility function* $u_i : C \to \mathbb{R}$ for each agent, specifying her preferences over outcomes.[1] In the most general case every profile has its own outcome, in which case we write $u_i(\mathbf{a})$ instead of $u_i(g(\mathbf{a}))$. The utility function of an agent is also called its *type*. The set of possible types for agent i is denoted by U_i.

A *mixed strategy* q_i is a probability distribution over actions in A_i. A *mixed profile* (or correlated profile) $\mathbf{q}$ is a probability distribution over profiles in $\mathbf{A}$. Note that if $\mathbf{q}$ is a product distribution $\times_{i \in N} q_i$ then it is equivalent to every agent i playing the mixed strategy q_i.

---

[1]The presentation of G as a table of utilities is also known as a *normal form game*.

Deviations, better-replies and best-replies   Given a game and a particular profile **a** (either pure or mixed), an agent $i \in N$ and an action $a'_i \in A_i$, we say that a'_i is a *better-reply* to **a** if $u_i(a'_i, a_{-i}) \geq u_i(\mathbf{a})$. a'_i is called a *deviation* from **a** if this holds with a strict inequality (which is only possible when $a'_i \neq a_i$). a'_i is called a *best-reply* if $a'_i \in \text{argmax}_{a \in A_i} u_i(a, a_{-i})$.

Note that a best-reply is not necessarily unique, and is not necessarily a deviation. Without loss of generality (w.l.o.g), the best-reply to **a** is always a pure strategy, and thus there is a pure deviation if and only if there is a deviation.

Nash equilibrium and other solution concepts   We say that the strategy profile **a** is a *Nash equilibrium* (NE) in G if there is no deviation from **a** for any agent i. Formally, this holds if for any agent i and any strategy $a'_i \neq a_i$, we have that $u_i(\mathbf{a}) \geq u_i(a_{-i}, a'_i)$. An NE **a** is called a *pure Nash equilibrium* (PNE) if it consists of pure strategies. Every game with a finite set of strategies has a Nash equilibrium, but does not necessarily have a PNE [Nash, 1950].

A Nash equilibrium and a pure Nash equilibrium are both examples of *solution concepts*. Formally, a solution concept φ can be any mapping from games to (sets of) outcomes. Of course, useful solution concepts are those that specify the outcomes that are made possible by a certain type of behavior.

Another important solution concept is *strong equilibrium*. This is similar to Nash equilibrium, but requires that no *coalition* can gain by deviating from the outcome. See Section 6.2 for a formal definition. It is important to emphasize that a particular solution concept may not exist in some games (like PNE), or may contain multiple outcomes; thus, it is only a "solution" in quite an abstract sense.

Dominant strategies $a^*_i \in A_i$ is a *dominant strategy* of i if agent i always prefers a^*_i, regardless of the choices of other agents. Formally, for all **a**, $u_i(a^*_i, a_{-i}) > u_i(\mathbf{a})$. Note that if some player has a dominant strategy, then it is unique, and all other players can assume that it will be played. If the above holds with a weak inequality, then a^*_i is called a *weakly dominant strategy*, and is not always unique.

Dominant strategies (and their variations) also give rise to solution concepts. They are *stronger* than NE in the sense that they are less likely to exist—in most games, players do not have dominant strategies. On the other hand, they require fewer assumptions regarding the behavior of players. Indeed, it is quite likely that a player will follow her dominant strategy if one is available to her.

Example 2.1 (Prisoner's Dilemma).   *In the Prisoner's Dilemma, two prisoners are tried for a robbery they committed together. The police offer each of them a deal, according to which the prisoner will testify against his partner. Since evidence against them is weak, the two decide to deny involvement in the crime, so that they can only be convicted for the lesser crime of trespassing. Each player must independently choose whether to* Cooperate, *by holding to the deal, or to* Defect, *by testifying. Thus $A_1 = A_2 = \{C, D\}$. The four possible outcomes are shown in Table 2.1.*

It can be easily verified that D is a strictly dominant strategy for each player. In particular, the unique Nash equilibrium of this game is $\mathbf{a} = (D, D)$. This is also the outcome where the sum of both players' prison time is maximal. In contrast, there is no strong equilibrium in this game, since both players gain by deviating from (D, D) to (C, C).

$u_1(\mathbf{a}), u_2(\mathbf{a})$	$a_1 = C$	$a_1 = D$
$a_2 = C$	-2,-2	0, -8
$a_2 = D$	-8,0	-5,-5

Table 2.1: $-u_i(\mathbf{a})$ is the number of years in prison for i.

Other solution concepts take into account the formation process of coalitions, uncertainty over the states of the world or over other players' types, and many other factors.

2.1.1 Mechanisms

A *mechanism* is a function f which receives inputs from participating agents $a_i \in A_i$ and returns an outcome from some set C.

Thus every mechanism f induces a game form GF_f. This game form, together with agents' types, composes a non-cooperative game G_f. The conceptual difference between a mechanism and other games is that in general a game is assumed to be merely a description of the environment. As explained in Chapter 1, a mechanism (like an algorithm) usually has a purpose or goal, for which it was designed.

We say that a mechanism f *implements* a certain property P according to a solution concept φ, if the following holds: for any selection of agents' types $\mathbf{u} \in \mathbf{U}$, there is an action profile $\mathbf{a} \in \mathbf{A}$ in $G_f = \langle GF_f, \mathbf{U} \rangle$ s.t. (1) $f(\mathbf{a})$ has property P; and (2) $\mathbf{a} \in \varphi(G_f)$. For example, f may implement the property "maximum social welfare in pure Nash equilibrium", which means that when agents face the (game induced by) mechanism f, there is always a PNE $\mathbf{a}$ which maximizes $\sum_{i \in N} u_i(\mathbf{a})$.

Some mechanisms require agents to reveal information about their type (elections, auctions, etc.). If every agent in G_f has a dominant strategy which is to reveal its true type, we say that f is *truthful*, or *strategyproof*.[2] We can also say that f *implements* the truthful outcome in dominant strategies.

Example of a mechanism whose goal is revenue   A very simple example is the Vickrey auction (also known as the *second price auction*) [Vickrey, 1961]. In this auction a single item is being sold, and agents are asked to "bid", i.e., to report the amount they are willing to pay. The highest bidder gets the item, but pays the price of the next highest bidder. It turns out that the Vickrey auction is strategyproof, and that under certain assumptions it also maximizes the revenue if a proper reserve price is set [Myerson, 1981]. Both the VCG auction mentioned in the Introduction, and the GSP auction, which is mentioned in Chapters 6 and 9, are generalizations of the Vickrey auction.

Examples of mechanisms whose goals are stability and social welfare   Consider a mechanism designed to place a facility as close as possible to agents according to their reported locations on a line. A mechanism selecting the *median* location is strategyproof. Further, it is also optimal w.r.t. social welfare. See Chapter 7 for details.

Next, consider a mechanism that is trying to increase the welfare of agents playing the Prisoner's Dilemma (Example 2.1), by taxing certain actions or outcomes. A sufficiently high tax on agents playing D will guarantee that C is a dominant strategy, rather than D.

2.1.2 Voting rules

Voting rules are a special class of mechanism, where the agents (also called "voters") are assumed to have ordinal or cardinal preferences over all candidates. There is a set C of m candidates, and a set V of n voters. Let $\mathcal{R}(C)$ be the set of all $m!$ total orders over C. A voting rule f allows each voter to submit his preferences over the candidates by selecting an action from the set A, where typically $A = \mathcal{R}(C)$. Then, f chooses a unique winning candidate—i.e., it is a function $f : A^n \to C$.[3] When referring to a voting rule we usually mean an infinite family of such functions, for every value of n and m. Unless explicitly mentioned otherwise, we do not allow mixed strategies in the game induced by the voting rule.

---

[2]The term strategyproof is only relevant for mechanisms where agents are asked to reveal private information. More generally, a mechanism is *straight-forward* if every agent has a dominant strategy that is based only on its type.

[3]The definition is sometimes extended so that f can return any nonempty subset of C as winners. See Chapter 5.

Examples of voting rules *Plurality* is the simplest example of a voting rule. Here $A = C$, i.e., every voter only reports his most-preferred candidate. The score of each candidate is the number of voters supporting it, and the candidate with the highest score is the winner. Note that a tie breaking rule (for example, lexicographic order over candidates) is required to make the winner unique.

More generally, *positional scoring rules* where each voter gives points to a candidate according to how it is ranked (like the *Borda* rule, or the Eurovision contest rule). Other voting rules look at pairwise comparisons between candidates. For example, in the *Maximin* rule the score of every candidate is the number of voters who prefer it over its strongest opponent, and the winner has the highest score. A *Condorcet winner* is a candidate that is preferred to any other candidate by a majority of voters.

We often seek voting rules that hold certain properties. For example, a rule is *Condorcet consistent* if a Condorcet winner (when one exists) is always elected. A rule is *onto* if for any candidate $c \in C$ there is some voting profile **a** s.t. $f(\mathbf{a}) = c$.

Strategic voting A fundamental question in voting is whether voters should or tend to report their true preferences (i.e., their type). It is easy to see that in some cases it is better for a voter to "lie" about his preferences. For example, under the Plurality rule if a voter supports some candidate a_1 but knows that this candidate is unpopular and has no chance of winning, it might be better for him to support one of the leading candidates.

On the other hand, consider a *dictatorial* rule, where the outcome is determined according to the preferences of a single voter (w.l.o.g. voter 1). Clearly voter 1 is always better off reporting his true type, whereas other voters cannot affect the outcome, and in particular cannot gain by lying. Thus a dictatorial rule is strategyproof.

A natural question is whether there is a way to characterize all strategyproof voting rules.

The Gibbard-Satterthwaite theorem (Gibbard [1973], Satterthwaite [1975]) . *An onto voting rule f for 3 or more candidates is strategyproof if and only if f is dictatorial.*

2.2 Cooperative Games

We consider games with the set of players $N = \{1, \ldots, n\}$. A *coalition* is simply a subset of N; N itself is referred to as the *grand coalition*. We denote by $\mathbb{R}_+$ the set of all nonnegative real numbers. Given two vectors $\mathbf{x} = (x_1, \ldots, x_n)$ and $\mathbf{y} = (y_1, \ldots, y_n)$, we write $\mathbf{x} \leq \mathbf{y}$ if $x_i \leq y_i$ for all $i = 1, \ldots, n$.

Definition 2.1. *A transferable utility (TU) game $G = \langle N, g \rangle$ is given by a set of players, or agents, $N = \{1, \ldots, n\}$ and a characteristic function $g : 2^N \to \mathbb{R}$, which for each subset of agents S outputs the payoff that the members of S can achieve by working together; we require $g(\emptyset) = 0, g(N) \neq 0$.*

In most TU games studied in the literature, the payoffs of all coalitions have the same sign, i.e., agents get together either to share costs (as in Example 3.1) or to earn profits (as in Example 2.2 below). In the former case, we say that G is an *expense-sharing game* and write $G = \langle N, c \rangle$, where $c \equiv -g$, and in the latter case we say that G is a *profit-sharing game* and write $G = \langle N, v \rangle$, where $v \equiv g$; note that both v and c only take values in $\mathbb{R}_+$.

An *outcome* of a TU game is a way of sharing the value (i.e., profit or expense) of the grand coalition among all players. Formally, a *payoff vector* for a TU game $G = \langle N, g \rangle$ is any vector $\mathbf{p} = (p_1, \ldots, p_n) \in \mathbb{R}^n$.

A payoff vector **p** is *budget balanced* if $\sum_{i \in N} p_i = |g(N)|$. That is, p_i is the profit received by (respectively, cost incurred by) player i. Note that there is no requirement that entries will be either positive or negative. We denote by $\mathbb{I}(G)$ the set of all balanced payoff vectors for the TU game G, also known as *preimputations*. Not all outcomes of coalitional games are equally attractive to the agents. In particular, an important consideration in the analysis of TU games is that of coalitional stability: a preimputation $\mathbf{p} \in \mathbb{I}(G)$ is said to be an *imputation* if it is *individually rational*, i.e., $G = \langle N, v \rangle$ is a profit-sharing game and $p_i \geq v(\{i\})$ for all $i \in N$, or $G = \langle N, c \rangle$ is an expense-sharing game and $p_i \leq c(\{i\})$ for all $i \in N$.

Individual rationality is only a preliminary requirement for stability. For an outcome to be *stable*, it should be the case that no *subset* of players has an incentive to deviate. Formally, given a profit-sharing game $G = \langle N, v \rangle$ (respectively, an expense-sharing game $G = \langle N, c \rangle$), we say that a coalition S *blocks* a payoff vector **p** if it can improve its payoff by deviating, i.e., if $v(S) > p(S)$ (respectively, $c(S) < p(S)$). A payoff vector **p** is said to be *stable* in a TU game $G = \langle N, g \rangle$ if it is not blocked by any coalition $S \subsetneq N$. We denote all stable payoff vectors by $\mathbb{S}(G)$.

Definition 2.2 (The core). $\mathbb{C}(G) = \mathbb{I}(G) \cap \mathbb{S}(G)$.

That is, a payoff vector **p** is in the core if **p** is both *stable* and *balanced*. The core is the most common solution concept that aims at capturing stability in cooperative games, and like strong equilibrium (in non-cooperative games) it requires that no *coalition* has an incentive to deviate. Unfortunately, the core may be empty in some games (see Example 2.2).

When $n = 3$ the core can be graphically demonstrated—see Figure 2.1. For simplicity we fix $v(1,2,3) = 1$ as the height of the simplex (triangle). (p_1, p_2, p_3) are the barycentric coordinates of the payoff vector **p**, and their sum always equals the height, which is 1. The core is in grey.

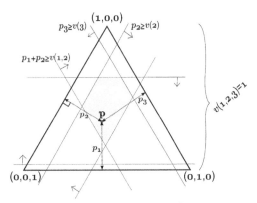

Figure 2.1: An illustration of the core.

2.2.1 Coalition structures

Following Aumann and Dréze [1974], we sometimes assume that agents may form *coalition structures*, where several disjoint coalitions may exist in parallel.

A *coalition structure* over N is a partition of N into disjoint subsets. We denote the set of all coalition structures over N by $\mathcal{CS}(\mathcal{N})$. Given a $CS \in \mathcal{CS}(\mathcal{N})$ we define its *value* $v(CS)$ as $g(CS) = \sum_{S \in CS} g(S)$ and set $CS_+ = \{S \in CS \mid g(S) > 0\}$.

For profit-sharing games (similar definitions hold for expense-sharing games), let **OPT**$(G) = \max\{v(CS) \mid CS \in \mathcal{CS}(\mathcal{N})\}$. A coalition structure CS is said to be *optimal* if $v(CS) = $ **OPT**(G). Stable payoff vectors and the core are defined in a similar way to the case without coalition structures, except transferring payoffs is only allowed within a coalition. See Section 3.5 for details.

Remark 2.1. *Since in the general case it is possible that $v(CS) > v(N)$, it is crucial which of them is used as the sum of potential preimputations, and may for example determine whether the* *core is empty or not. Unless explicitly stated otherwise (e.g., in most of Chapter 4), we assume that coalition structures are not allowed, and thus that preimputations have to sum up to $v(N)$.*

2.2.2 Subclasses of TU Games

We will now define several important classes of TU games that are induced by restrictions on the characteristic function, such as monotonicity and superadditivity.

Monotone games A TU game $G = \langle N, g \rangle$ is called *monotone* if $|g(S)| \leq |g(T)|$ for all $S \subseteq T$. Monotonicity means that adding agents to a coalition can only increase its profit in a profit-sharing game, or its expenses in an expense-sharing game.

Superadditive and Subadditive games A profit-sharing game $\langle N, v \rangle$ is said to be *superadditive* if $v(S \cup T) \geq v(S) + v(T)$ for all $S, T \subseteq N$ such that $S \cap T = \emptyset$. An expense-sharing game $\langle N, c \rangle$ is said to be *subadditive* if $c(S \cup T) \leq c(S) + c(T)$ for all $S, T \subseteq N$ such that $S \cap T = \emptyset$. Intuitively, in superadditive profit-sharing games and subadditive expense-sharing games it is never harmful to merge two non-overlapping coalitions. In particular, if G is superadditive, then $\{N\}$ is optimal and $g(N) = \mathbf{OPT}(G)$. In what follows, we will refer to superadditive profit-sharing games and subadditive expense-sharing games as *s-additive* games.

Anonymous games A TU game $G = \langle N, g \rangle$ is called *anonymous* if the payoff of a coalition depends only on its size, i.e., $g(S) = g(T)$ whenever $|S| = |T|$. Given an anonymous game $G = \langle N, g \rangle$, for every $k = 1, \ldots, n$ we define $g_k = g(\{1, \ldots, k\})$; we have $g_k = g(S)$ for every $S \subseteq N$ of size k.

Simple games A profit TU game $G = \langle N, v \rangle$ is called *simple* if $v(S) \in \{0, 1\}$ for all $S \subseteq N$, and $v(N) = 1$.[4] In a simple game we say that a coalition $S \subseteq N$ *wins* if $v(S) = 1$, and *loses* if $v(S) = 0$. A player i in a simple game G is called a *veto* player if he is necessary to form a winning coalition, i.e., we have $v(S) = 0$ for all $S \subseteq N \setminus \{i\}$. The notion of a veto player turns out to be useful for characterizing the core of a simple monotone game: it is well known that the core is non-empty if and only if there are veto players.

An important subclass of simple games is that of *weighted voting games* (WVGs). In these games, each agent has a weight, and a coalition of agents wins the game if the sum of the weights of its members meets or exceeds a certain quota. Formally, a *weighted voting game* is given by a set of agents $N = \{1, \ldots, n\}$, a vector of agents' *weights* $\mathbf{w} = (w_1, \ldots, w_n) \in (\mathbb{R}_+)^n$ and a *quota* $q \in \mathbb{R}_+$; we write $G = [\mathbf{w}; q]$. The *weight* of a coalition $S \subseteq N$ is $w(S)$; we require $q \leq w(N)$. The characteristic function of a weighted voting game is given by $v(S) = 1$ if $w(S) \geq q$, and $v(S) = 0$ otherwise. Weighted voting games are simple monotone games; however, they are not necessarily superadditive.

Example 2.2. Four contractors $N = \{1, 2, 3, 4\}$ compete for a construction project. The project requires at least 10 trucks, whereas the contractors have $2, 5, 8$, and 12 trucks, respectively. This situation corresponds to a weighted voting game $[2, 5, 8, 12; 10]$. In this game, $\{4\}$ and $\{1, 2, 3\}$ are winning coalitions (with value 1), whereas $\{1, 2\}$ is a losing coalition (with value 0). Note that there are no veto players in this game, and thus the core is empty, which means that if all four contractors cooperate, they have no stable way to divide the project's profits. For instance, the payoff vector $\mathbf{p} = (0, 1/4, 1/4, 1/2)$ is blocked by the coalition $S = \{2, 3\}$, since $p(\{2, 3\}) =$

---

[4]Simple games are sometimes required to also be monotone. We make no such requirement, and state explicitly when a game (simple or not) is assumed to be monotone.

$1/2 < 1 = v(\{2,3\})$. In contrast, if we allow the formation of coalition structures (meaning that several construction projects can be performed independently by disjoint contractors), the structure $CS = \{\{1,2,3\},\{4\}\}$ can be stabilized (for example, with a payoff of $p_3 = 10$ and $p_4 = 10$).

Part I

Stability

Chapter 3

The Cost of Stability

Subsidies in Cooperative Games

Abstract. We study the minimal external subsidy required to stabilize the core of a coalitional game, known as the *Cost of Stability* (CoS) [Bachrach et al., 2009a]. The CoS is used both as a measure of the inherent (in)stability of a game, and as a design tool for an external party that wishes agents to reach a stable outcome. In this chapter we prove tight upper and lower bounds on the CoS, and compare the extended core induced by subsidies with the least core of the game. The relation between the CoS and the least core is then used to further improve the bounds for a large class of games.

3.1 Introduction

Coalitional games, or *cooperative games* deal with the allocation of profit (or cost) that results from cooperation. The most prominent solution concept that aims to formalize the idea of stability in coalitional games is the *core* (see Section 2.2). However, this concept has an important drawback: the core of a game may be empty. In games with empty cores, any outcome is unstable, and therefore there is always a group of agents that is tempted to abandon the existing plan.

In this chapter we focus on *subsidies* by an external authority as a mechanism-design approach to stabilize games with an empty core. An external party can provide a subsidy that increases the profit of the grand coalition in a profit-sharing game or lowers the cost of the grand coalition in an expense-sharing game. This subsidy is given to the grand coalition as a whole, and is conditional on agents forming the grand coalition. The minimal subsidy that stabilizes a given game is known as its *cost of stability* [Bachrach et al., 2009a] (see Section 3.6 for more related work).

The following example demonstrates how subsidies can induce stability.

Example 3.1 (Sharing the cost). *Three private hospitals in a large city plan to purchase an X-ray machine. The standard X-ray machine costs $5 million, and can fulfill the needs of up to two hospitals. There is also a more advanced machine, which is capable of serving all three hospitals, but costs $9 million. The hospital managers understand that the right thing to do is to buy the more expensive machine, which will serve all three hospitals and cost less than two standard machines, but cannot agree on how to allocate the cost of the more expensive machine among the hospitals:*

there will always be a pair of hospitals that (together) need to pay at least $6 million, and would then rather split off and buy the cheaper machine for themselves. The generous mayor decides to solve the problem by subsidizing the more advanced X-ray machine: she agrees to contribute $3 million, and let each hospital add $2 million. Pairs of hospitals now have no incentive to buy the less efficient machine, as each pair (together) pays only $4 million.

3.1.1   Results in this Chapter

After presenting the definitions and initial results by Bachrach *et al.* [2009a], we prove tight bounds on the cost of stability in expense-sharing games, anonymous games, and games where coalition sizes are bounded (Section 3.3). We then turn to study the relation between the cost of stability and the least core (Section 3.4), which enables us to improve the bounds for a broad class of games. Finally, in Section 3.5 we extend our analysis to coalition structures. Our results on this chapter are summarized in Table 3.1. The most important and surprising results regarding the cost of stability require some more definitions and appear in the next chapter.

3.2   Preliminaries

3.2.1   The Cost of Stability

Recall the definitions of transferable utility (TU) games from Section 2.2, and in particular the definition of the core. Following Bachrach *et al.* [2009a], we present the formal definitions of the *cost of stability* and minimal subsidies. Given a TU game $G = \langle N, g \rangle$ and a real value Δ, the *adjusted coalitional game* $G(\Delta) = \langle N, g' \rangle$ is given by

$$g'(S) = \begin{cases} g(S) & \text{if } S \neq N \\ g(S) + \Delta & \text{if } S = N. \end{cases}$$

We say that $g'(N) = g(N) + \Delta$ is the *adjusted payoff* of the grand coalition. We assume that Δ is always non-negative for profit sharing games, and always non-positive for expenses sharing games, and will refer to the quantity $|\Delta|$ as the *subsidy* for the game G. Note that if $\Delta \neq 0$, a preimputation $\mathbf{p}'$ for the adjusted game $G(\Delta)$ is *not* a preimputation for the original game G, since $p'(N) \neq |g(N)|$.

We say that a subsidy Δ *stabilizes* the game G if the adjusted game $G(\Delta)$ has a non-empty core. We emphasize that a payoff vector $\mathbf{p}$ is stable in $G(\Delta)$ iff it is stable in G, since $\mathbb{S}(G(\Delta)) = \mathbb{S}(G)$.

Example   To illustrate the concepts introduced in the previous paragraph, consider Example 3.1. In this example, $c(N)$ was reduced from 9 (million) to $c'(N) = 6$ (i.e., by $\Delta = 3$), while for every other non-empty coalition S we have $c'(S) = c(S) = 5$. Thus, $\mathbf{p}' = (2, 2, 2)$ is a payoff vector for the new game $G(3)$. In fact, $\Delta = 3$ stabilizes the game G: in particular, $\mathbf{p}' = (2, 2, 2)$ is in the core of $G(3)$.

We observe that *any TU game* can be stabilized by an appropriate choice of Δ. Indeed, if $G = \langle N, c \rangle$ is an expense-sharing game, it suffices to set $\Delta = -c(N)$; then the payoff vector $(0, \ldots, 0)$ is in the core of $G(\Delta)$. Similarly, if $G = \langle N, v \rangle$ is a profit-sharing game, we can set $\Delta = n \max_{S \subseteq N} v(S)$ and distribute the profits so that each player receives at least $\max_{S \subseteq N} v(S)$.[1]

---

[1]For monotone games adding $(n - 1)v(N)$ is sufficient.

However, the central authority typically wants to spend as little money as possible. Hence, we are interested in the *smallest* subsidy that stabilizes the grand coalition. We will refer to this quantity as the *cost of stability*. We will consider both the subsidy $|\Delta|$ and the total payout obtained/distributed by the central authority relative to the value of the grand coalition, thus distinguishing between *additive* and *multiplicative* cost of stability.

Definition 3.1 (Additive CoS, Bachrach *et al.* [2009a]).

$$\text{addCoS}(G) = \inf\{|\Delta| \in \mathbb{R}_+ \mid \mathbb{C}(G(\Delta)) \neq \emptyset\} \equiv \inf_{\mathbf{p} \in \mathbb{S}(G)} |p(N) - g(N)|. \qquad (3.1)$$

The multiplicative cost of stability For expense-sharing games, the multiplicative cost of stability is also known as the *cost recovery ratio* (CRR) and has a natural economic interpretation [Xu and Du, 2006]: this is the maximal fraction of the cost of providing the service to the grand coalition that can be collected without giving the agents an incentive to deviate.

Similarly, we term the multiplicative CoS in profit sharing games as the *required subsidy ratio* (RSR), i.e., the ratio between the minimal total payoff that guarantees stability, and the available payoff.[2] Formally:

Definition 3.2 (Multiplicative CoS).

$$\text{RSR}(G) = \text{multCoS}(G) = \frac{|v(N) + \text{addCoS}(G)|}{|v(N)|} \equiv \inf_{\mathbf{p} \in \mathbb{S}(G)} \frac{p(N)}{v(N)} \qquad (3.2)$$

for profit sharing games, and

$$\text{CRR}(G) = \text{multCoS}(G) = \frac{|c(N) - \text{addCoS}(G)|}{|c(N)|} \equiv \sup_{\mathbf{p} \in \mathbb{S}(G)} \frac{p(N)}{c(N)} \qquad (3.3)$$

for expense sharing games (recall that we assume that $g(N) \neq 0$ throughout).

In what follows, we will alternate between the additive and the multiplicative notation; obviously, all results formulated for the additive cost of stability can be restated for its multiplicative sibling, and vice versa. Note that we have $\text{RSR}(G) \geq 1$ and $0 \leq \text{CRR}(G) \leq 1$. We will denote the game $G(\text{addCoS}(G))$ by $\overline{G}$. A simple continuity argument implies that $\overline{G}$ has a non-empty core.

Consider the following class of simple monotone games defined by finite projective planes; Bachrach *et al.* [2009a] provided this example to prove lower bounds on the cost of stability. We describe it here for completeness, and also since we will later use similar examples.

Example 3.2 (Bachrach *et al.* [2009a]). Consider a finite projective plane P of order q, where q is a prime number. It has $q^2 + q + 1$ points and the same number of lines, every line contains $q + 1$ points, every two lines intersect, and every point belongs to exactly $q + 1$ lines. We construct a simple game $G_q = \langle N, v \rangle$ as follows. We let N be the set of points in P, and for every $S \subseteq N$ we let $v(S) = 1$ if S contains a line and $v(S) = 0$ otherwise. Observe that this game is superadditive: since any two lines intersect, there do not exist two disjoint winning coalitions.

Now, consider a stable payoff vector $\mathbf{p}$. For each line R we have $p(R) \geq 1$. Summing over all q^2+q+1 lines, and using the fact that each point belongs to $q+1$ lines, we obtain $(q+1)\sum_{i \in N} p_i \geq q^2 + q + 1$, i.e., $p(N) \geq \frac{q^2+q+1}{q+1} = q + \frac{1}{q+1}$. Since $n = |N| = q^2 + q + 1$, we have $q + 1 > \sqrt{n}$ and hence $\text{RSR}(G_q) \geq p(N) > q > \sqrt{n} - 1$.

---

[2] In hindsight, the term *cost of stability* was not the best selection, as the pattern "cost of X" is overloaded, and the term is somewhat vague. To maintain consistency with published papers we keep the term (additive) CoS, but use the more natural CRR and RSR when referring to the multiplicative CoS.

The extended core   The notion of cost of stability presupposes that the subsidy is provided *before* the agents decide how to share profits/expenses. Alternatively, one can ask if a given preimputation can be transformed into a stable payoff vector by providing a subsidy of Δ for some $\Delta \geq 0$. Formally, given a profit-sharing game $G = \langle N, v \rangle$ and a vector $\mathbf{p} \in \mathbb{I}(G)$, we define the *cost of stability* of $\mathbf{p}$ as the smallest payment required to extend $\mathbf{p}$ to a stable payoff vector, i.e.,

$$\mathrm{addCoS}(\mathbf{p}, G) = \inf\{\Delta \geq 0 \mid \text{ there exists a } \mathbf{p}' \geq \mathbf{p} \text{ s.t. } \mathbf{p}' \in \mathbb{C}(G(\Delta))\}; \qquad (3.4)$$

for expense-sharing games, the definition has to be modified by replacing the inequality $\mathbf{p}' \geq \mathbf{p}$ in (3.4) with $\mathbf{p}' \leq \mathbf{p}$. In general, we have $\mathrm{addCoS}(\mathbf{p}, G) \geq \mathrm{addCoS}(G)$. The *extended core* of a TU game G consists of all payoff vectors for which this inequality holds with equality. We define:

$$\mathbb{EC}(G) = \{\mathbf{p} \in \mathbb{I}(G) \mid \mathrm{addCoS}(\mathbf{p}, G) = \mathrm{addCoS}(G)\}.$$

3.2.2   Cost of Stability: A Linear Programming Formulation

We will now give two alternative definitions of the cost of stability, which can be expressed in terms of linear programming and will prove to be useful later in this chapter. We formulate our results for profit-sharing games only; similar results can be derived for expense-sharing games.

   The core of every cooperative game can be described as a linear feasibility program over the variables $p_1, \ldots, p_n$, with a single linear constraint $\sum_{i \in S} p_i \geq v(S)$ for every coalition S, and additional constraints to guarantee that $\mathbf{p}$ is balanced (i.e., $\sum_{i \in N} p_i = v(N)$). Similarly, Bachrach *et al.* [2009a] defined an *optimization* linear program $\mathcal{LP}^*$, which finds the minimal Δ s.t. $\sum_{i \in N} p_i = v(N) + \Delta$, subject to the same feasibility constraints.

   Clearly the optimal value of this linear program is exactly $\mathrm{addCoS}(G)$. Moreover, any optimal solution of $\mathcal{LP}^*$ corresponds to an imputation in the core of $\overline{G}$. It will be convenient to modify this linear program by replacing the objective function with $p_1 + \cdots + p_n$ (which equals to $v(N) + \Delta$, rather than Δ): if the core of G is empty, the optimal value of the resulting linear program, which we will denote by $\mathcal{LP}'$, is exactly $\mathrm{addCoS}(G) + v(N)$.

   The cost of stability can also be written in a closed form, using the Bondareva–Shapley characterization of the core. To state the Bondareva–Shapley theorem, we first need to introduce the notion of a (minimal) balanced collection of subsets.

Definition 3.3. *A collection $\mathcal{D}$ of subsets of a finite set N is said to be* balanced *if there exists a vector $\{\delta_S\}_{S \in \mathcal{D}}$ such that $\delta_S \in \mathbb{R}_+$ for every $S \in \mathcal{D}$ and for every agent $i \in N$ it holds that $\sum_{S \in \mathcal{D}: i \in S} \delta_S = 1$; the vector $\{\delta_S\}_{S \in \mathcal{D}}$ is called the* balancing weight vector *for $\mathcal{D}$. We denote the set of all balanced collections of subsets of N by $\mathcal{BC}(N)$; the collection of all balancing weight vectors for a balanced collection $\mathcal{D}$ is denoted by $\mathcal{B}(\mathcal{D})$.*

   A balanced collection of subsets $\mathcal{D}$ is called minimal *if there exists no $\mathcal{D}' \subsetneq \mathcal{D}$ such that $\mathcal{D}'$ is balanced.*

Theorem 3.3 (Bondareva–Shapley Theorem). *A profit-sharing game $G = \langle N, v \rangle$ has a non-empty core if and only if for every [minimal][3] balanced collection $\mathcal{D}$ and every balancing weight vector $\{\delta_S\}_{S \in \mathcal{D}}$ for $\mathcal{D}$ it holds that $\sum_{S \in \mathcal{D}} \delta_S v(S) \leq v(N)$.*

   For a full proof and a more detailed discussion of this characterization, see, e.g., the textbook by Peleg and Sudhölter [2003].

---

[3]There are versions of the theorem with and without the minimality requirement.

Now, fix a profit-sharing game $G = \langle N, v \rangle$ with an empty core and consider the game $\overline{G}$. It is not hard to see that for $\overline{G}$ there exists a collection $\mathcal{D}$ with a balancing weight vector $\{\delta_S\}_{S \in \mathcal{D}}$ for which the inequality in the statement of the Bondareva–Shapley theorem holds with equality. Thus, we can write the multiplicative cost of stability of the game G as follows:

$$\text{RSR}(G) = \frac{1}{v(N)} \max \left\{ \sum_{S \in \mathcal{D}} \delta_S v(S) \mid \mathcal{D} \in \mathcal{BC}(N), \{\delta_S\}_{S \in \mathcal{D}} \in \mathcal{B}(\mathcal{D}) \right\}. \qquad (3.5)$$

Equivalently, $\text{addCoS}(G) = \max \left\{ \sum_{S \in \mathcal{D}} \delta_S v(S) \mid \mathcal{D} \in \mathcal{BC}(N), \{\delta_S\}_{S \in \mathcal{D}} \in \mathcal{B}(\mathcal{D}) \right\} - v(N)$. Furthermore, let $\mathcal{D}$ be a collection of sets with a balancing weight vector $\{\delta_S\}_{S \in \mathcal{D}}$ such that $\text{RSR}(G) = \frac{1}{v(N)} \sum_{S \in \mathcal{D}} \delta_S v(S)$; we can assume without loss of generality that $\mathcal{D} = 2^N$ by setting $\delta_S = 0$ for $S \notin \mathcal{D}$.

Unfortunately, in general neither the linear program $\mathcal{LP}^*$ nor equation (3.5) provide an efficient way to compute the cost of stability. This remains true even if the value of each coalition can be easily computed. See [Bachrach et al., 2009a] for more details on computational complexity of related problems.

3.3   Bounds on the Cost of Stability

3.3.1   The Cost of Stability in Profit-Sharing Games

Consider an arbitrary profit-sharing game $G = \langle N, v \rangle$ with an empty core. We start with some general bounds on the required subsidy ratio (RSR) that have been shown by Bachrach *et al.* [2009a]. The subsequent results are newer contributions.

Let $G = \langle N, v \rangle$ be a monotone profit-sharing game. As noted in Section 3.2.1, $\text{RSR}(G) \leq n$. This bound is tight, even if G is simple and anonymous (consider a game where $v(S) = 1$ for every non-empty coalition).

For superadditive profit-sharing games, the upper bound of n can be strengthened considerably.[4]

Theorem 3.4 (Bachrach *et al.* [2009a]). *Let $G = \langle N, v \rangle$ be a superadditive profit-sharing game. Then $\text{RSR}(G) \leq \sqrt{n}$, and this bound is asymptotically tight.*

We note that the lower bound is due to Example 3.2. If we assume both superadditivity and anonymity, we can strengthen Theorem 3.4 considerably.

Theorem 3.5 (Bachrach *et al.* [2009a]). *Let $G = \langle N, v \rangle$ be an anonymous superadditive profit-sharing game. Then $\text{RSR}(G) \leq 2$, and this bound is asymptotically tight.*

While Bachrach *et al.* provided a direct proof for Theorem 3.5, a simple alternative proof uses the following lemma (see proof of the symmetric case of expense sharing games in Section 3.3.2).

Lemma 3.6. *Let $G = \langle N, v \rangle$ be an anonymous profit-sharing game. Then $\text{RSR}(G) = \frac{n}{v_n} \cdot \max_{k \leq n} \frac{v_k}{k}$.*

---

[4]We note that the cost of stability of *subadditive* profit-sharing games (as well as that of superadditive expense-sharing games), is not an interesting quantity. In such games it is never beneficial to form a coalition, and thus the cheapest way to stabilize them is to ensure that agent i gets exactly $v(\{i\})$ (or pays exactly $c(\{i\})$).

Stability with small coalitions In many scenarios it is not realistic to assume that an arbitrary group of players can deviate from the grand coalition. In particular, deviations by large groups of players may be infeasible due to communication, coordination or trust issues (see next chapter where more intricate restrictions are considered). In such cases, it is meaningful to ask whether the game in question has an outcome that is resistant to deviations by coalitions of size at most k (where k is a given parameter), or whether it can be made resistant to such deviations by a subsidy of at most Δ.

Formally, given a profit-sharing game $G = \langle N, v \rangle$ and an integer k, $1 \leq k \leq n$, we define a game $G|_k = \langle N, v|_k \rangle$ by setting $v|_k(S) = v(S)$ for every S such that $|S| \leq k$ or $S = N$ and $v|_k(S) = 0$ otherwise. Our first result in this chapter bounds the subsidy in size-restricted superadditive games.

Theorem 3.7. *Let $G = \langle N, v \rangle$ be a superadditive profit-sharing game. Then for any positive integer $k < |N|$ we have $\mathrm{RSR}(G|_k) \leq k$. This bound is asymptotically tight for any $k \leq \sqrt{n}$.*

Combining Theorem 3.4 and Theorem 3.7, we conclude that for any superadditive profit-sharing game G it holds that $\mathrm{RSR}(G|_k) \leq \min\{\sqrt{n}, k\}$.

3.3.2 The Cost of Stability of Expense-Sharing Games

Having covered profit-sharing games in detail, we now turn to study expense-sharing games. The cost recovery ratio (CRR) can be characterized via the Bondareva–Shapley theorem, similarly to equation (3.5): for a game $G = \langle N, c \rangle$ with an empty core, we have

$$\mathrm{CRR}(G) = \frac{1}{c(N)} \min \left\{ \sum_{S \in \mathcal{D}} \delta_S c(S) \mid \mathcal{D} \in \mathcal{BC}(N), \{\delta_S\}_{S \in \mathcal{D}} \in \mathcal{B}(\mathcal{D}) \right\}. \tag{3.6}$$

We will use equation (3.6) to prove bounds on the cost of stability for several classes of expense-sharing games. We note that in expense-sharing games $\mathrm{mult CoS}(G) = \mathrm{CRR}(G)$ also coincides with the maximal γ for which the γ-core of G is non-empty [Jain and Mahdian, 2007]. We describe some relevant results from the literature in the context of our setting, and compare with additional results we obtain. Clearly $\mathrm{CRR}(G) \geq 0$ and this is tight in a simple game where $c(S) = 0$ for all $S \neq N$.

Subadditive expense-sharing games A well-studied class of expense-sharing games is that of *set cover games* [Devanur et al., 2005]. Briefly, a set cover game is described by an instance of the set cover problem: the agents are elements of the ground set, and the cost of a coalition S is the cost of the cheapest collection of subsets that covers all elements of S. More formally, a set cover game is an expense-sharing game given by a tuple $\langle N, \mathcal{F}, w \rangle$, where $N = \{1, \ldots, n\}$ is a set of agents, $\mathcal{F}$ is a collection of subsets of N that satisfies $\bigcup_{F \in \mathcal{F}} F = N$, and $w : \mathcal{F} \to \mathbb{R}_+$ is a mapping that assigns a non-negative weight to each set in $\mathcal{F}$. The cost of a coalition $S \subseteq N$ is given by $c(S) = \min \left\{ \sum_{F \in \mathcal{F}'} w(F) \mid \mathcal{F}' \subseteq \mathcal{F}, S \subseteq \cup_{F \in \mathcal{F}'} F \right\}$. We will write $\mathcal{F}^*(S)$ to denote a cheapest cover of the set S.

It is easy to see that the hospital game described in Example 3.1 is a set cover game with three agents (the hospitals). Indeed, every subadditive expense-sharing game can be represented as a set cover game.

Observation 3.8. *Set cover games are subadditive. Furthermore, every subadditive expense-sharing game can be described as a set cover game (by adding to $\mathcal{F}$ one set per each coalition).*

We remark that the construction in the proof of Observation 3.8 produces a set cover game with exponentially many sets. However, sometimes the number of sets can be reduced. In particular, if $c(S) = c(S_1) + \cdots + c(S_k)$ for some partition $\{S_1, \ldots, S_k\}$ of S, then the set S can be removed from $\mathcal{F}$ (this observation is inspired by the *synergy coalition groups* representation for superadditive profit-sharing games [Conitzer and Sandholm, 2006]).

The cost of stability in set cover games is closely related to the integrality ratio of the standard linear program for the set cover problem. Specifically, consider an instance $\langle N, \mathcal{F}, w \rangle$ of the set cover problem. The cost of the grand coalition in the corresponding game G can be written as the following integer linear program (ILP) over the variables $\{y_j\}_{F_j \in \mathcal{F}}$:

$$\min \sum_{F_j \in \mathcal{F}} w(F_j) y_j \qquad \text{subject to:}$$

$$\sum_{j : i \in F_j} y_j \geq 1 \text{ for each } i \in N, \tag{3.7}$$

$$y_j \in \{0, 1\} \text{ for each } F_j \in \mathcal{F}. \tag{3.8}$$

In this ILP, setting $y_j = 1$ corresponds to picking the set F_j for the cover. The linear relaxation of this program is obtained by replacing condition (3.8) with the condition $y_j \geq 0$ for each $F_j \in \mathcal{F}$ (clearly, in the optimal solution we will have $y_j \leq 1$ for each $F_j \in \mathcal{F}$); we will denote the resulting linear program by $\mathcal{LP}(G, N)$.

For a given instance of the set cover problem, the ratio between the value of its optimal integer solution and that of its optimal fractional solution is known as the *integrality gap*. Formally, let $\text{ILP}(G, N)$ and $\text{LP}(G, N)$ denote, respectively, the values of optimal integer and fractional solutions of the linear program $\mathcal{LP}(G, N)$ corresponding to the set cover game G. The integrality gap of G is defined as $\text{IG}(G) = \text{ILP}(G, N)/\text{LP}(G, N)$; note that $\text{ILP}(G, N) = c(N)$. The following theorem relates the integrality gap of a set cover game to its multiplicative cost of stability.

Theorem 3.9 (Deng *et al.* [1999], Jain and Mahdian [2007]). *Let G be a set cover game. Then* $\text{CRR}(G) = 1/\text{IG}(G)$.

The proof of Theorem 3.9 can be obtained by modifying the proof of Theorem 1 in [Deng et al., 1999]; an alternative proof using the Bondareva-Shapley condition is given in [Jain and Mahdian, 2007] (Corollary 15.9). For completeness, we provide a direct proof in Appendix A, and also demonstrate how an optimal stable payoff vector can be computed efficiently.

The integrality gap of the set cover problem is well-studied in the literature: it is known to be bounded from above by $H_n = \sum_{i=1}^{n} 1/i < \ln n + 1$, and that n can be replaced with k when sets sizes are bounded [Chvatal, 1979]. Moreover, these bounds are essentially tight, even when the sets are non-weighted [Slavík, 1996]. Thus, we obtain the following corollary.

Corollary 3.10. *Let $G = \langle N, c \rangle$ be a subadditive expense-sharing game. Then* $\text{CRR}(G|_k) \geq \frac{1}{\ln(k)+1}$, *and this bound is asymptotically tight. In particular,* $\text{CRR}(G) \geq \frac{1}{\ln(n)+1}$.

It is interesting to note that the worst-case bounds on the multiplicative cost of stability for subadditive expense-sharing games (Corollary 3.10) are much stronger than the ones for superadditive profit-sharing games (Theorems 3.4 and 3.7), and depend on $\ln n$ rather than $\sqrt{n}$.

Anonymous Expense-Sharing Games

As with profit-sharing games, anonymity allows us to simplify equation (3.6).

Lemma 3.11. *Let $G = \langle N, c \rangle$ be an anonymous expense-sharing game. Then* $\mathrm{CRR}(G) = \frac{n}{c_n} \cdot \min_{k \leq n} \frac{c_k}{k}$.

Without further assumptions, the cost recovery ratio of an anonymous expense-sharing game can still be as low as 0: consider, for instance, the game $G = \langle N, c \rangle$ given by $c_n = 1$, $c_k = 0$ for every $k \leq n$. However, if we assume both anonymity and subadditivity, we get a tight lower bound.

Theorem 3.12. *Let $G = \langle N, c \rangle$ be an anonymous subadditive expense-sharing game. Then* $\mathrm{CRR}(G) \geq 1/2 + \frac{1}{2n-2}$, *and this bound is tight.*

In particular, we get that $\mathrm{CRR}(G) \geq 1/2$, which is symmetric to the result on expense sharing games (Theorem 3.5). Note however that our bound on the CRR is exactly tight and not just asymptotically.

3.4   The Cost of Stability and the Least Core

In this section we explore the relationship between the cost of stability and another common measure of stability in coalitional games, namely, the value of the least core. We will focus on profit-sharing games.

We start by formally defining two variants of the least core: the *strong* and the *weak* least core. Consider a profit-sharing game $G = \langle N, v \rangle$ and some $\epsilon \geq 0$. Following Maschler *et al.* [1979], the *strong ϵ-core* of G is the set $\mathrm{SC}_\epsilon(G)$ of all pre-imputations for G such that *no coalition* can gain more than ϵ by deviating:

$$\mathrm{SC}_\epsilon(G) = \{ \mathbf{p} \in \mathbb{I}(G) \mid p(S) \geq v(S) - \epsilon \text{ for all } S \subseteq N \}.$$

Clearly, for a large enough ϵ the set $\mathrm{SC}_\epsilon(G)$ is non-empty. The quantity $\epsilon_\mathbf{S}(G) = \inf\{\epsilon \geq 0 \mid \mathrm{SC}_\epsilon(G) \neq \emptyset\}$ is called the *value of the strong least core* of G.

One particular payoff vector of interest is the *pre-nucleolus* $\mathbf{pn}(G)$, which minimizes the excess $v(S) - p(S)$ of the least satisfied coalition, then the next one, and so on [Schmeidler, 1969; Maschler et al., 1979].

The strong $\epsilon_\mathbf{S}$-core of G is referred to as the *strong least core* of G, and is denoted by $\mathbb{SLC}(G)$; a simple continuity argument shows that for every profit-sharing game G the set $\mathbb{SLC}(G)$ is non-empty. It always holds that $\mathbf{pn}(G) \in \mathbb{SLC}(G)$, and the pre-nucleolus can be thought of as the "most stable" preimputation of G.

In contrast, the *weak ϵ-core* of G (see e.g., in [Bejan and Gómez, 2009]) consists of payoff vectors such that no coalition can deviate in a way that profits *each deviator* by more than ϵ:

$$\mathrm{WC}_\epsilon(G) = \{ \mathbf{p} \in \mathbb{I}(G) \mid p(S) \geq v(S) - \epsilon|S| \text{ for all } S \subseteq N \}.$$

Just as for the strong least core, we define the *value of the weak least core* of G as $\epsilon_\mathbf{W}(G) = \inf\{\epsilon \geq 0 \mid \mathrm{WC}_\epsilon(G) \neq \emptyset\}$; the *weak least core* (denoted by $\mathbb{WLC}(G)$) is the weak $\epsilon_\mathbf{W}$-core of G. Again, a continuity argument shows that every profit-sharing game has a non-empty weak least core.

Similarly to the additive cost of stability, both the value of the weak least core and the value of the strong least core can be obtained as optimal values of certain linear programs. We can think of all three notions as different *measures* of (in)stability. For instance, it is clear that conditions $\epsilon_\mathbf{S}(G) > 0$, $\epsilon_\mathbf{W}(G) > 0$, and $\mathrm{addCoS}(G) > 0$ are pairwise equivalent, as each of them holds if and only if the core of G is empty. We will now discuss the relationship between the weak least core, the strong least core, and the cost of stability in more detail.

3.4.1 The Strong Least Core

The goal of this section is to establish upper and lower bounds on $\mathrm{addCoS}(G)$ in terms of $\epsilon_{\mathbf{S}}(G)$. We start by showing that their ratio never exceeds the number of players n. This proof is simply by adding $\epsilon_{\mathbf{S}}(G)$ to each agent.

Proposition 3.13. *Let $G = \langle N, v \rangle$ be a profit-sharing game. Then* $\mathrm{addCoS}(G) \leq n\epsilon_{\mathbf{S}}(G)$, *and this bound is tight even for simple games.*

For the remainder of this section, we use the following construction. Given a game G with an empty core, we set $\epsilon = \epsilon_{\mathbf{S}}(G)$ and define a new game $G_\epsilon = \langle N, v_\epsilon \rangle$, where $v_\epsilon(S) = v(S) - \epsilon$ for all $S \subsetneq N$, and $v_\epsilon(N) = v(N)$. Intuitively, G_ϵ is obtained by imposing the minimum penalty on deviating coalitions that ensures stability, just as $\overline{G}$ is obtained by providing the minimum subsidy that ensures stability. Clearly, $\mathbb{C}(G_\epsilon) = \mathbb{SLC}(G)$.

We will now show when the upper bound shown in Proposition 3.13 can be improved.

Theorem 3.14. *Let $G = \langle N, v \rangle$ be a superadditive profit-sharing game, Then* $\mathrm{addCoS}(G) \leq \sqrt{n} \cdot \epsilon_{\mathbf{S}}(G)$, *and this bound is tight up to a small additive constant.*

An immediate corollary that follows by Equation (3.2), is that $\mathrm{RSR}(G) \leq 1 + \frac{\mathrm{addCoS}(G)}{v(N)} \leq 1 + \frac{\sqrt{n}\epsilon_{\mathbf{S}}(G)}{v(N)}$. Since $\epsilon_{\mathbf{S}}(G) \leq v(N)$ and it is usually significantly smaller, Theorem 3.14 strengthens Theorem 3.4 for almost every game.

We now focus on establishing a lower bound on $\mathrm{addCoS}(G)/\epsilon_{\mathbf{S}}(G)$. We begin with a simple example. Consider a game $G = \langle N, v \rangle$ with $N = \{1, 2\}$, and suppose that the core of G is empty. This means that $v(\{1\}) + v(\{2\}) > v(\{1, 2\})$. Clearly, we have $\mathrm{addCoS}(G) = v(\{1\}) + v(\{2\}) - v(\{1, 2\})$. On the other hand, it is not hard to see that for $n = 2$ the strong least core coincides with the weak least core, and $\epsilon = \epsilon_{\mathbf{W}}(G) = \epsilon_{\mathbf{S}}(G)$ satisfies $\epsilon = v(\{1\}) - p_1 = v(\{2\}) - p_2$, where (p_1, p_2) is a payoff vector in the strong least core. Together with the constraint $p_1 + p_2 = v(\{1, 2\})$ this implies $2\epsilon = \mathrm{addCoS}(G)$.

This is illustrated in Fig-

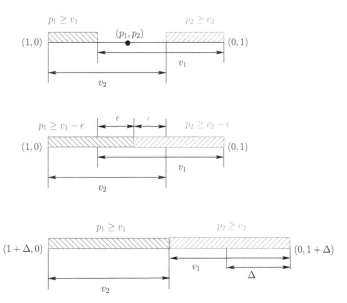

Figure 3.1: The core, the strong least core, and the additive cost of stability in a two-player game.

ure 3.1, where we scale the characteristic function so that $v(N) = 1$ and set $v_1 = v(\{1\})$, $v_2 = v(\{2\})$; the space of all pre-imputations for G corresponds to the one-dimensional simplex (i.e., the segment $[0, 1]$); and each of the core constraints corresponds to a halfspace of this space. The core is empty if and only if these halfspaces do not intersect (top figure). To find the

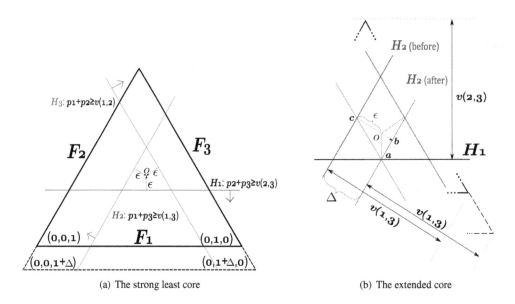

(a) The strong least core   (b) The extended core

Figure 3.2: In Fig. 3.2(a), the three hyperplanes in the figure contradict one another. The point o is the least-core, induced by moving all three hyperplanes an equal distance of ϵ. The dashed line shows the new simplex induced by increasing the value of the grand coalition. In Fig. 3.2(b), we can see the locations of all three hyperplanes before and after translation. H_1 is fixed, and H_2, H_3 move to the intersection point a. We see that H_2 moved exactly Δ as its distance from the opposing vertex is fixed to $v(1,3)$, thus $\overline{ab} = \Delta$. Also, $\overline{ao} = \overline{co} = \epsilon$, and $\overline{ob} = \frac{1}{2}\overline{ao} = \frac{\epsilon}{2}$, since the angle $\angle bao$ is 30°. Thus $\Delta = \overline{ab} = \overline{ao} + \overline{ob} = \epsilon + \frac{\epsilon}{2} = 1\frac{1}{2}\epsilon$.

strong least core, we move both halfspaces towards each other at the same rate until they meet, i.e., we increase ϵ until the ϵ-core is no longer empty (middle figure). To find the additive cost of stability, we stretch our segment from $[0,1]$ to $[0, 1 + \Delta]$, while the constraints remain "locked" to its endpoints; we increase Δ until the halfspaces that correspond to the core constraints intersect (bottom figure).

The graphical approach described above builds on the geometric representation of the least core that was proposed by Maschler, Peleg, and Shapley [1979], and can be extended to an arbitrary number of players. Specifically, we can think of every payoff vector $\mathbf{p} \in \mathbb{I}(G)$ as a point in an $(n-1)$-dimensional simplex of height $v(N)$, where each agent corresponds to a face of the simplex, and p_i is the distance from $\mathbf{p}$ to face i (an illustration of the core of a game with three players appears in Figure 2.1). Note that $\sum_{i \in N} p_i$ is always equal to the height of the simplex.

Every core constraint corresponds to some coalition, and defines a halfspace of admissible payoff vectors. The core is then the intersection of all such halfspaces. To find the strong least core of a game with an empty core, we move all halfspaces until they intersect (see Figure 3.2).

Similarly, to determine the additive cost of stability, we keep one vertex fixed to its location, and move only the other $n-1$ vertices. Halfspaces are "locked" to their corresponding faces, and move with them. Thus the halfspaces converge somewhat more slowly towards their intersection point. By formalizing this analysis, we obtain the following lower bound on addCoS(G).

Theorem 3.15. *Let $G = \langle N, v \rangle$ be a profit-sharing game. Then* $\mathrm{addCoS}(G) \geq \frac{n}{n-1} \epsilon_{\mathbf{S}}(G)$, *and this bound is tight.*

Proposition 3.13 and Theorem 3.15 establish a quantitative relationship between the additive cost of stability and the value of the strong least core. We conjecture that the strong least core is also closely related to the extended core.

Conjecture 3.16. *For every profit-sharing game G with an empty core we have* $\mathbb{SLC}(G) \subseteq \mathbb{EC}(G)$.

In other words, we conjecture that payoff vectors in the strong least core are also the ones that are the easiest to stabilize: for every $\mathbf{p} \in \mathbb{SLC}(G)$ it holds that $\mathrm{addCoS}(\mathbf{p}, G) = \mathrm{addCoS}(G)$. It is possible to verify that Conjecture 3.16 holds for $n = 2$ and $n = 3$ (see Prop. A.3 in the appendix); proving it for $n \geq 4$ is an interesting open problem. Note that the conjecture implies that the pre-nucleolus $\mathbf{pn}(G)$ (which is contained in the strong least core) is also the easiest vector to stabilize. Yet a stronger conjecture would be that the nucleolus of $\overline{G}$ would itself be a non-negative extension of $\mathbf{pn}(G)$.

3.4.2 The Weak Least Core

Consider a game with an empty core G. A simple observation is that the additive Cost of Stability equals n times the value of the weak least core (see also [Bejan and Gómez, 2009]).

To see why this is true, let $\Delta > 0$, take any pre-imputation $\mathbf{p} \in \mathbb{I}(G)$, and add $\epsilon = \Delta/n$ to every agent, s.t. $\mathbf{p}' = \mathbf{p} + \mathbf{1} \cdot \epsilon$. For any coalition $S \subsetneq N$, $p(S) \geq v(S) - |S|\epsilon$ if and only if $p'(S) \geq v(S)$.[5] In particular, $\mathbf{p} \in \mathrm{WC}_\epsilon(G)$ if and only if $\mathbf{p}' \in \mathbb{C}(G(\Delta))$, and thus

$$n\epsilon_{\mathbf{W}}(G) = n\min\{\epsilon \geq 0 \mid \mathrm{WC}_\epsilon(G) \neq \emptyset\} = \min\{n\epsilon \geq 0 \mid \mathbb{C}(G(n\epsilon)) \neq \emptyset\} = \mathrm{addCoS}(G).$$
(3.9)

Clearly, this also entails that $\mathbb{WLC}(G) \subseteq \mathbb{EC}(G)$, as any payoff vector $\mathbf{z} \in \mathbb{WLC}(G)$ can be transformed into a stable payoff vector in $\mathbb{S}(G)$ by adding ϵ to every coordinate.

For superadditive games, Eq. (3.9) allows us to derive the following bounds.

Corollary 3.17 (from Theorems 3.14 and 3.15). *Let $G = \langle N, v \rangle$ be a superadditive profit-sharing game. Then*
$$\sqrt{n}\epsilon_{\mathbf{W}}(G) \leq \epsilon_{\mathbf{S}}(G) \leq (n-1) \cdot \epsilon_{\mathbf{W}}(G).$$

3.5 The Cost of Stability in Games with Coalition Structures

So far, we have tacitly assumed that the only possible outcome of a coalitional game is the formation of the grand coalition. This makes sense in s-additive games or when the context dictates that only one coalition can be formed (as with companies competing for a contract).

The situations where agents can split into teams to work on several tasks can be modeled as *TU games with coalition structures* [Aumann and Dréze, 1974]. In this section, we consider the problem of stabilizing TU games with coalition structures. See Section 2.2.1 for basic definitions.

---

[5] Note that payoff vectors in the least core may have negative entries.

The core of games with coalition structures   Given a TU game $G = \langle N, g \rangle$, we extend the notation $\mathcal{CS}(N)$ to subsets of N: given a set $S \subseteq N$, we denote by $\mathcal{CS}(S)$ the set of all partitions of S.

A *pre-imputation* for a coalition structure $CS = (S^1, \ldots, S^m)$ in a coalitional game $G = \langle N, g \rangle$ is a vector $\mathbf{p} = (p_1, \ldots, p_n)$ that satisfies $\sum_{i \in S^j} p_i = |g(S^j)|$ for every $j = 1, \ldots, m$. That is, just as in the setting without coalitions structures, p_i is the profit received by (respectively, cost incurred on) player i. We emphasize that the profit (expenses) of each coalition in a coalition structure is distributed among the coalition members. We denote the set of all pre-imputations for a coalition structure CS by $\mathbb{I}(CS)$.

An *outcome* of a TU game $G = \langle N, g \rangle$ with coalition structures is a pair $(CS, \mathbf{p})$, where $CS \in \mathcal{CS}(N)$ and $\mathbf{p} \in \mathbb{I}(CS)$. Just as for games without coalition structures, we are interested in outcomes that are stable. Such outcomes are said to form the *CS-core* of G. More formally, an outcome $(CS, \mathbf{p})$ is said to be in the *CS-core* of G if $\mathbf{p}$ is not blocked by any coalition, i.e., $\mathbf{p} \in \mathbb{S}(G)$. Note that stability constraints are the same regardless of the coalition structure being formed, that is $\mathbb{S}(G)$ is the same whether coalition structures are allowed or not. We will denote the CS-core of a game G by $\mathbb{CSC}(G)$. Also, for a particular structure CS we set

$$\mathbb{C}(G, CS) = \{\mathbf{p} \in \mathbb{I}(CS) \mid (CS, \mathbf{p}) \in \mathbb{CSC}(G)\} = \mathbb{I}(CS) \cap \mathbb{S}(G).$$

Note that $\mathbf{p}$ is in the core of G if and only if $(N, \mathbf{p})$ is in the CS-core of G.

In Example 2.2, for instance, allowing coalition structures means that contractors do not compete over a single project, but rather that any group of contractors with 10 trucks can take on a project and share its profits. As shown, under this interpretation (of multiple projects) the CS-core of the game is non-empty (in contrast to the core), and contains $(CS = \{\{1, 2, 3\}, \{4\}\}, \mathbf{p} = (0, 0, 10, 10))$.

3.5.1   Subsidizing the socially optimal coalition structure

As in [Bachrach et al., 2009a], the quantity $\mathrm{addCoS_{cs}}(G)$, which we will call the *additive coalitional cost of stability* of G, is the minimal subsidy needed to stabilize G if agents are allowed to form coalition structures. Since the only difference from $\mathrm{addCoS}(G)$ is the amount that agents can generate without the subsidy, $\mathrm{addCoS_{cs}}(G) = \mathrm{addCoS}(G) - (\mathbf{OPT}(G) - v(N))$. The *multiplicative coalitional cost of stability* of G can be similarly defined as in Definition 3.2. For example, $\mathrm{RSR}_{CS}(G) = \mathrm{RSR}(G)\frac{v(N)}{\mathbf{OPT}(G)} = \frac{\mathbf{OPT}(G) + \mathrm{addCoS_{cs}}(G)}{\mathbf{OPT}(G)}$ for profit sharing games.

Following Aumann and Drèze [1974], we define the *superadditive cover* of a profit-sharing game $G = \langle N, v \rangle$ as a game $G^* = \langle N, v^* \rangle$ given by $v^*(S) = \max_{CS \in \mathcal{CS}(S)} v(CS)$. Note that for $S = N$ we get $v^*(N) = v(\widehat{CS})$. It is easy to see that G^* is a superadditive game: for every pair of non-overlapping coalitions, S^1, S^2 we have $(S^1, S^2) \in \mathcal{CS}(S^1 \cup S^2)$ and hence $v^*(S^1 \cup S^2) \geq v(S^1) + v(S^2)$. The *subadditive cover* $G^* = \langle N, c^* \rangle$ of an expense-sharing game $G = \langle N, c \rangle$ is defined similarly: we have $c^*(S) = \min_{CS \in \mathcal{CS}(S)} c(CS)$. Clearly, $G^* = \langle N, c^* \rangle$ is subadditive. We will refer to both the superadditive covers of profit-sharing games and the subadditive covers of expense-sharing games as *s-additive covers* of the respective games.

We will now show that the coalitional cost of stability of a given game equals the cost of stability of its s-additive cover.

Proposition 3.18. *Let $G = \langle N, g \rangle$ be a coalitional game, and let $G^* = \langle N, g^* \rangle$ be its s-additive cover. Then $\mathrm{addCoS_{cs}}(G) = \mathrm{addCoS}(G^*)$ and $\mathrm{multCoS_{cs}}(G) = \mathrm{multCoS}(G^*)$.*

Proposition 3.18 follows almost immediately from in [Greco et al., 2011b, Theorem 3.5].[6]

By Proposition 3.18 we can directly translate all of the upper bounds in this chapter (e.g., in Theorem. 3.4) to bounds on $\text{multCoS}_{cs}(G)$ *omitting the super/subadditivity requirement.*

3.6 Related Work

The term "cost of stability" was introduced in a joint paper with Yoram Bachrach, Michael Zuckerman, Jörg Rothe and Jeffrey S. Rosenschein, who defined this concept formally, proved several bounds on the additive cost of stability, and presented computational complexity results for the cost of stability in weighted voting games [Bachrach et al., 2009]. This short paper was later extended by Bachrach *et al.* [2009a], who studied general classes of games (see results in Section 3.3.1), and showed for example that computing the CoS is NP-complete under natural assumptions on the representation of the game.

Recent research on subsidies and the CoS Since the first papers on the CoS, several groups of researchers studied the cost of stability, focusing mainly on computational questions. Aadithya *et al.* [2011] showed that for coalitional games represented by algebraic decision diagrams, the cost of stability can be computed in polynomial time. Greco *et al.* [2011c] proved bounds on the complexity of computing the cost of stability, for games with and without coalition structures. Bounds in other classes of games have been studied in [Resnick et al., 2009; Aziz et al., 2010; Bachrach et al., 2013; Bachrach and Shah, 2013].

A model for subsidies in coalitional games was independently suggested by Bejan and Gómez [2009], who focused (as we do in Section 3.4) on the relationship between subsidies and other solution concepts. We adopted some of their notation, which is useful in our case as well. However, in their work the additional payment required to stabilize a game is collected from the participating agents by means of a specific *taxation* system, rather than injected into the game by an external authority, whereas we do not assume any form of taxation. The taxation approach was extended by Zick *et al.* [2013], who also studied the connections between taxes and the CoS. The relation between the CoS and another property of TU games (which aims to measure how far a game is from being a weighted voting game), was studied in [Freixas and Kurz, 2011].

Approximate core Several other researchers studied subsidies and other issues about incentives in expense-sharing games using different terminology. Specifically, Deng *et al.* [1999] show that a coalitional game whose characteristic function is given by an integer program of a certain form has a non-empty core if and only if the linear relaxation of this problem has an integer solution. Their argument can be used to relate the multiplicative cost of stability in such games and the integrality gap of the respective program. The connection between the integrality gap and the multiplicative cost of stability is made explicit in the work of Goemans and Skutella [2004] in the context of facility location games.

An application that has drawn much attention is routing in networks, which was initially formulated as a minimum spanning tree game [Claus and Kleitman, 1973]. In the minimum spanning tree game the agents are nodes of a graph, and each edge is a connection that has a fixed price. The cost of a coalition is the price of the cheapest tree that connects all participating nodes to the source node. The additive cost of stability in this particular game is always 0, as its core is never empty [Granot and Huberman, 1981]. However, there is a more realistic variation of this game known as the Steiner tree game, where nodes are allowed to route through nodes that are not part

---

[6]Our work preceded that of Greco at al. [2011b]. See [Meir et al., 2010].

	Any	s-additive games / Games with coalition structures		
		all	k-size	anonymous
Profit (upper bound on RSR)	n (#)	$\sqrt{n}$ (#)	$\min\{k, \sqrt{n}\}$ (Thm. 3.7)	2 (#)
Expense (lower bound on CRR)	0	$\frac{1}{\ln n + 1}$ (Cor. 3.10)	$\frac{1}{\ln k + 1}$ (Cor. 3.10)	$1/2$ (Thm. 3.12)

Table 3.1: The multiplicative cost of stability for different classes of TU games. All bounds are asymptotically tight. #—[Bachrach et al., 2009a].

of their coalition. Megiddo [1978] showed that the core of the Steiner tree game may be empty, and therefore its cost of stability is nontrivial. Jain and Vazirani [2001] proposed a mechanism for the Steiner tree game with cost recovery ratio of $1/2$, under the stronger requirements of group strategyproofness.[7]

A different line of research [Skorin-Kapov, 1995] suggested a cost-sharing mechanism for Steiner trees that does not guarantee strategyproofness, and showed *empirically* that it allocates at least 92% of the cost on all tested instances. This finding indicates that the average-case CoS may be much lower than the worst-case in other classes of TU games as well.

Other cost-sharing mechanisms for many different games have been suggested. For example, Moulin and Shenker [2001] studied the tradeoff between efficiency and the CRR in subadditive expense-sharing games; see [Pál and Tardos, 2003; Jain and Mahdian, 2007; Immorlica et al., 2005] for an overview.

3.7 Conclusion

We provided bounds on the cost of stability for general games and under various restrictions on the characteristic function, such as super- and subadditivity and anonymity, and extended our results to the case where the goal is to stabilize some coalition structure rather than the grand coalition. Our results are summarized in Table 3.1. We have also explored the relationship between the cost of stability and the (strong and weak) least core, leaving some interesting open questions for future research, especially regarding the minimal subsidy required to stabilize the prenucleolus.

In the next chapter, we show how the RSR can be further bounded by considering finer restrictions on valid coalitions. Bounding the cost of stability of a game is important as a metric to how "unstable" the game is. Thus, for example, we now know that all subadditive anonymous games cannot be very unstable. The CoS is also useful as a design tool for an external authority interested in a stable outcome. Such an authority may ponder the effectiveness of subsidies, perhaps comparing the induced level of stability to other forms of intervention that change the game.

---

[7]More precisely, Jain and Vazirani [2001] demanded full cost recovery and relaxed stability constraints. The bound on the cost of stability is achieved if we divide their proposed payments by 2.

Chapter 4

Subsidies, Stability, and Restricted Cooperation

Abstract. We study the stability of cooperative games played over an interaction network, in a model that was introduced by Myerson [1977]. We show that the cost of stability of such games (CoS, the subsidy required to stabilize the game) can be bounded in terms of natural parameters of their underlying interaction networks. Specifically, we prove that if the treewidth of the interaction network H is k, then the relative cost of stability of *any* game played over H is at most $k + 1$ and this is tight in the worst case. We then provide similar results for the pathwidth, and show how our results can be used to derive bounds on the CoS in many classes of games from the literature.

4.1 Introduction

In the previous chapter, we considered the problem of games with empty cores, and suggested the *cost of stability* both as a measure to the instability of a game, and as a design tool that enables an external party to incentivize cooperation between agents who would otherwise be reluctant to join in one coalition. Specifically, we showed how stability may be achieved via *subsidies*: an external party may try to stabilize the game by offering a lump sum to the agents if they form some desired coalition structure. The minimum subsidy required to guarantee stability is known as the *cost of stability (CoS)* [Bachrach et al., 2009a]. Several other ways have been proposed in order to capture the intuition behind the notion of the core, while relaxing the core constraints—the *least-core*, for example (see Section 3.4).

Another approach, pioneered by Myerson [1977], assumes that interaction among agents may be limited, and that agents cannot deviate unless they can communicate with one another. In more detail, the game has an underlying interaction network, called the *Myerson graph*: agents are nodes, and an edge indicates the presence of a communication link. Permissible coalitions correspond to connected subgraphs of the Myerson graph. Myerson's model is a type of restriction scheme known as a *partition system* [Bilbao, 2000, Chapter 5].

In this chapter, we study the interplay between restricted interaction and the cost of stability. Our goal is to bound the relative cost of stability in terms of structural properties of the interaction network (represented by the Myerson graph). One such property is the *treewidth*: this is a combinatorial measure of graph structure that, intuitively, says how close a graph is to being a tree. Breton, Owen and Weber [1992] have demonstrated a connection between structure and stability by showing that if the Myerson graph is a tree, then the core of the game is non-empty. This result was later independently reproduced by Demange [2004], who also provided an efficient algorithm for constructing a core imputation. It is thus natural to ask if the CoS of games whose Myerson graphs have small treewidth, is low.

4.1.1 Related Work

Literature on subsidies has been covered in the previous chapter (Section 3.6). A survey of restricted cooperation in TU games is in [Grabisch, 2009]. Recently, Greco *et al.* [2011b] studied questions related to the CoS in games with restricted cooperation in the Myerson model, mainly from a computational complexity perspective. Extension of the Myerson model to directed graphs have also been suggested [Li and Li, 2011; Khmelnitskaya, 2010]. Other effects of network structure on subsidies have also been studied in fairly different settings, as in [Elliott and Golub, 2013].

It is well-known that many graph-related problems that are computationally hard in the general case become tractable once the treewidth of the underlying graph is bounded by a constant (see, e.g., [Courcelle, 1990]). There are several graph-based representation languages for cooperative games, and for many of them the complexity of computational questions that arise in cooperative game theory (such as finding an outcome in the core or an optimal coalition structure) can be bounded in terms of the treewidth of the corresponding graph [Ieong and Shoham, 2005; Aziz et al., 2009; Bachrach et al., 2010; Greco et al., 2011a; Voice et al., 2012]. Bounding the treewidth of the Myerson graph however, *does not* lead to a tractable solution for these computational questions,[1] as shown by Greco *et al.* [2011b] and later by Chalkiadakis *et al.* [2012].

4.1.2 Results in this chapter

In Section 4.3 we provide a complete characterization of the relationship between the treewidth of the interaction network and the worst-case cost of stability. We prove that for *any game G* played over a network of treewidth k, its *required subsidy ratio* (RSR, also known as the multiplicative cost of stability) is at most $k + 1$. This is done by first showing the bound for simple games, and then extending it to general games. We emphasize that throughout the chapter we assume that agents may form *coalition structures* (as in Section 3.5). We further show that the bound of $k + 1$ is tight whenever $2 \leq k \leq \sqrt{n}$.

In Section 4.4 we prove a similar result with respect to the *pathwidth* of the interaction network, showing that the RSR is bounded by the pathwidth k (without the additional 1), and that this bound is also tight.

In both sections we provide algorithms that explicitly construct a stable payoff vector. The runtime of these algorithms may be exponential in n in the general case, but for simple monotone games an outcome can be computed efficiently. Some important implications of our result for various classes of cooperative games are drawn in Section 4.5.

Finally, we show in Section 4.6 that bounded treewidth (even $k = 2$) does not enable efficient algorithms for computing optimal coalition structures. This (together with a similar negative result by Greco *et al.* [2011b] regarding the computation of the CoS) leads to the conclusion that bounding the treewidth of the Myerson graph has little impact from a computational perspective, but great significance from an economic perspective.

---

[1]Except for the special case of width 1 mentioned above.

To the best of our knowledge, our work is the first to employ treewidth in order to prove a game-theoretic result that is not algorithmic in nature.

4.2   Preliminaries

For the standard notations of cooperative games, see Sections 2.2 and 3.2. Following Aumann and Dréze [1974], we assume that agents may form coalition structures. We follow the definitions of Section 3.5, and refresh some of the concepts we will use.

Payoffs and Stability   Recall that $\mathbf{OPT}(G) = \max\{v(CS) \mid CS \in \mathcal{CS}(\mathcal{N})\}$. A payoff vector $\mathbf{x}$ is a *pre-imputation* for a coalition structure CS if for all $S \in CS$ it holds that $x(S) = v(S)$. A pair of the form $(CS, \mathbf{x})$, where $CS \in \mathcal{CS}(\mathcal{N})$ and $\mathbf{x}$ is a pre-imputation for CS, is referred to as an *outcome* of the game $G = \langle N, v \rangle$. Recall that $\mathbb{S}(G)$ denotes the set of all payoff vectors (not necessarily pre-imputations) that satisfy the stability constraints.

We say that an outcome $(CS, \mathbf{x})$ of a game $G = \langle N, v \rangle$ is *stable* if $\mathbf{x}$ is a pre-imputation for CS and $\mathbf{x} \in \mathbb{S}(G)$. The set of all stable outcomes of G is called the *core* of G, and is denoted $\mathbb{CSC}(G)$.

The *required subsidy ratio* (denoted by RSR, and also known as the multiplicative cost of stability) of a game G, is the ratio between smallest total payoff that stabilizes the game, and the maximal available payoff:

$$\mathrm{RSR}_{CS}(G) = \inf_{\mathbf{x} \in \mathbb{S}(G)} \frac{x(N)}{\mathbf{OPT}(G)}. \quad \text{(compare with Eq. (3.2))}$$

Since we assume coalition structures are used throughout the chapter, we replace the terms $\mathbb{CSC}(G)$ and $\mathrm{RSR}_{CS}(G)$ with $\mathbb{C}(G)$ and $\mathrm{RSR}(G)$, respectively.

4.2.1   Interaction graphs and their treewidth

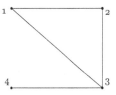

An *interaction network* (also called a *Myerson graph*) over N is a graph $H = \langle N, E \rangle$. Given a game $G = \langle N, v \rangle$ and an interaction network over N, we define a game $G|_H = \langle N, v|_H \rangle$ by setting $v|_H(S) = v(S)$ if S is a connected subgraph of H, and $v|_H(S) = 0$ otherwise; that is, in $G|_H$ a coalition $S \subseteq N$ may form if and only if its members are connected (See Fig. 4.1).

Figure 4.1: The graph H. The coalition $\{1, 2, 3\}$ is allowed, but $\{1, 2, 4\}$ is not.

A *tree decomposition* of H is a tree $\mathcal{T}$ over the nodes $V(\mathcal{T})$ such that:
- Each node of $\mathcal{T}$ is a subset of N.
- For every pair of nodes $X, Y \in V(\mathcal{T})$ and every $i \in N$, if $i \in X$ and $i \in Y$ then for any node Z on the (unique) path between X and Y in $\mathcal{T}$ we have $i \in Z$.
- For every edge $e = \{i, j\}$ of E there exists a node $X \in V(\mathcal{T})$ such that $e \subseteq X$.

The *width* of a tree decomposition $\mathcal{T}$ is $tw(\mathcal{T}) = \max_{X \in V(\mathcal{T})} |X| - 1$; the *treewidth* of H is

$$tw(H) = \min\{tw(\mathcal{T}) \mid \mathcal{T} \text{ is a tree decomposition of } H\}.$$

If a graph H has a treewidth of at most k, then it is possible to find a tree decomposition of H whose width is k in $f(k)O(n)$ time, for some function f. Examples of graphs with low treewidth include trees (whose treewidth is 1) and series-parallel graphs (whose treewidth is at most 2); see, e.g., [Bodlaender and Kloks, 1996; Bodlaender and van Antwerpen-de Fluiter, 2001].

Given a subtree $\mathcal{T}'$ of a tree decomposition $\mathcal{T}$ (we use the term "subtree" to refer to any connected subgraph of $\mathcal{T}$), we denote the agents that appear in the nodes of $\mathcal{T}'$ by $N(\mathcal{T}')$. Conversely, given a set of agents $S \subseteq N$, let $\mathcal{T}(S)$ denote the subgraph of $\mathcal{T}$ induced by nodes $\{X \in V(\mathcal{T}) \mid X \cap S \neq \emptyset\}$; it is not hard to check that $\mathcal{T}(S)$ is a subtree of $\mathcal{T}$ for every $S \subseteq N$. Given a tree decomposition $\mathcal{T}$ of H and a node $R \in V(\mathcal{T})$, we can set R to be the root of $\mathcal{T}$. In this case, we denote the subtree rooted in a node $S \in V(\mathcal{T})$ by $\mathcal{T}_S$.

A tree decomposition of a graph H such that $\mathcal{T}$ is a path is called a *path decomposition* of H. The *pathwidth* of H is $pw(H) = \min\{tw(\mathcal{T}) \mid \mathcal{T}$ is a path decomposition of $H\}$.

For any graph H, $tw(H) \leq pw(H)$ and $pw(H) = tw(H) \cdot O(\log(n))$.

4.2.2   Cost of stability and the degree of H

Before we head to our main results on the treewidth, we test the natural conjecture that the multiplicative cost of stability (RSR) of a game is related to the *degree* of the Myerson graph (as low degree means sparser graph and fewer valid coalitions).

Let $d(H)$ be the maximum degree of a node in H. Is it true that $\mathrm{RSR}(G|_H) \leq g(d(H))$, for some function g? Our next proposition shows that this conjecture is false. The proof (see appendix) shows that *any* superadditive simple game can be embedded in a 3-dimensional grid network.

Proposition 4.1. *For any $k \in \mathbb{N}$ there exists an interaction network H with $d(H) = 6$ and a simple superadditive game G with $\mathrm{RSR}(G|_H) \geq k$.*

4.3   Treewidth and the Cost of Stability

Our goal in this section is to provide a general upper bound on the cost of stability for TU games whose interaction networks have bounded treewidth. We start by proving a bound for simple games; we then show how to extend it to the general case.

4.3.1   Simple Games

We now show that for any simple game $G = \langle N, v \rangle$ and an interaction network H over N, $\mathrm{RSR}(G|_H) \leq tw(H) + 1$. Our proof is constructive: we show that Algorithm 1, whose input is a simple game $G = \langle N, v \rangle$, a network H, a parameter k, and a tree decomposition $\mathcal{T}$ of H of width at most k, outputs a stable payoff vector $\mathbf{x}$ for $G|_H$ such that $x(N) \leq (tw(H) + 1) \cdot \mathbf{OPT}(G|_H)$.

Superadditive simple games   Before presenting the full algorithm, we will provide some intuition by describing a simpler algorithm for the superadditive case (i.e., games such that $G|_H$ is superadditive). Since G is also simple, this means that any two winning coalitions in $G|_H$ intersect. Hence, for every pair of winning coalitions $S_1, S_2 \subseteq N$ the subtrees $\mathcal{T}(S_1)$ and $\mathcal{T}(S_2)$ intersect. This implies that there exists a node $A \in V(\mathcal{T})$ that belongs to the intersection of *all* subtrees that correspond to winning coalitions in $\mathcal{T}$, and hence intersects every winning coalition. Therefore we can stabilize the game by paying 1 to every agent in A. Thus, our total payment is $|A| \leq tw(\mathcal{T}) + 1 \leq k + 1$.

We now turn to the more general case of arbitrary simple games. Briefly, Algorithm 1 picks an arbitrary node $R \in V(\mathcal{T})$ to be the root of $\mathcal{T}$ and traverses the nodes of $\mathcal{T}$ from the leaves towards the root. Upon arriving at a node A, it checks whether the subtree $\mathcal{T}_A$ contains a coalition that is winning in $G|_H$ (note that we have to check every subset of $N(\mathcal{T}_A) \cap N_t$, since $G|_H$ is not

---

Mechanism 1 STABLE-TW$(G = \langle N, v \rangle, H, k, \mathcal{T})$

Fix an arbitrary $R \in V(\mathcal{T})$ to be the root
$t \leftarrow 0 \quad N_1 \leftarrow N \quad \mathbf{x} \leftarrow 0^n$
for $A \in V(\mathcal{T})$, traversed from the leaves upwards **do**
    $t \leftarrow t + 1$
    if $\exists S \subseteq N(\mathcal{T}_A) \cap N_t$ s.t. $v|_H(S) = 1$ **then**
        for $i \in A \cap N_t$ **do**
            $x_i \leftarrow 1$
        end for
        $N_{t+1} \leftarrow N_t \setminus N(\mathcal{T}_A)$
    else
        $N_{t+1} \leftarrow N_t$
    end if
end for **return** $\mathbf{x} = (x_1, \ldots, x_n)$

---

necessarily monotone). If this is the case, it pays 1 to all agents in A and removes all agents in $\mathcal{T}_A$ from every node of $\mathcal{T}$. Note that every winning coalition in $\mathcal{T}_A$ has to be connected, so either it is fully contained in a proper subtree of $\mathcal{T}_A$ or it contains agents in A. The reason for deleting the agents in $\mathcal{T}_A$ is simple: every winning coalition that contains members of $\mathcal{T}_A$ is already stable (one of its members is getting a payoff of 1). The algorithm then continues up the tree in the same manner until it reaches the root. We note that Algorithm 1 is similar in spirit to the one proposed by Demange [2004]; however, Algorithm 1 may pay $2 \cdot \mathbf{OPT}(G|_H)$ if H is a tree. Moreover, unlike Demange's algorithm for trees, Algorithm 1 may require exponential time. However, if the simple game given as input is *monotone*, a straightforward modification (check whether $v|_H(S) = 1$ only for $S = N(\mathcal{T}_A)$ rather than for every $S \subseteq N(\mathcal{T}_A)$) makes it run in polynomial time.

Theorem 4.2. *For every simple game $G = \langle N, v \rangle$ and every interaction network H over N,* $\mathrm{RSR}(G|_H) \leq tw(H) + 1.$

Proof. Let $\mathcal{T}$ be a tree decomposition of H such that $tw(\mathcal{T}) = k$. Let $\mathbf{x}$ be the output of Algorithm 1. We claim that $\mathbf{x}$ is stable and $x(N) \leq (k+1)\mathbf{OPT}(G|_H)$.

To prove stability, consider a coalition S with $v|_H(S) = 1$; we need to show that $x(S) > 0$. Suppose for the sake of contradiction that $x(S) = 0$; this means that each agent in S is deleted before he is allocated any payoff. Consider the first time-step when an agent in S is deleted; suppose that this happens at step t when a node $A \in V(\mathcal{T})$ is processed. Clearly for an agent in S to be deleted at this step it has to be the case that $\mathcal{T}(S) \cap \mathcal{T}_A \neq \emptyset$. Further, it cannot be the case that $S \cap (A \cap N_t) \neq \emptyset$, since each agent in $A \cap N_t$ is assigned a payoff of 1 at step t, and we have assumed that $x(S) = 0$. Therefore, $\mathcal{T}(S)$ must be a proper subtree of $\mathcal{T}_A$. Let B be the root of $\mathcal{T}(S)$, and consider the time-step $t' < t$ when B is processed. At time t', all agents in S are still present in $\mathcal{T}$, so the node B meets the **if** condition in Algorithm 1, and therefore each agent in B gets assigned a payoff of 1. This is a contradiction, since B is the root of $\mathcal{T}(S)$, and therefore $B \cap S \neq \emptyset$, which implies $x(S) > 0$.

It remains to show that $x(N) \leq (k+1)\mathbf{OPT}(G|_H)$. To this end, we will construct a specific coalition structure CS^* and argue that $x(N) \leq (k+1)v|_H(CS^*)$. The coalition structure CS^* is constructed as follows. Let A_t be the node of the tree considered by Algorithm 1 at time t, and let $S_t = N(\mathcal{T}_{A_t}) \cap N_t$, i.e., S_t is the set of all agents that appear in $\mathcal{T}_{A_t}$ at time t. Let T^* be the set of all values of t such that A_t meets the **if** condition in Algorithm 1. For each $t \in T^*$ the set S_t

contains a winning coalition; let W_t be an arbitrary winning coalition contained in S_t. Finally, let $L = N \setminus (\cup_{t \in T^*} W_t)$, and set $CS^* = \{L\} \cup \{W_t \mid t \in T^*\}$.

Observe that CS^* is a coalition structure, i.e., a partition of N. Indeed, $L \cap W_t = \emptyset$ for all $t \in T^*$, and, moreover, if $i \in W_t$ for some $t > 0$, then i was removed from $\mathcal{T}$ at time t, and cannot be a member of coalition $W_{t'}$ for $t' > t$. Further, we have $v_H(CS^*) \geq |T^*|$.

To bound the total payment, we observe that no agent is assigned any payoff at time $t \notin T^*$, and each agent that is assigned a payoff of 1 at time $t \in T^*$ is a member of A_t. Hence we have

$$x(N) = \sum_{t \in T^*} x(A_t) \leq \sum_{t \in T^*} |A_t| \leq (k+1)|T^*| \leq (k+1)v|_H(CS^*) \leq (k+1)\mathbf{OPT}(G),$$

which proves that $\mathrm{RSR}(G) \leq k + 1$. $\qquad\qquad\qquad\qquad\qquad\qquad\qquad\qquad\qquad\qquad\square$

4.3.2 The General Case

Using Theorem 4.2, we are now ready to prove our main result.

Theorem 4.3. *For every game* $G = \langle N, v \rangle$ *and every interaction network* H *over* N *it holds that* $\mathrm{RSR}(G|_H) \leq tw(H) + 1$.

Proof. Given a game $G' = \langle N, v' \rangle$, let $\#(G') = |\{S \subseteq N \mid v'(S) > 0\}|$. We prove the theorem by induction on $\#(G|_H)$. If $\#(G|_H) = 1$ then $\mathrm{RSR}(G|_H) = 1$: any outcome of this game where the positive-value coalition forms is stable. Now suppose that our claim is true whenever $\#(G|_H) < m$; we will show that it holds for $\#(G|_H) = m$. To simplify notation, we identify v with $v|_H$, i.e., we write v in place of $v|_H$ throughout the proof.

We define a simple game $G' = \langle N, v' \rangle$ by setting $v'(S) = 1$ if $v(S) > 0$ and $v'(S) = 0$ otherwise. By Theorem 4.2, there exists a payoff vector $\mathbf{x}'$ such that $x'(S) \geq v'(S)$ for all $S \subseteq N$ and $x'(N) \leq (tw(H) + 1)v(CS')$, where CS' is an optimal coalition structure for G'. Moreover, we can assume that $\mathbf{x}' \in \{0,1\}^n$, as Algorithm 1 outputs such a payoff vector.

We set $\epsilon = \min\{v(S) \mid v(S) > 0\}$ and define a game $G'' = \langle N, v'' \rangle$ by setting $v''(S) = \max\{0, v(S) - \epsilon x'(S)\}$. Intuitively, we "split" G to a simple game $\epsilon G'$ and a remainder G'', and stabilize each one independently.

Consider a coalition S with $v(S) = \epsilon$. We have $v'(S) = 1$ and hence $x'(S) = 1$. Therefore, $v''(S) = 0$ and hence $\#(G'') < m$, so the induction hypothesis applies to G''. Therefore, there is a stable payoff vector $\mathbf{x}''$ such that $x''(N) \leq (tw(H) + 1)\mathbf{OPT}(G'')$, We set $\mathbf{x} = \epsilon \mathbf{x}' + \mathbf{x}''$. We will now show that $x(N) \leq (tw(H) + 1)\mathbf{OPT}(G)$ and $x(S) \geq v(S)$ for all $S \subseteq N$.

We have $x(S) = \epsilon x'(S) + x''(S) \geq \epsilon x'(S) + v''(S) \geq \epsilon x'(S) + v(S) - \epsilon x'(S) = v(S)$ for all $S \subseteq N$, so $\mathbf{x}$ is a stable payoff vector for G.

Let CS'' be an optimal coalition structure for G''. We can assume without loss of generality that there is only one coalition of value 0 in CS''; we denote this coalition by S_0.

Let $N^* = N \setminus S_0$; $t^* = |\{S \in CS'_+ \mid S \cap N^* \neq \emptyset\}|$; and $t_0 = |\{S \in CS'_+ \mid S \subseteq S_0\}|$. We have that $v'(CS') = |CS'_+| = t^* + t_0$, and

$$\sum_{S \in CS''_+} x'(S) = x'(N^*) \geq \sum_{S \in CS'_+} x'(S \cap N^*) \geq \sum_{S \in CS'_+} v'(S \cap N^*) \geq |\{S \in CS'_+ \mid S \cap N^* \neq \emptyset\}|.$$

We are now ready to bound $x(N)$. Using the last inequality, we obtain

$$x(N) = \epsilon x'(N) + x''(N) \le \epsilon(tw(H) + 1)v'(CS') + (tw(H) + 1)v''(CS'')$$

$$= (tw(H) + 1)\left(\epsilon|CS'_+| + \sum_{S \in CS''_+} (v(S) - \epsilon x'(S))\right)$$

$$\le (tw(H) + 1)\left(\epsilon|CS'_+| + v(CS''_+) - \epsilon t^*\right) = (tw(H) + 1)\left(v(CS''_+) + \epsilon t_0\right).$$

Further, $t_0 = \sum_{S \in CS'_+ : S \subseteq S_0} v'(S) \le \sum_{S \in CS'_+ : S \subseteq S_0} \frac{1}{\epsilon} v(S)$, thus

$$x(N) \le (tw(H) + 1)\left(v(CS''_+) + \sum_{S \in CS'_+ : S \subseteq S_0} v(S)\right).$$

The coalitions in the right-hand side of this expression form a partition of (a subset of) N, so their total value under v does not exceed $\mathbf{OPT}(G|_H)$. $\qquad\square$

The multiplicative cost of stability of any TU game, even with unrestricted cooperation, is at most $\sqrt{n}$ (see Chapter 3). Thus, we obtain $\mathrm{RSR}(G|_H) \le \min\{tw(H) + 1, \sqrt{n}\}$, assuming that coalition structures are allowed. For superadditive games Theorem 4.3 implies that there is some stable payoff vector $\mathbf{x}$ such that $x(N) \le (tw(H) + 1)v(N)$.[2]

4.3.3 Tightness

We will now show that if the treewidth of the interaction network is at least 2, then the upper bound of $tw(H) + 1$ proved in Theorem 4.3 is tight.

Theorem 4.4. *For every $k \ge 2$ there is a simple superadditive game $G = \langle N, v \rangle$ and an interaction network H over N such that $tw(H) = k$ and $\mathrm{RSR}(G|_H) = k + 1$.*

Proof sketch. Instead of defining H directly, we will describe its tree decomposition $\mathcal{T}$. There is one central node $A = \{z_1, \ldots, z_{k+1}\}$. For every unordered pair $I = \{i, j\}$, where $i, j \in \{1, \ldots, k+1\}$ and $i \ne j$, we define a set D_I that consists of 7 agents and set $N = A \cup \bigcup_{i \ne j \in \{1, \ldots, k+1\}} D_{\{i,j\}}$.

The tree $\mathcal{T}$ is a star, where leaves are all sets of the form $\{z_i, z_j, d\}$, where $d \in D_{\{i,j\}}$. That is, there are $7 \cdot \binom{k+1}{2}$ leaves, each of size 3. Since the central node of $\mathcal{T}$ is of size $k+1$, it corresponds to a network of treewidth at most k. We set $\mathcal{D}_i = \bigcup_{j \ne i} D_{\{i,j\}}$; observe that for any two agents $z_i, z_j \in A$ we have $\mathcal{D}_i \cap \mathcal{D}_j = D_{\{i,j\}}$. Given $\mathcal{T}$, it is now easy to construct the underlying interaction network H: there is an edge between z_i and every $d \in D_{\{i,j\}}$ for every $j \ne i$; see Figure 4.2 for more details.

For every unordered pair $I = \{i, j\} \subseteq \{1, \ldots, k+1\}$, let $\mathcal{Q}_I$ denote the projective plane of dimension 3 (a.k.a. the Fano plane, marked by dotted lines in Fig. 4.2) over D_I. That is, $\mathcal{Q}_I$ contains seven triplets of elements from D_I, so that every two triplets intersect, and every element $d \in D_I$ is contained in exactly 3 triplets in $\mathcal{Q}_I$. Winning sets are defined as follows. For every $i = 1, \ldots, k+1$ the set $\{z_i\} \cup \bigcup_{j \ne i} \mathcal{Q}_{\{i,j\}}$ is winning. Thus for every z_i there are 7^k winning coalitions containing z_i, each of size $1 + 3k$.

---

[2]Note that, while the proof for *simple* superadditive games is straightforward, we cannot use the inductive argument made in Theorem 4.3 directly, as superadditivity may not be preserved.

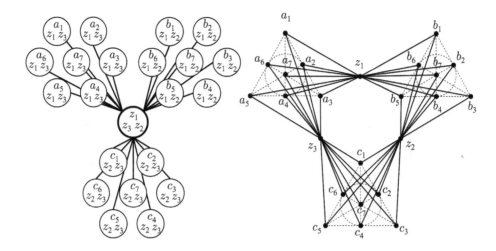

Figure 4.2: The interaction network of Theorem 4.4 for $k = 2$ (left), and its tree decomposition (right). Here, $D_{1,3} = \{a_1, \ldots, a_7\}$, $D_{1,2} = \{b_1, \ldots, b_7\}$ and $D_{2,3} = \{c_1, \ldots, c_7\}$. An edge connects z_1 to all agents in $D_{1,3}$ and $D_{1,2}$, z_2 to $D_{1,2}$ and $D_{2,3}$, and z_3 to $D_{1,3}$ and $D_{2,3}$. Agent z_1 forms winning coalitions with triplets of agents from $D_{1,2}$ and $D_{1,3}$ that are on a dotted line; z_2 and z_3 form winning coalitions with their respective sets as well.

We can observe that all winning coalitions intersect, which implies that the simple game induced by these winning coalitions is indeed superadditive and has an optimal value of 1. It remains to verify that every stable payoff vector must pay at least $k + 1$ to the agents (see appendix). $\square$

The proof of Theorem 4.4 is not applicable when $k = 1$, since the width of our construction is at least 2 (each leaf is of size 3). Indeed, if Theorem 4.4 were to hold for $k = 1$, we would obtain a contradiction with Demange's result.

4.4   Pathwidth and the Cost of Stability

For some graphs we can bound not just their treewidth, but also their pathwidth. For example, for a simple cycle graph both the treewidth and the pathwidth are equal to 2. For games over networks with bounded pathwidth, the bound of $tw(H) + 1$ shown in Section 3 can be tightened.

Theorem 4.5. *For every TU game $G = \langle v, N \rangle$ and every interaction network H over N it holds that $\mathrm{RSR}(G|_H) \leq pw(H)$, and this bound is tight.*

Proof Sketch. We argue that, given a simple game G and a network H, Algorithm 5 (see Appendix B.2) outputs a stable payoff vector $\mathbf{x}$ such that $x(N) \leq pw(H) \cdot \mathbf{OPT}(G|_H)$. First, Algorithm 5 pays 1 to all winning singletons and removes them from the game; it can be shown that this step does not increase the cost of stability. Next, we proceed in a manner similar to Algorithm 1; however, when processing a node A_j such that $N(\mathcal{T}_{A_j})$ contains a winning coalition, we do not pay any agent $i \in A_j$ such that $i \notin N(\mathcal{T}_{A_j}) \setminus A_j$. Paying such agents is not necessary, as any winning coalition that contains them must contain some other agent in A_j that is paid 1 by the algorithm. It can be shown that such agents are guaranteed to exist, thus not all agents in A_j are paid. We then employ an inductive argument similar to the one in Theorem 4.3. To show tightness, we use a slight modification of the construction from Section 3. $\square$

4.5 Implications for Games on Graphs

Our results apply to several well-studied classes of cooperative games. The following definition, which appears in [Potters and Reijnierse, 1995], becomes useful in showing this.

Let $H = \langle N, E \rangle$ be an interaction network. We say that two coalitions $S, T \subseteq N$ are *connected* in H if there exists an edge $(i, j) \in E$ such that $i \in S$, $j \in T$; otherwise S and T are said to be *disconnected*. A TU game $G = \langle N, v \rangle$ is said to be *H-component additive* if for every pair of coalitions S, T that are disconnected in H, it holds that $v(S \cup T) = v(S) + v(T)$. If G is H-component additive then G is essentially equivalent to $G|_H$: these games can only differ in values of infeasible coalitions.

There are many classes of combinatorial TU games defined over graphs, where every game in the class is component-additive with respect to the graph on which it is defined; our results hold for all of these classes. Some examples include induced subgraph games [Deng and Papadimitriou, 1994]; matching games, edge cover games, coloring games and vertex connectivity games [Deng et al., 1999]; and social distance games [Brânzei and Larson, 2011].[3] While some of these games are known to have a non-empty core, our results hold for unstable variants of them as long as they maintain component-additivity.

Games over hypergraphs Another two classes of games—Synergy Coalition Groups [Conitzer and Sandholm, 2006] and Marginal Contribution Nets [Ieong and Shoham, 2005]—are defined over collections of subsets, i.e., hypergraphs. Now, the notion of an interaction network can be naturally extended to that of an interaction hypergraph, an idea suggested by Myerson himself as well as by others (see [Bilbao, 2000], p. 112): a coalition can form only if for any two coalition members i and j there is a sequence of overlapping hyperedges that connect them.

The concepts of treewidth and tree decomposition of a hypergraph coincide with the corresponding definitions applied to its *primal graph* [Gottlob et al., 2001]. Therefore, all of our proofs work for games whose interaction networks are hypergraphs with bounded treewidth. The notion of a component-additive game can be extended to games on hypergraphs, and it is not hard to show that both Synergy Coalition Groups and Marginal Contribution Nets are component-additive with respect to their underlying hypergraphs. Hence, our results hold for these models as well.

4.6 Structure and Computational Complexity

We define the decision problem OPTCS as follows: it receives as input a game $G = \langle N, v \rangle$, an interaction network H and some value $\alpha \in \mathbb{R}$; it outputs yes if and only if there is some partition $S_1, \ldots, S_k$ of N such that $\sum_{j=1}^{k} v|_H(S_j) \geq \alpha$. We assume oracle access to v.[4]

It is known that if H is a tree and G is a simple monotone game then there is a polynomial algorithm for OPTCS . This is by selecting an arbitrary root and iteratively isolate winning coalitions from the leafs upwards (similarly to the procedure of Algorithm 1, see [Demange, 2004; Meir et al., 2012]).

We next show that the conditions of tree-structure, monotonicity, and simple game are minimal.

Proposition 4.6. OPTCS *(G, H) is NP-hard even in the following cases:*
(a) $tw(H) = pw(H) = 2$, G is simple and monotone.

---

[3]Brânzei and Larson [2011] define an NTU version of social distance games; however a TU version can be naturally defined.

[4]This means that for every $S \subseteq N$ we can access $v(S)$ in constant time.

(b) H is a tree, G is simple but not monotone.
(c) H is a tree, G is monotone but not simple.

Proof sketch of (a). Our reduction is from an instance of the PARTITION problem [Garey and Johnson, 1979]. Given a PARTITION instance $(a_1, \ldots, a_n)$ we define a weighted voting game with $n+2$ players, setting $w_i = a_i$ for $i \leq n$, $w_x = w_y = 0$. The threshold is $q = \frac{1}{2} \sum_{i \leq n} w_i$. Our interaction network H over the player set is defined as follows: there are edges (i, x) and (i, y) for all $1 \leq i \leq n$; observe that $tw(H) = 2$. Thus a coalition wins iff its weight is at least q, and it contains either x or y (for connectivity). Thus $\mathbf{OPT}(G|_H) = 2$ if and only if the weights can be partitioned into two equal sets. $\square$

Computing the CoS It is well known that in the general case computing the exact CoS of a game, is an NP-hard problem [Bachrach et al., 2009a]. It is therefore a natural question whether a restricted interaction structure helps in that respect. While it was shown by Greco *et al.* [2011b] that the answer is affirmative in case the network H is a tree, they also showed that the problem remains NP-hard even for graphs with tree-width (and path-width) of 2.

We find it quite remarkable that, contrary to the common wisdom, the treewidth of the Myerson graph plays no role from an algorithmic perspective (except for the special case of a tree), but does have significant game-theoretic implications.

4.7 Conclusion

We saw that the required subsidy ratio (RSR) of any cooperative game is bounded by the treewidth of the social network by which players are connected. Simply put, as the network of social connections becomes "simpler" and with fewer cycles, the game becomes easier to stabilize. To the best of our knowledge, this is the first time that the notion of treewidth has been used to obtain results that are purely game-theoretic rather than algorithmic in nature.[5]

While we provide a stronger bound with respect to pathwidth, the bound on the treewidth is more significant; indeed, Theorem 4.5 improves upon Theorem 4.3 only when the treewidth equals the pathwidth, which is uncommon.

Our results imply a separation between games whose interaction networks are acyclic (i.e., with treewidth 1), which have been shown to be stable [Demange, 2004] (i.e., RSR of 1), and other games. For any higher value of treewidth, the RSR is somewhat higher than the treewidth. In particular, the result of Demange *is not* a special case of our theorem, although a slight modification of our algorithm can be used to provide an alternative proof for Demange's theorem.

Hypertreewidth We have argued in Section 4.5 that our results can be extended to hypergraphs, giving a bound on the RSR in terms of the treewidth of the interaction hypergraph. Gottlob *et al.* [2001] describe a stronger notion of width for hypergraphs, called *hypertreewidth*. This definition can result in a much lower width for general hypergraphs, and it is an open question whether it can provide us with a better bound on the RSR.

---

[5] Interestingly, game-theory has been useful in characterizing hypergraphs with low hypertreewidth [Gottlob et al., 2003]. We establish a novel connection in the opposite direction.

The least core   In Chapter 3 we saw that the value of both the strong least core and the weak least core of a cooperative game can be bounded in terms of its additive cost of stability. Our combined results imply that any bound on the treewidth or pathwidth of the interaction graph translates into a bound on this other well-known measure of inherent instability.

Chapter 5

Convergence of Iterative Voting

Abstract. In this chapter we consider voting scenarios where voters cannot coordinate their actions, but are allowed to *change their vote* after observing the current outcome. Such scenarios are common in small committees and in online polls (for example on Facebook). We focus on the Plurality voting rule, and study the conditions under which this iterative game is guaranteed to converge to a Nash equilibrium (i.e., to a decision that is stable against further unilateral changes). Our main result is that if voters restrict their behavior to natural best-response, the game always converges. We conclude with an extensive discussion of iterative voting and its prospects.

5.1 Introduction

In this chapter we consider a game where players should reach a joint decision (say, select a candidate for a tenure track position), using the Plurality voting rule. While it is known that no reasonable voting rule is completely immune to strategic behavior, Plurality has been shown to be particularly susceptible, both in theory and in practice [Saari, 1990; Forsythe et al., 1996; Friedgut et al., 2008]. This makes the analysis of any voting scenario—even one where the simple and common Plurality rule is used—a challenging task. As voters may speculate and counter-speculate, it would be beneficial to have formal tools that would help us understand (and perhaps predict) the final outcome.

Natural tools for this task include well-studied solution concepts developed for non-cooperative games. While voting is not always presented as a game, several natural formulations have been proposed (see Sections 5.6 and 2.1.2 for related work). Moreover, such formulations are extremely simple in Plurality voting games, where voters only have a few available ways to vote.

The most prominent solution concept for games—the Nash equilibrium—has typically been overlooked when it comes to voting, mainly because it appears to be too weak: there are typically many Nash equilibria in a voting game, and most of them are trivial. For example, if all voters vote for the same candidate, then this is clearly an equilibrium, since any single agent cannot change the result.

The lack of a single prominent solution for the game suggests that in order to fully understand the outcome of the voting procedure, it is not sufficient to consider voters' preferences. The strategies voters' choose to adopt, as well as the information available to them, are necessary for the analysis of possible outcomes. To play an equilibrium strategy for example, voters must have some beliefs about the preferences of others. Partial knowledge (as well as a communication method) is also required in order to collude with other voters.

We make no assumption about the beliefs of the voters, who may be completely oblivious about the preferences of others. We do assume however that voters cannot or will not coordinate their actions. Such situations may arise, for example, when voters do not trust one another or have restricted communication abilities. Thus, even if two voters have exactly the same preferences, they may be reluctant or unable to share this information, and hence they will each vote independently. Voters may still try to vote strategically, based on their current information, which may be partial or wrong. The analysis of such settings is of particular interest to AI as it tackles the fundamental problem of multi-agent decision making, where autonomous agents (that may be distant, self-interested and/or unknown to one another) have to choose a joint plan of action or allocate resources or goods. The central questions are (i) whether, (ii) how fast, and (iii) on what alternative the agents will agree.

In our (Plurality) voting model, voters start from some announcement (e.g., the truthful one), but can change their votes after observing the announcements of other voters and the current outcome. The game proceeds in turns, where a single voter changes his vote at each turn. This process is similar to online polls via Doodle or Facebook, where users can log-in at any time and change their vote.

5.1.1 Results in this Chapter

We study different versions of this game, varying tie-breaking rules, weights and policies of voters, and the initial profile. Our main result shows that in order to guarantee convergence under deterministic tie-breaking from any initial state, it is sufficient that voters restrict their actions to natural best replies, and that this restriction cannot be relaxed. A similar result still holds under randomized tie-breaking, provided that voters start from the truthful state.

5.2   Preliminaries

We denote the set of n voters by V. The alternatives, or *candidates* are denoted by C where $|C| = m$.

As explained in detail in Chapter 2, every voting rule induces a *game form*. In the case of the Plurality rule, this game form is particularly simple, as every voter only needs to specify his top candidate, and the game form is a function $f : C^n \to 2^C \setminus \emptyset$.

We extend this game form by including the possibility that only k out of the n voters may play strategically. We denote by $K \subseteq V$ the set of k strategic voters, which are called *agents*, or *manipulators*. The set $B = V \setminus K$ contains the $n - k$ additional voters who have already cast their votes, and are not participating in the game. Thus, the outcome is $f(a_1, \ldots, a_k, b_{k+1}, \ldots, b_n)$, where $b_{k+1}, \ldots, b_n$ are fixed as part of the game form. This separation of the set of voters does not affect generality, but allows us to encompass situations where only some of the voters behave strategically.

The Plurality game form   According to the Plurality rule, the winner is the candidate (or a set of those) with the most votes, where votes may be weighted. The weight of voter $i \le n$ is denoted by $w_i \in \mathbb{N}$. The *initial score* $\hat{s}(c)$ of a candidate c is defined as the total weight of the fixed voters who selected c—i.e., $\hat{s}(c) = \sum_{j \in B: b_j = c} w_j$. The *final score* of c for a given joint action $\mathbf{a} \in C^k$ (also called a *voting profile*) is the total weight of voters that chose c (including the fixed set B):

v_1, v_2	a	b	c
a	$(14, 9, 3)$ $\{a\}$	$(10, 13, 3)$ $\{b\}$	$(10, 9, 7)$ $\{a\}$
b	$(11, 12, 3)$ $\{b\}$	$(7, 16, 3)$ $\{b\}$	$(7, 12, 7)$ $\{b\}$
c	$(11, 9, 6)$ $\{a\}$	$(7, 13, 6)$ $\{b\}$	$(7, 9, 10)$ $\{c\}$

Table 5.1: There is a set $C = \{a, b, c\}$ of candidates with initial scores $\hat{s} = (7, 9, 3)$. Voter 1 has weight 3 and voter 2 has weight 4. Thus, $GF_T = \langle\{a, b, c\}, \{1, 2\}, (3, 2), (7, 9, 3)\rangle$. The table shows the outcome vector $s(a_1, a_2)$ for every joint action of the two voters, as well as the set of winning candidates $GF_T(a_1, a_2)$. In this example there are no ties, and it thus fits both tie-breaking schemes.

$s(c, \mathbf{a}) = \hat{s}(c) + \sum_{i \in K : a_i = c} w_i$. We sometimes write $s(c)$ if the joint action is clear from the context. We write $s(c) >_p s(c')$ if either $s(c) > s(c')$ or the score is equal and c has a higher priority (lower index). We denote by PL_R the Plurality rule with randomized tie breaking, and by PL_D the Plurality rule with deterministic tie breaking in favor of the candidate with the lower index. We have that

$$PL_R(\hat{s}, \mathbf{w}, \mathbf{a}) = \text{argmax}_{c \in C}\, s(c, \mathbf{a}), \text{ and}$$
$$PL_D(\hat{s}, \mathbf{w}, \mathbf{a}) = \{c \in C \text{ s.t. } \forall c' \neq c, s(c, \mathbf{a}) >_p s(c', \mathbf{a})\}.$$

Note that $PL_D(\hat{s}, \mathbf{w}, \mathbf{a})$ is always a singleton, whereas $PL_R(\hat{s}, \mathbf{w}, \mathbf{a})$ is a set.

For any joint action, its *outcome vector* $\mathbf{s}(\mathbf{a})$ contains the score of each candidate: $\mathbf{s}(\mathbf{a}) = (s(c_1, \mathbf{a}), \ldots, s(c_m, \mathbf{a}))$. For a tie-breaking scheme T $(T \in \{D, R\})$ the *Game Form* $GF_T = \langle C, K, \mathbf{w}, \hat{s}\rangle$ specifies the winner for any joint action of the agents—i.e., $GF_T(\mathbf{a}) = PL_T(\hat{s}, \mathbf{w}, \mathbf{a})$. Table 5.1 demonstrates a game form with two weighted manipulators.

5.2.1 Incentives

We now complete the definition of our voting game, by adding incentives to the game form. The order $\succ_i \in \mathcal{R}$ reflects the preferences of voter i, where $\mathcal{R}$ is the set of all strict orders over C. The vector containing the preferences of all k agents is called a *preference profile*, and is denoted by $\mathbf{r} = (\succ_1, \ldots, \succ_k)$. The game form GF_T, coupled with a preference profile $\mathbf{r}$, define a normal form game $G_T = \langle GF_T, \mathbf{r}\rangle$ with k agents. agent i prefers outcome $GF_T(\mathbf{a})$ over outcome $GF_T(\mathbf{a}')$ if $GF_T(\mathbf{a}) \succ_i GF_T(\mathbf{a}')$.

Note that for deterministic tie-breaking, every pair of outcomes can be compared. If ties are broken randomly, $\succ_i$ does *not* induce a complete order over outcomes, which are *sets* of candidates. A natural solution is to augment agents' preferences with cardinal utilities, where $u_i(c) \in \mathbb{R}$ is the utility of candidate c to agent i. This definition naturally extends to multiple winners by setting $u_i(W) = \frac{1}{|W|} \sum_{c \in W} u_i(c)$.[1] A utility function u is *consistent* with a preference relation $\succ_i$ if $u(c) > u(c') \Leftrightarrow c \succ_i c'$.

Lemma 5.1. *For any utility function u which is consistent with preference order $\succ_i$, the following holds:*

1. *$a \succ_i b \Rightarrow \forall W \subseteq C \setminus \{a, b\}, u(\{a\} \cup W) > u(\{b\} \cup W)$;*

---

[1] One interpretation is that we randomize the final winner from the set W. For a thorough discussion of cardinal and ordinal utilities in normal form games, see [Borgers, 1993].

v_1, v_2	a	b	* c
* a	$\{a\}$ **3, 2**	$\{b\}$ 2, 1	* $\{a\}$ **3, 2**
b	$\{b\}$ 2, 1	$\{b\}$ **2, 1**	$\{b\}$ 2, 1
c	$\{a\}$ 3, 2	$\{b\}$ 2, 1	$\{c\}$ 1, 3

Table 5.2: A game $G_T = \langle GF_T, \mathbf{r} \rangle$, where GF_T is as in Table 5.1, and $\mathbf{r}$ is defined by $a \succ_1 b \succ_1 c$ and $c \succ_2 a \succ_2 b$. The table shows the ordinal utility of the outcome to each agent (the final score is not shown). **Bold** outcomes are the NE points. Here the truthful vote (marked with *) is also a NE.

v_1, v_2	a	b	* c
* a	$\{a\}$ 3, 1	$\{b\}$ **1, 2**	* $\{a\}$ 3, 1
b	$\{b\}$ 1, 2	$\{b\}$ **1, 2**	$\{b\}$ 1, 2
c	$\{a\}$ 3, 1	$\{b\}$ 1, 2	$\{c\}$ 2, 3

Table 5.3: This game has the same game form as in Table 5.1, and the preference profile $a \succ_1 c \succ_1 b$ and $c \succ_2 b \succ_2 a$. In this case, the truthful vote is not a NE.

2. $\forall b \in W, a \succ_i b \Rightarrow u(a) > u(\{a\} \cup W) > u(W)$.

By Lemma 5.1, any order $\succ_i$ induces a partial preference order on the set of outcomes, but this order is not complete if the cardinal utilities are not specified. For instance, the order $a \succ_i b \succ_i c$ does not determine if i will prefer $\{b\}$ over $\{a, c\}$. When utilities are given explicitly, every pair of outcomes can be compared, and we will slightly abuse the notation by using $GF_R(\mathbf{a}) \succ_i GF_R(\mathbf{a}')$ to note that i prefers the outcome of action $\mathbf{a}$ over that of $\mathbf{a}'$.

5.2.2 Manipulation and Stability

Having defined a normal form game, we can now apply standard solution concepts. Let $G_T = \langle GF_T, \mathbf{r} \rangle$ be a Plurality voting game, and let $\mathbf{a} = (a_{-i}, a_i)$ be a joint action in G_T. We say that $a_i \xrightarrow{i} a_i'$ is an *improvement step* of agent i if $GF_T(a_{-i}, a_i') \succ_i GF_T(a_{-i}, a_i)$. A joint action $\mathbf{a}$ is a *Nash equilibrium* (NE), if no agent has an improvement step from $\mathbf{a}$ in G_T. That is, no agent can gain by changing his vote, provided that others keep their votes unchanged. A priori, a game with pure strategies does not have to admit any NE. However, in our voting games there are typically (but not necessarily) many such points.

Now, observe that the preference profile $\mathbf{r}$ induces a special joint action $\mathbf{a}^*$, termed the *truthful vote*, such that $\mathbf{a}^*(\mathbf{r}) = (a_1^*, \ldots, a_k^*)$, where $a_i^* \succ_i c$ for all $c \neq a_i^*$. We also call $\mathbf{a}^*(\mathbf{r})$ the *truthful state* of G_T, and refer to $GF_T(\mathbf{a}^*(\mathbf{r}))$ as the *truthful outcome* of the game. If i has an improvement step in the truthful state, then this is a *manipulation*.[2] Thus, $\mathbf{r}$ cannot be manipulated if and only if $\mathbf{a}^*(\mathbf{r})$ is a Nash equilibrium of $G_T = \langle GF_T, \mathbf{r} \rangle$. However, the truthful vote may or may not be included in the NE points of the game, as can be seen from Table 5.2 and 5.3 that demonstrate games that are induced by adding incentives to the game form shown in Table 5.1, and indicate the truthful states and the NE points in these games.

---

[2]This definition of manipulation coincides with the standard definition from social choice theory.

5.2.3 Game Dynamics

We finally consider natural *dynamics* in Plurality voting games. Assume that agents start by announcing some initial vote, and then proceed and change their votes until no one has objections to the current outcome. It is not clear how rational agents would act to achieve a stable decision, especially when there are multiple equilibrium points. However, one can make some plausible assumptions about their behavior. First, the agents are likely to only make improvement steps, and to keep their current strategy if such a step is not available. Thus, the game will end when it first reaches a NE. Second, it is often the case that the initial state is truthful, as agents know that they can reconsider and vote differently, if they are not happy with the current outcome.

We start with a simple observation that if the agents may change their votes simultaneously, then convergence is not guaranteed, even if the agents start with the truthful vote and use best replies—that is, vote for their most preferred candidate out of potential winners in the current round.

Proposition 5.2. *If agents are allowed to re-vote simultaneously, the game may never converge.*

Example 5.2. The counterexample is the game with 3 candidates $\{a, b, c\}$ with initial scores given by $(0, 0, 2)$. There are 2 voters $\{1, 2\}$ with weights $w_1 = w_2 = 1$ and the following preferences: $a \succ_1 b \succ_1 c$, and $b \succ_2 a \succ_2 c$. The two agents will repeatedly swap their strategies, switching endlessly between the states $\mathbf{a(r)} = (a, b)$ and (b, a). Note that this example works for both tie-breaking schemes. ◇

We therefore restrict our attention to dynamics where simultaneous improvements are not available. That is, given the initial vote $\mathbf{a}_0$, the game proceeds in steps, where at each step t, a single agent may change his vote, resulting in a new state (joint action) $\mathbf{a}_t$. The process ends when no agent has objections, and the outcome is set by the last state. Such a restriction makes sense in many computerized environments, where voters can log-in and change their vote at any time.

5.2.4 Types of moves

Let us first provide some useful notation. We denote the outcome at time t by $o_t = PL(\mathbf{a}_t) \subseteq C$, and its score by $s(o_t)$. Suppose that agent i has an improvement step at time t, and as a result the winner switched from o_{t-1} to o_t. The possible steps of i are given by one of the following types (an example of such a step appears in parentheses):

type 1 from $a_{i,t-1} \notin o_{t-1}$ to $a_{i,t} \in o_t$; (step 1 in Ex.5.4a.)

type 2 from $a_{i,t-1} \in o_{t-1}$ to $a_{i,t} \notin o_t$; (step 2 in Ex.5.4a.)

type 3 from $a_{i,t-1} \in o_{t-1}$ to $a_{i,t} \in o_t$; (step 1 in Ex.5.4b.),

where inclusion is replaced with equality for deterministic tie-breaking. We refer to each of these steps as a *better reply* of agent i. If $a_{i,t}$ is i's most preferred candidate capable of winning, then this is a *best reply*.

Remark 5.1. *Any rational move of a myopic agent in the normal form game corresponds to exactly one of the three types of better-reply. In contrast, our definition of best-reply is somewhat different from the traditional definition in game theory, which allows the agent to choose any strategy that guarantees him a best possible outcome. For example, a voter could possibly make o_t become a winner by just removing his vote from o_{t-1} and voting for some other candidate with the lower score. We refer to this type of move as an* extended best-reply. *In this work, we assume the improver* *makes the more natural response by actually voting for o_t. Thus, under our definition, the best reply is always unique.*

Note that there are no best replies of type 2. Finally, we denote by $s_t(c)$ the score of a candidate c *without the vote of the currently playing agent*; thus, it always holds that $s_{t-1}(c) = s_t(c)$.

5.3 Deterministic Tie-Breaking

Our first result (which is also the main result of this chapter) shows that under the most simple conditions, the game must converge.

Theorem 5.3. *Let G_D be a Plurality game with deterministic tie-breaking. If all agents have weight 1 and use best replies, then the game will converge to a NE from any state.*

Proof. We first show that there can be at most $(m-1) \cdot k$ sequential steps of type 3. Note that at every such step $a \xrightarrow{i} b$ it must hold that $b \succ_i a$. Thus, each voter can only make $m-1$ such subsequent steps.

Now suppose that a step $a \xrightarrow{i} b$ of type 1 occurs at time t. We claim that at any later time $t' \geq t$: (I) there are at least two candidates whose score is *at least* $s(o_{t-1})$; (II) the score of a will not increase at t'. We use induction on t' to prove both invariants. Right after step t we have that

$$s_t(b) + 1 = s(o_t) >_p s(o_{t-1}) >_p s_t(a) + 1 . \tag{5.1}$$

Thus, after step t we have at least two candidates with scores of at least $s(o_{t-1})$: $o_t = b$ and $o_{t-1} \neq b$. Also, at step t the score of a has decreased. This proves the base case, $t' = t$.

Assume by induction that both invariants hold until time $t'-1$, and consider step t' by voter j. Due to (I), we have at least two candidates whose score is at least $s(o_{t-1})$. Due to (II) and Equation (5.1) we have that $s_{t'}(a) \leq_p s_t(a) <_p s(o_{t-1}) - 1$. Therefore, no single voter can make a a winner and thus a cannot be the best reply for j. This means that (II) still holds after step t'. Also, j has to vote for a candidate c that can beat $o_{t'}$—i.e., $s_{t'}(c) + 1 >_p s(o_{t'}) >_p s(o_{t-1})$. Therefore, after step t' both c and $o_{t'} \neq c$ will have a score of at least $s(o_{t-1})$—that is, (I) also holds. $\square$

The proof also supplies us with a polynomial bound on the rate of convergence. At every step of type 1, at least one candidate is ruled out permanently, and there at most k times a vote can be withdrawn from a candidate. Also, there can be at most mk steps of type 3 between such occurrences. Hence, there are in total at most m^2k^2 steps until convergence. It can be further shown that if all voters start from the truthful state then there are no type 3 steps at all. Thus, the score of the winner never decreases, and convergence occurs in at most mk steps. The proof idea is similar to that of the corresponding randomized case in Theorem 5.8.

We now show that the restriction to best replies is necessary to guarantee convergence.

Proposition 5.4. *If agents are not limited to best replies, then: (a) there is a counterexample with two agents; (b) there is a counterexample with an initial truthful vote.*

Example 5.4a. $C = \{a, b, c\}$. We have a single fixed voter voting for a, thus $\hat{s} = (1, 0, 0)$. The preference profile is defined as $a \succ_1 b \succ_1 c$, $c \succ_2 b \succ_2 a$. The following cycle consists of better replies (the vector denotes the votes (a_1, a_2) at time t, the winner appears in curly brackets):

$$(b, c)\{a\} \xrightarrow{2} (b, b)\{b\} \xrightarrow{1} (c, b)\{a\} \xrightarrow{2} (c, c)\{c\} \xrightarrow{1} (b, c) \quad \Diamond$$

Example 5.4b. $C = \{a, b, c, d\}$. Candidates a, b, and c have 2 fixed voters each, thus $\hat{s} = (2, 2, 2, 0)$. We use 3 agents with the following preferences: $d \succ_1 a \succ_1 b \succ_1 c$, $c \succ_2 b \succ_2 a \succ_2 d$ and $d \succ_3 a \succ_3 b \succ_3 c$. Starting from the truthful state (d, c, d) the agents can make the following two improvement steps (showing only the outcome): $(2, 2, 3, 2)\{c\} \xrightarrow{1} (2, 3, 3, 1)\{b\} \xrightarrow{3} (3, 3, 3, 0)\{a\}$,
after which agents 1 and 2 repeat the cycle shown in (5.4a). $\diamond$

In fact, it can be easily verified that Example 5.4a shows that convergence from an arbitrary state is not guaranteed even under extended best-reply. However, Reijngoud and Endriss [2012] later showed that if voters start from the *truthful* state, then extended best-reply is guaranteed to converge as well.

5.3.1   Weighted voters

While using the best reply strategies guaranteed convergence for equally weighted agents, this is no longer true for non-identical weights:

Proposition 5.5. *There is a counterexample with four candidates and three weighted agents that start from the truthful state and use best replies.*

However, if there are *only two* weighted voters, either restriction is sufficient to guarantee convergence.

Theorem 5.6. *Let G_D be a Plurality game with deterministic tie-breaking. If $k = 2$ and both agents (a) use best replies **or** (b) start from the truthful state, a NE will be reached.*

5.4   Randomized Tie-Breaking

The choice of tie-breaking scheme has a significant impact on the outcome, especially when there are few voters. A randomized tie-breaking rule has the advantage of being neutral—no specific candidate or voter is preferred over another.

In order to prove convergence under randomized tie-breaking, we must show that convergence is guaranteed for *any* utility function which is consistent with the given preference order. That is, we may only use the relations over outcomes that follow directly from Lemma 5.1. To disprove, it is sufficient to show that for a specific assignment of utilities, the game forms a cycle. In this case, we say that there is a *weak counterexample*. When the existence of a cycle will follow only from the relations induced by Lemma 5.1, we will say that there is a *strong counterexample*, since it holds for any profile of utility scales that fits the preferences.

In contrast to the deterministic case, the weighted randomized case does not always converge to a Nash equilibrium or possess one at all, even with (only) two strategic agents.

Proposition 5.7. *There is a strong counterexample G_R for two weighted agents with randomized tie-breaking, even if both agents start from the truthful state and use best replies.*

Example 5.7. $C = \{a, b, c\}$, $\hat{s} = (0, 1, 3)$. There are 2 agents with weights $w_1 = 5$, $w_2 = 3$ and preferences $a \succ_1 b \succ_1 c$, $b \succ_2 c \succ_2 a$ (in particular, $b \succ_2 \{b, c\} \succ_2 c$). The resulting 3×3 normal form game contains no NE states. $\diamond$

Nevertheless, the conditions mentioned are sufficient for convergence if all agents have the same weight.

Theorem 5.8. *Let G_R be a Plurality game with randomized tie-breaking. If all agents have weight 1 and use best replies, then the game will converge to a NE from the truthful state.*

Proof. Our proof shows that in each step, the current agent votes for a *less* preferred candidate. Clearly, the first improvement step of every agent must hold this invariant.

Assume, toward deriving a contradiction, that $b \xrightarrow{i} c$ at time t_2 is the first step s.t. $c \succ_i b$. Let $a \xrightarrow{i} b$ at time $t_1 < t_2$ be the previous step of the same agent i. We denote by $M_t = o_t$ the set of all winners at time t. Similarly, L_t denotes all candidates whose score is $s(o_t) - 1$.

We claim that for all $t < t_2$, $M_t \cup L_t \subseteq M_{t-1} \cup L_{t-1}$, i.e., the set of "almost winners" can only shrink. Also, the score of the winner cannot decrease. Observe that in order to contradict any of these assertions, there must be a step $x \xrightarrow{j} y$ at time t, where $\{x\} = M_{t-1}$ and $y \notin M_{t-1} \cup L_{t-1}$. In that case, $M_t = L_{t-1} \cup \{x, y\} \succ_j \{x\}$, which means either that $y \succ_j x$ (in contradiction to the minimality of t_2) or that y is not a best reply.

From our last claim we have that $s(o_{t_1-1}) \leq s(o_{t'})$ for any $t_1 \leq t' < t_2$. Now consider the step t_1. Clearly $b \in M_{t_1-1} \cup L_{t_1-1}$ since otherwise voting for b would not make it a winner.

Case 1: $c \notin M_{t_1-1} \cup L_{t_1-1}$. We have that $s_{t_1}(c) \leq s(o_{t_1-1}) - 2$. Let t' be any time s.t. $t_1 \leq t' < t_2$, then $c \notin M_{t'} \cup L_{t'}$. By induction on t', $s_{t'}(c) \leq s_{t_1}(c) \leq s(o_{t_1-1}) - 2 \leq s(o_{t'}) - 2$, and therefore c cannot become a winner at time $t' + 1$, and the improver at time $t' + 1$ has no incentive to vote for c. In particular, this holds for $t' + 1 = t_2$; hence, agent i will not vote for c.

Case 2: $c \in M_{t_1-1} \cup L_{t_1-1}$. It is not possible that $b \in L_{t_1-1}$ or that $c \in M_{t_1-1}$: since $c \succ_i b$ and i plays best reply, i would have voted for c at step t_1. Therefore, $b \in M_{t_1-1}$ and $c \in L_{t_1-1}$. After step t_1, the score of b equals the score of c plus 2; hence, we have that $M_{t_1} = \{b\}$ and $c \notin M_{t_1} \cup L_{t_1}$, and we are back in case 1.

In either case, voting for c at step t_2 leads to a contradiction. Moreover, as agents only vote for a less-preferred candidate, they make at most $m - 1$ steps each, and at most $(m - 1) \cdot k$ steps in total. $\square$

However, in contrast to the deterministic case, convergence is no longer guaranteed, if agents start from an arbitrary profile of votes. The following example shows that in the randomized tie-breaking setting even best reply dynamics may have cycles, albeit for specific utility scales.

Proposition 5.9. *If agents start from an arbitrary voting profile, there is a weak counterexample with 3 unweighted agents, even if they use best replies.*

As in the previous section, if we relax the requirement for best replies, there may be cycles even from the truthful state.

Proposition 5.10. *(a) If agents use arbitrary better replies, then there is a strong counterexample with 3 agents of weight 1. Moreover, (b) there is a weak counterexample with 2 agents of weight 1, even if they start from the truthful state.*

5.5 Truth-Biased Agents

So far we assumed purely rational behavior on the part of the agents, in the sense that they were indifferent regarding their chosen action (vote), and only cared about the outcome. Thus, for example, if an agent cannot affect the outcome at some round, he simply keeps his *current vote*. This assumption is indeed common when dealing with normal form games, as there is no reason to prefer one strategy over another if outcomes are the same. However, in voting theory it is typically assumed that a voter will vote *truthfully* unless she has an incentive to do otherwise. As our model incorporates ideas from both domains, it is important to clarify the exact assumptions that are necessary for convergence.

Consider a variation of our model where agents always prefer their higher-ranked outcomes, but will vote honestly if the outcome remains the same—i.e., the agents are *truth-biased*. Formally, let $W = PL_T(\hat{\mathbf{s}}, \mathbf{w}, a_i, \mathbf{a}_{-i})$ and $Z = PL_T(\hat{\mathbf{s}}, \mathbf{w}, a_i', \mathbf{a}_{-i})$ be two possible outcomes of i's voting. Then, the action a_i' is *better than* a_i if either $Z \succ_i W$, or $Z = W$ and $a_i' \succ_i a_i$. Note that with this definition there is a strict preference order over all possible actions of i at every step. Unfortunately, truth-biased agents may not converge even in the simplest settings (see Proposition C.1 in the appendix).

5.6   Related Work

Equilibrium analysis   As explained in Section 1.1.1, almost every voting profile is a Nash equilibrium, so other solution concepts should be considered when analyzing voting. Strong equilibrium in voting was studied by Sertel and Sanver [2004], whereas a variation of strong equilibrium for the Plurality rule was suggested by Messner and Polborn [2002]. Another solution concept that is based on coalitions is *stability scores*. For details on stability scores in Plurality voting see the next chapter and in particular Section 6.5. A different approach was suggested by Myerson [1993], who modeled to the uncertainty regarding the preferences of other voters in elections with a very large number of voters.

Another highly relevant work is that of Dhillon and Lockwood [2004] whose game formulation is identical to our deterministic setting (without iterations). They prove a necessary and sufficient condition to remove dominated voting strategies. Unfortunately, their analysis shows that this rarely occurs, making dominance perhaps a too-strong solution concept for actual situations.

Crucially, all of the aforementioned papers assume that voters have some prior knowledge regarding the preferences of others. In contrast, our model in this chapter applies to a finite number of voters, that have no knowledge regarding the distribution of other voters' preferences.

Models of iterative voting   A different type of iterative voting procedures investigated in the literature, is where voting is presented as an extensive form game with one turn for each voter. Strategic considerations in such settings have been studied by multiple researchers [Farquharson, 1969; McKelvey and Niemi, 1978; Desmedt and Elkind, 2010; Xia and Conitzer, 2010]. Since in such a game each voter plays at most once, there is no notion of "convergence". Note that in order to play optimally, the voters must have full information not only about the current state, but also about the preferences of voters who have not voted yet. Chopra *et al.* [2004] consider a variation of this model, where voters have different levels of information. In the lowest level agents are myopic and are assumed to follow a simple best-reply behavior (as we assume as well).

The convergence of best-response dynamics to a pure equilibrium in games is often showed via a *potential function* [Monderer and Shapley, 1996]. However, Kukushkin [2011] showed that the only (deterministic) voting rules that possess a potential function are dictatorial.

When considering various solution concepts for games in general and for voting in particular, a line can be drawn between *deductive* and *inductive* methods. This distinction of behavior types goes back to the works on bounded rationality [Arthur, 1994]. In deductive methods, which assume perfect rationality as in [Myerson and Weber, 1993; Messner and Polborn, 2002; Desmedt and Elkind, 2010; Xia and Conitzer, 2010] and in fact in most work in game theory, the players/voters derive their optimal action (or vote) *backward* from the equilibrium outcome. Inductive reasoning assumes that agents are not involved in complicated strategic reasoning, and are simply following some myopic policy, or a "rule of thumb" that requires little information and effort. While in a one-shot voting game it is not clear how inductive voting policies can be formulated, an iterated process is a fertile ground for the development of voting heuristics and myopic policies. The current work, as well as its extensions that are briefly summarized in the next paragraph examples of such inductive methods.

A different example of a voting procedure as an iterative game was offered by Airiau and Endriss [Airiau and Endriss, 2009]. In their paper, they study the outcome of a sequence of majority contests, each held between the incumbent winner and an offered challenger.

Recent follow-up work   Since the publication of this work [Meir et al., 2010], our iterative voting model was employed by other researchers, who further developed the model in various directions.

Iterative voting under additional voting rules, which is the most natural extension of this work, was studied independently by Lev and Rosenschein [2012] and by Reyhani and Wilson [2012]. Both papers showed that in contrast to Plurality, most standard voting rules (except Veto) do not guarantee convergence.

This observation triggered attempts to modify the voting dynamics so that convergence is guaranteed (keeping the dynamics simple when possible). Indeed, Grandi et al. [2013] offered several such myopic behaviors, and proved they must converge for various voting rules. Similarly, Gohar [2012] proved convergence and bounded the number of iterations under particular dynamics, focusing on Plurality with weighted voters.

A different study by Reijngoud and Endriss [2012] placed our model of iterative voting within a wider framework of *voting with polls*. A poll reveals some information on the current state to some voters, who in turn respond to this information in an optimal way. They also perform initial experiments (under the *impartial culture* assumption) that demonstrate how such dynamics can lead to improved efficiency. More specifically, they show that the iterative procedure leads more often to the election of the Condorcet winner, when exists. Similar experiments have also been performed by Grandi et al. [2013].

Brânzei et al. [2013] look at a different criterion of efficiency, namely the *price of anarchy*, using the social welfare of the truthful outcome as a baseline. We highlight that under their definition, the truthful outcome is necessarily optimal and thus welfare can only decrease as the dynamics takes the voters "far" from the truthful outcome.

Finally, the effect of *truth-bias* on a single-round voting game was studied empirically by Thompson et al. [2013], and theoretically by Obraztsova et al. [Obraztsova et al., 2013], who showed that such bias dramatically reduces the number of Nash equilibria in the game.

5.7   Conclusion

We summarize the results in Table 5.4. We can see that in most cases convergence is not guaranteed unless the agents restrict their strategies to "best replies"—i.e., always select their most-preferred candidate that can win. Also, deterministic tie-breaking seems to encourage convergence more often. This makes sense, as the randomized scheme allows for a richer set of outcomes, and thus agents have more options to "escape" from the current state. Neutrality can be maintained (in expectation) by randomizing a tie-breaking order and publicly announcing it *before* the voters cast their votes.

We saw that if voters are non-weighted, begin from the truthful announcement and use best reply, then they always converge within a polynomial number of steps (in both schemes), but to what outcome? The proofs show that the score of the winner can only increase, and by at most 1

Deterministic Tie breaking

Dynamics Initial state	Best reply from		Ex. best reply from		Any better reply from	
	Truth	Anywhere	Truth	Anywhere	Truth	Anywhere
Weighted ($k > 2$)	X (Ex. 5.5)	X	X	X	X	X
Weighted ($k = 2$)	V	V (Thm. 5.6a)	V	X	V (Thm. 5.6b)	X (Ex. 5.4a)
Non-weighted	V	V (Thm. 5.3)	V (#)	X (Ex. 5.4a)	X (Ex. 5.4b)	X

Randomized Tie breaking

Dynamics Initial state	Best reply from		Any better reply from	
	Truth	Anywhere	Truth	Anywhere
Weighted	X (Ex. 5.7)	X	X	X
Non-weighted	V (Thm. 5.8)	X (Ex. 5.9)	X (Ex. 5.10)	X (Ex. 5.10)

Table 5.4: We highlight cases where convergence is guaranteed. The number in brackets refers to the index of the corresponding theorem (marked with **V**) or counterexample (X). Entries with no index follow from other entries in the table. We added the newer results on extended best-reply from [Reijngoud and Endriss, 2012] so they can be compared with ours (marked with #). Also note that for truth-biased agents, convergence is not guaranteed under any of the above settings (Example C.1).

in each iteration. Thus possible winners are only candidates that are either tied with the (truthful) Plurality winner, or fall short by one vote. In other words, the winner of Plurality under iterative voting is either a Plurality winner herself, or very close to it. This intuitive finding was later formalized by Brânzei *et al.* [2013], who showed that the *dynamic price of anarchy* of Plurality is low.

A new voting rule   We observe that the improvement steps induced by the best reply policy are unique. If, in addition, the order in which agents play is fixed, we get a *new voting rule*—Iterative Plurality. In this rule, agents submit their full preference profiles, and the center simulates an iterative Plurality game, applying the best replies of the agents according to the predetermined order. It may seem at first glance that Iterative Plurality is somehow resistant to manipulations, as the outcome was shown to be an equilibrium. This is not possible of course, and indeed agents can still manipulate the new rule by submitting false preferences. Such an action can cause the game to converge to a different equilibrium (of the Plurality game), which is better for the manipulator.

Prediction and design   Two of the most important goals of social choice research, which are also the hardest, are *predicting* human voter behavior, and the *design* of artificial agents with strategic voting capabilities. The best-reply dynamics is natural, straight-forward, and requires little information. As such, and due to the convergence properties demonstrated in this work, it is an attractive "baseline" candidate both for prediction and design purposes. However, the clear disadvantage of this approach is that in the vast majority of cases (especially when there are more than a handful of voters), almost every voting profile (including the truthful one) is already a Nash equilibrium.

Our analysis is particularly suitable when the number of voters is small, for two main reasons. First, it is more practical to perform an iterative voting procedure with few participants. Second, the question of convergence is only relevant when cases of tie or near-tie are common. An analysis in the spirit of [Myerson and Weber, 1993] would be more suitable when the number of voters increases, as it rarely happens that a single voter would be able to influence the outcome, and almost any outcome is a Nash equilibrium. This limitation of our formulation is due to the fact that the behaviors of voters encompass only myopic improvements.

Chapter 6

Stability Scores

Quantifying Coalitional Stability

Abstract. We introduce a measure for the level of stability against coalitional deviations, called *stability scores*, which generalizes widely-used notions of stability in non-cooperative games. Stability scores allow for the comparison of various Nash equilibria within a particular game, and can be used to quantify the effect of game parameters on coalitional stability. We demonstrate both uses on simple congestion games. For our main results, we apply stability scores to analyze and compare the Vickrey-Clarke-Groves (VCG) and the Generalized Second Price (GSP) ad auctions, showing that the latter is far more stable.

6.1   Introduction

A *group* of individuals can often coordinate their actions in a way that will benefit the entire group—perhaps at the expense of other players. In cases where such coalitions can easily form, the stability conveyed by the Nash equilibrium as a solution concept is insufficient, and equilibria concepts that take coalitions into account are required.

A profile is a *strong equilibrium* (SE) if no coalition of agents can jointly deviate in a way that strictly increases the payoff of each coalition member [Aumann, 1959]. Intermediate levels of coalitional stability have also been suggested, such as stability against deviations of small coalitions (see, e.g., [Andelman et al., 2007]), and in particular pairs. An even more appealing solution concept than SE is the *Super-Strong Equilibrium* (SSE) that considers deviations in which no member loses while at least one member makes a positive gain (see, for example, [Feldman and Tennenholtz, 2009]).

A major problem with these proposed solutions is that they seldom exist. Indeed, SSE rarely exist even in cases where strong equilibria do exist (e.g., in simple congestion games [Holzman and Law-Yone, 1997; Andelman et al., 2007]), and even if only deviations by pairs are considered.

In this chapter we relax the requirement that no coalition will have an incentive to deviate, and suggest a quantitative measure to coalitional stability. Assuming we have a Nash equilibrium profile of a game where some pairs of agents can still deviate, we may still wish to measure its stability by referring to the *number* of pairs that have beneficial deviations from that profile. More generally, given a game and a strategy profile, we can associate with it a tuple in which the r-th entry in the tuple is the number of coalitions of size r that can gain by a deviation. This tuple determines the *stability score* of the strategy profile.

Given two strategy profiles, we need a way to decide which one is more stable. Since small coalitions are more likely to form and maintain cooperation, a natural extension is to compare stability scores of games with associated strategy profiles using a *lexicographic* ordering of the corresponding vectors.[1] For example, given an n-person game G and two Nash equilibria a and a' in G, the stability score of the former will be *better* if the number of beneficial deviations by pairs from a is *smaller* than the number of beneficial deviations by pairs from a'. Note that we could compare in the same way a pair of equilibrium profiles in *different games* (say, G and G'), as long as both games have n players.

While the existence of, say, 19 coalitions that can deviate rather than 15 does not have much significance, we usually care about the behavior of stability scores in some parameterized family of games where parameters may include number of players, size of the strategy space, etc. If the score of a is *asymptotically lower* than the score of a' (w.r.t. one of the parameters), then this may indicate that a' is substantially more prone to coalitional deviations. Moreover, when studying such a parameterized family, stability scores may assist us in understanding how the parameters of the game affect coalitional stability. This holds even if there is a unique or a prominent equilibrium.

Stability scores are particularly useful in the context of *mechanism design*, as they allow us to quantify the coalitional stability of various mechanisms and to compare mechanisms that operate in a specific domain. To illustrate this point, we consider two central mechanisms in what is perhaps the most widely studied economic scenario in recent years: ad auctions. We analyze in detail the Generalized Second Price (GSP) auction and the Vickrey-Clarke-Groves (VCG) auction, and compare their stability scores.

6.1.1   Related work

A recent application of stability scores to voting games is in [Falik et al., 2012]; see Section 6.5.

Related solution concepts in games   In the context of non-cooperative games, approximate stability is typically measured by the strength of the incentive required to convince an agent to deviate, captured for example by the concept of ϵ-Nash equilibrium [Nisan et al., 2007, p. 45]. As discussed above, stability against collusion is captured by concepts such as SE and SSE, but these often do not allow a fine distinction between various outcomes.

In addition, coalitions are the key component in *cooperative* game theory, and many variations of coalitional stability have been studied. While we are unaware of solutions concepts that quantify stability by counting coalitional deviations, models of restricted cooperation capture social constraints that may prevent the formation of some coalitions (see [Myerson, 1977], and Chapter 4 in this work). However, even if some coalition *can* gain by deviation, it may or may not do so: members of the coalition might intentionally avoid cooperation based on far-sighted prediction (an assumption underlying *coalition-proofness* for example [Bernheim et al., 1987]), or just fail to recognize the benefit in deviating. This is especially true if the coalition is large. Stability scores do not assume a particular social context or incentive structure, but simply try and minimize the number of coalitions with profitable deviations.

---

[1]There are many ways to compare stability score vectors (see [Falik et al., 2012]). Choosing the "right" one highly depends on the context and underlying assumptions. However in this work we avoid such complications by only comparing deviations of coalitions of the same size.

Collusion and equilibria in ad auctions Major results of previous work on ad auctions, characterized a special family of equilibria of the GSP auction, termed *symmetric Nash equilibria*, or SNE . SNEs have many attractive properties which make them a natural choice as outcomes of the GSP auction (see Section 6.4.1 for details). Moreover, it has been shown that the SNE leading to the lowest revenue for the seller (termed *Lower Equilibrium* (LE)), coincides with the natural equilibrium of VCG where all bidders report their true values [Varian, 2007; Edelman et al., 2007].

The above results led to a surge of papers comparing VCG and the various equilibrium outcomes of GSP, under both public information and private information settings [Kuminov and Tennenholtz, 2009; Thompson and Leyton-Brown, 2009; Edelman and Schwarz, 2010; Lucier et al., 2012]. However, these comparisons focused mainly on revenue (and occasionly on welfare), rather than on coalitional stability. The VCG mechanism was shown to be vulnerable to collusion in various domains (see, e.g., [Conitzer and Sandholm, 2006; Bachrach, 2010] for relatively recent work), compared to a simple first-price (pay-your-bid) auction. The formal literature on collusion in second-price auctions goes back to Graham and Marshall [1987], while the literature on the more involved matter of collusion in first-price auctions goes back to McAfee and McMillan [1987].

6.1.2   Results in this chapter

Stability scores are formally defined in Section 6.2, where we show how they generalize well known solution concepts. In Section 6.3 we study stability scores in a simple family of congestion games. The main purpose of this study is to demonstrate how stability scores can be used in order to compare different Nash equilibria, and to measure how stability is affected by game's parameters. Moreover, while the studied family itself is quite simple, it is often used to model real world situations such as load balancing. Our analysis can give some intuition as to the main factors affecting coalitional stability in such games.

The main results are in Section 6.4, where we present the VCG and GSP mechanisms for ad auctions, and show bounds on stability scores in these auctions. In particular, we study how the stability of GSP varies as a function of the distributions of agents' valuations and slots' click-through rates, thereby showing that under certain reasonable conditions GSP is far more stable than VCG.

6.2   Preliminaries

We follow the notation of non-cooperative games as defined in Section 2.1. Recall that a *deviation* of agent i from profile $\mathbf{a}$ is an action $b_i \in A_i$ s.t. $u_i(b_i, a_{-i}) > u_i(a_i, a_{-i})$.

Coalitional deviations We now extend the notion of deviations to coalitions. Given an action profile $\mathbf{a}$, we denote by a_S the profile of agents in S, and by A_S the set of all such joint actions. The profile of all agents in $N \setminus S$ is denoted by a_{-S}.

Given a profile of actions $\mathbf{a} \in \mathbf{A}$, $b_S \in A_S$ is a *strict deviation* from $\mathbf{a}$ if $u_i(b_S, a_{-S}) > u_i(a_S, a_{-S})$ for every $i \in S$. The profile $\mathbf{a}$ is termed a *strong equilibrium* (SE) if there are no $S \subseteq N$ and $b_S \in A_S$, such that b_S is a strict deviation from $\mathbf{a}$.

One can also consider the following weaker notion of deviation. Given a profile of actions $\mathbf{a} \in A$, $b_S \in A_S$ is a *deviation* from $\mathbf{a}$ if $u_i(b_S, a_{-S}) \geq u_i(a_S, a_{-S})$ for every $i \in S$ and there exists $j \in S$ such that $u_j(b_S, a_{-S}) > u_j(a_S, a_{-S})$. The profile $\mathbf{a}$ is termed a *super-strong equilibrium* (SSE) if there is no $S \subseteq N, b_S \in A_S$ that is a deviation from $\mathbf{a}$. Since every strict deviation is clearly a deviation, every SSE is also a SE.

SSE captures the natural requirement that we should resist even situations in which a deviation only benefits some of the deviators without hurting others. A strategy profile is r-SE (respectively, r-SSE) if there are no coalitions of size at most r that have strict deviations (resp., deviations).

Stability scores The stability score of the profile $\mathbf{a}$ in game G is defined as a vector with n entries. For every $1 \le r \le n$, let $\mathcal{D}_r(G, \mathbf{a}) \in \mathbb{N}$ (respectively, $\mathcal{SD}_r(G, \mathbf{a}) \in \mathbb{N}$) be the *number* of coalitions of size r that have deviations (resp., strict deviations) from $\mathbf{a}$ in G. While there are many ways to impose an order based on vectors, we believe that the following lexicographic order is particularly natural.

Given two n-player games G and G' and two profiles $\mathbf{a}$ and $\mathbf{a}'$ in the respective games, we say that the pair $(G, \mathbf{a})$ is *more resistant to deviations* (or *more stable*) than $(G', \mathbf{a}')$, if there exists some $r \le n$ such that $\mathcal{D}_r(G, \mathbf{a}) < \mathcal{D}_r(G', \mathbf{a}')$ and the terms are equal for every $r' < r$. We can similarly compare strict stability scores to one another.

Our definition of stability scores generalizes some widely used notions of stability. For example, $\mathbf{a}$ is a Nash equilibrium (NE) of G iff $\mathcal{D}_1(G, \mathbf{a}) = \mathcal{SD}_1(G, \mathbf{a}) = 0$. This means that the score of a NE (by either definition) is always strictly better than the score of any profile that is not a NE. Further, any profile that is r-SE has a better strict-stability score than any non r-SE profile. A similar property holds w.r.t. r-SSE. As a different example, a profile $\mathbf{a}$ is *Pareto efficient* in G iff $\mathcal{D}_n(G, \mathbf{a}) = 0$.

6.3 Resource Selection Games

In this section we demonstrate how stability scores can be used to measure and compare the stability of different outcomes in a given game. To this end we focus on a very simple parametrized family, where games are known to posses at least one pure equilibrium. A natural choice is the simple class of *resource selection games* (RSG) with identical resources.

In a RSG there is a set of resources $F = \{1, \ldots, m\}$, and a non-decreasing cost function $c : [n] \to \mathbb{R}_+$, where $[n] = \{1, \ldots, n\}$. Each agent $i \in N$ can select exactly one resource j, and suffers a cost (negative utility) of $c(n_j)$, where n_j is the number of agents that selected resource j. RSGs are *potential games* and thus always admit a pure Nash equilibrium. In fact, any NE $\mathbf{a}$ of a RSG $G = \langle F, N, c \rangle$ is a *strong equilibrium* [Holzman and Law-Yone, 1997], and thus all equilibria have the same (strict) stability score. However, this is no longer true if the games are concatenated in a sequence.

Formally, a *sequential* RSG (SRSG) is a RSG with k steps. A strategy $a_i \in F^k$ of agent i requires selecting one resource in each step.[2] We next show that the number of coalitional deviations significantly depends on the played equilibrium. We consider games where $m, n, k \ge 2$, focusing mainly on games with 2 steps.

6.3.1 Counting deviations: an example

Suppose that $m = 4, n = 6, k = 2$ and that $c(t) = t$ for all $t \le n$. Any profile in which there are exactly 1 or 2 agents on each resource (in each step) is a Nash equilibrium. However, these equilibria differ in their stability against strict deviation of pairs. Suppose that in the first step agents are partitioned $\{1, 2\}, \{3, 4\}, \{5\}, \{6\}$, and repeat the same actions in the second step. Denote this profile by $\mathbf{a}$. In this case the pair $\{1, 2\}$ can strictly gain as follows: agent 1 joins

---

[2]Equivalently, the game can be described as a *congestion game* [Rosenthal, 1973], with k sequential parts and m parallel edges in each part.

agent 5 (or 6) in the first step, and agent 2 joins 5 in the second. Thus the cost for each of the two agents drops from 4 to 3. Only pair $\{3, 4\}$ can do the same, thus $\mathcal{SD}_2(G, \mathbf{a}) = 2$.

On the other hand, consider the profile $\mathbf{b}$ where players play in the first step as in $\mathbf{a}$, and in the second step are partitioned $\{1, 3\}, \{2, 4\}, \{5\}, \{6\}$; then no pair can strictly gain by deviating. Notice though, that this is still not a strong equilibrium, as the coalition $\{1, 2, 3, 4\}$ can still gain (agents $2, 3$ deviate in the first step, and $1, 4$ in the second), thus $\mathcal{SD}_2(G, \mathbf{b}) = 0$ and $\mathcal{SD}_4(G, \mathbf{b}) = 1$.

Finally, in the profile $\mathbf{c}$ agents are partitioned $\{1, 5\}, \{2, 6\}, \{3\}, \{4\}$ (in the second step), and this is a strong equilibrium, i.e., $\mathcal{SD}_r(G, \mathbf{c}) = 0$ for all r. It therefore follows that w.r.t strict stability scores $\mathbf{c}$ is *more stable* than $\mathbf{b}$, which is more stable than $\mathbf{a}$.

Note however that none of these profiles is an SSE or even 2-SSE. More generally, in *any* profile in G there is at least one pair (in fact two) that shares a resource and thus they have a (weak) deviation where just one of them gains. Thus for every profile $\mathbf{p}$ in G, we have that $\mathcal{D}_2(G, \mathbf{p}) \geq 2$.

6.3.2 Bounding stability scores in two-step RSG

The example above shows that different NE profiles in a particular game may differ in their stability to deviations of pairs or larger coalitions. We want to get a better picture of the gap between the most and least stable NE profiles, focusing on pair deviations. For the results in this section, we will restrict our cost function to be convex.

A nondecreasing cost function $c : [n] \to \mathbb{R}$ is said to be *convex* if it has an increasing marginal loss; i.e., $c(i + 1) - c(i) \leq c(j + 1) - c(j)$ for every $i < j$. Note that when facing a convex cost function, agents in an RSG try to minimize the maximal number of agents using a single resource. If the number of agents on every resource is the same, we say that the partition is *balanced*. If these numbers differ by at most one, we say that the partition is *nearly balanced*. Note that in our simple class of games, every NE is nearly balanced in all steps, and thus maximizes the social welfare.

Let G be a two-step game with a convex cost function. Note that when $n \mod m = 0$, any NE is a balanced partition of agents to resources (in each step). In such partition, no coalition can gain by deviating, as at least one deviating agent will end up paying more in expectation. If, in addition, costs are *strictly* convex, then even weak deviations are impossible. Since in this case every NE is an SE (and even an SSE), stability scores are trivial. We therefore assume in the remainder of this section that $n \mod m = q > 0$.

Let $\hat{\mathbf{a}}$ be the profile with the highest number of pair deviations, and let $\mathbf{a}^*$ be the profile with the lowest number of pair deviations. interestingly, the stability score of the various profiles we study is completely independent in the cost functions—except for the convexity assumption.

Proposition 6.1. $\mathcal{SD}_2(G, \hat{\mathbf{a}}) = \Theta\left(\frac{qn^2}{m^2}\right)$.

Proof sketch of lower bound. We note that in $\hat{\mathbf{a}}$ agents play some nearly balanced partition in the first step, and repeat the same partition in the second step. Thus some resources (called *full*) will have $\lceil n/m \rceil$ agents, and the others will have $\lfloor n/m \rfloor$ agents. A crucial observation used in the proof (and in the proofs of the other propositions in this section), is that a pair has a strict deviation if and only if it shares a full resource in both steps. Then (similarly to the example above) one agent switches to a non-full resource in the first step, and the other does the same in the second step. $\square$

Proposition 6.2. $\mathcal{SD}_2(G, \mathbf{a}^*) = O\left(\frac{n^2}{m^2}\right)$. *Further, if either $n < m^2$ or $q \leq \frac{m}{2}$, then $\mathcal{SD}_2(G, \mathbf{a}^*) = 0$, i.e., $\mathbf{a}^*$ is 2-SE.*

Note that the best NE $\mathbf{a}^*$ is significantly more stable than $\hat{\mathbf{a}}$: either $\mathbf{a}^*$ has no deviations at all, or $\hat{\mathbf{a}}$ has more deviations by a factor of $\Theta(q) = \Theta(m/2) = \Theta(m)$.

In order to achieve the upper bound asserted in Proposition 6.2, we define a profile that tries to scatter in the second step agents that shared a resource in the first step. As a qualitative conclusion, we see that in order to minimize possible deviations, agents should form a partition in the second step that *differs as much as possible* from the partition in the first step.

6.3.3   SRSGs with multiple steps

The following proposition quantifies the stability score of a random pure NE in a RSG with k steps. Note that the set of pure NEs coincides with the set of profiles that are nearly balanced in each step.

Proposition 6.3. *Let G be an SRSG with k steps and a convex cost function, and let $\mathbf{a}$ be a random NE in G. The expected number of deviating pairs in G is $\mathcal{SD}_2(G, \mathbf{a}) \cong \binom{n}{2}(1 - (1 + \alpha)e^{-\alpha})$, where $\alpha = \frac{q(k-1)}{m^2}$.*

We can summarize how the parameters affect stability as follows. If the number of steps k is small, and the number of resources m increases, then $\alpha \to 0$, and thus $\mathcal{SD}_2(G, \mathbf{a}) \to 0$ as well (i.e., there are very few pairs that can deviate). Conversely, when the number of steps grows (in particular when $k \gg \frac{m^2}{q}$), then almost every pair can deviate with a high probability.

As a corollary of Proposition 6.3 when $k = 2$, we get the lower bound of Proposition 6.1 for the case $q = \Theta(m)$, as $\mathcal{SD}_2(G, \hat{\mathbf{a}}) \geq \binom{n}{2}\left(1 - \left(1 - \frac{1}{m}\right)\left(1 + \frac{1}{m}\right)\right) = \Omega\left(\frac{n^2}{m}\right).$

6.4   Stability Scores in Ad Auctions

Having showed how stability scores can be used to analyze coalitional stability in simple games, we next turn to prove our main results. We compute the stability scores of the VCG and GSP ad auctions, which are central to the recent literature on economic mechanism design. Since both auctions admit strong equilibria, we do not consider strict deviations, and instead focus our analysis on non-strict deviations and the scores they induce.

6.4.1   Ad auctions: model and notations

Following [Varian, 2007], an *ad auction* has s slots to allocate, and $n \geq 2s$ bidders,[3] each with valuation v_i per click. Every slot $1 \leq j \leq s$ is associated with a click-through rate (CTR) $x_j > 0$, where $x_j \geq x_{j+1}$. For mathematical convenience, we define $x_j = 0$ for every $j > s$. Throughout the paper we make the simplifying assumptions that CTRs are strictly decreasing (i.e., $x_j > x_{j+1}$), and that $v_i \neq v_j$ for all $i \neq j$. We denote by bold letters the corresponding vectors of valuations, CTRs, and bids (e.g., $\mathbf{b} = (b_1, \ldots, b_n)$).

A bidder i that has been allocated slot j gains v_i per click (regardless of the slot), and is charged p_j per click. Thus, her total utility is given by $u_i = (v_i - p_j)x_j$.

---

[3]When discussing deviating pairs it is sufficient to assume $n > s$, which is a typical situation. Also, all of our results can be easily adjusted to cases with fewer bidders.

VCG In the Vickrey-Clark-Groves (VCG) mechanism every bidder i submits a bid b_i, and the mechanism allocates the j'th slot, $j = 1, \ldots, s$, to the j'th highest bidder. Each bidder j is charged (per click) for the "harm" she poses to the other bidders, i.e., the difference between the welfare of bidders $k \neq j$ if j is omitted and their welfare when j exists.

It is well known that the VCG mechanism is *truthful*, meaning that reporting true valuations $b_j = v_j$ is a (weakly) dominant strategy for all bidders. In particular, it is a Nash equilibrium.

Suppose that bidders' valuations are sorted in non-increasing order. Assuming truthful bidding (i.e., $b_j = v_j$ for all j), each bidder $i \leq s$ is allocated slot i (which means that the allocation maximizes the social welfare), and pays

$$p_i^{VCG} = \sum_{s+1 \geq j \geq i+1} \frac{x_{j-1} - x_j}{x_i} \cdot v_j. \tag{6.1}$$

GSP In the Generalized Second Price (GSP) auction, slot j is given to the j'th highest bidder (as in the VCG auction). Denote by j the bidder who is getting slot j. The price to bidder $j = 1, \ldots, s$ equals to the bid of the next bidder; i.e., $p_j = b_{j+1}$. For mathematical convenience, we define $b_{j+1} = 0$ for $j \geq n$.

GSP equilibria Varian [2007] identifies a set of natural Nash equilibria of the GSP auction, termed *envy free NE* or *Symmetric NE* (SNE), which are characterized by a set of recursive inequalities. Varian shows that all SNE's satisfy some very convenient properties. First, in SNE no bidder wants to swap slots with any other bidder.[4] Second, SNEs are efficient in the sense that bidders with higher valuations always bid higher (and thus get better slots, which means that social welfare is maximized as in VCG). This allows us to assume that valuations are also sorted in non-decreasing order $v_1 \geq v_2 \geq \cdots \geq v_n$. Lastly, SNEs can be easily computed by a recursive formula, which makes them especially attractive for computerized and online settings.

The two equilibria that reside on the boundaries of the SNE set, referred to as *Lower Equilibrium* (LE) and *Upper Equilibrium* (UE), are of particular interest. We denote the LE and UE profiles by $\mathbf{b}^L = (b_i^L)_{i \in N}$ and $\mathbf{b}^U = (b_i^U)_{i \in N}$, respectively. The bids in the LE, for every $2 \leq i \leq s+1$, are given by

$$b_i^L x_{i-1} = v_i(x_{i-1} - x_i) + b_{i+1}^L x_i = \sum_{s+1 \geq j \geq i} v_j(x_{j-1} - x_j). \tag{6.2}$$

In particular, since CTRs are strictly decreasing, we get that $b_i > b_{i+1}$ for all $i \leq s$. A central result by Varian [2007] is that the LE equilibrium induces payments, utilities, and revenue equal to those of the truthful outcome in VCG. It is therefore of great interest to compare the stability of these seemingly identical outcomes in both mechanisms.

The bids in the UE, for every $2 \leq i \leq s+1$, are given by

$$b_i^U x_{i-1} = v_{i-1}(x_{i-1} - x_i) + b_{i+1}^U x_i = \sum_{s+1 \geq j \geq i} v_{j-1}(x_{j-1} - x_j). \tag{6.3}$$

6.4.2 Deviations in VCG

Recall that the payment for bidder i is a weighted average of the reported (and by truthfulness, the actual) values of bidders $i + 1 \leq j \leq s + 1$ (see Eq. (6.1)).

---

[4]When swapping with a bidder in a worse slot, this requirement coincides with the one implied by NE. However when swapping with a bidder in a better slot, envy-freeness is slightly stronger.

We next characterize the structure of a set of deviators R of size r. We say that a coalition R of r bidders has a *potential to deviate* under VCG (or that it is a *potential coalition*), if either: (a) the group R contains exactly r *winners* (i.e., bidders that are allocated a slot $j \leq s$); or (b) the set R is composed of $t < r$ winners, the first loser, and the $r - t - 1$ bidders that directly follow (i.e., bidders $s + 1$ through $s + r - t$). We denote the number of potential coalitions of size r by M_r, and argue that it only makes sense to count potential coalitions when considering a deviation.

To see why, note first that all bidders ranked $s + r$ or worse have no effect on the payment of any other bidder, and can be ignored. Second, the bidders ranked $s + 2, \ldots, s + r - 1$ are only effective if they allow the bidder allocated slot $s + 1$ to lower her bid. Thus non-potential coalitions always contain at least one bidder that has no contribution at all to the deviation, and can therefore be ignored. Note for example that while adding dummy bidders (with valuation 0) increases the total number of coalitions, the number of potential coalitions remains unchanged.

It is easy to verify that there are $\binom{s}{r}$ coalitions of type (a), and $\sum_{t=1}^{r-1} \binom{s}{t}$ coalitions of type (b). Thus $M_r = \sum_{t=1}^{r} \binom{s}{t}$. Interestingly, in VCG every potential coalition can actually deviate.

Proposition 6.4. *Under the truthful equilibrium of VCG, denoted by T, any potential coalition has a deviation, i.e., $D_r(VCG, T) = M_r$ for all $2 \leq r \leq s$.*

Proof. Let R be some potential coalition, and $i^* \in \mathrm{argmin}_{i \in R} v_i$. We call i^* the *indifferent bidder*. Suppose that every agent $i \in R$ reports v_i' so that $v_i > v_i' > v_{i+1}$. Clearly, this has no effect on slot allocation. In coalitions that include only winners, all the agents except agent i^* (which is indifferent) pay strictly less than their original payments, as the payment monotonically depends on the valuations of the other members of R. In potential coalitions of the other type, where R includes t winners and $r - t$ losers, all t winners strictly gain.   □

6.4.3 Deviations in GSP

Since LE is a Nash equilibrium, we have that $\mathcal{D}_1(GSP, LE) = \mathcal{SD}_1(GSP, LE) = 0$. In fact, as in the VCG mechanism, no coalition has a strict deviation from the LE profile in GSP. This statement is not as trivial in the GSP mechanism, but it follows from Lemma D.3 in the appendix. We next turn to evaluate the resistance of GSP to (non-strict) deviations, focusing on the lower equilibrium. As in the previous section, we only count potential coalitions as all other coalitions necessarily contain redundant participants.

Characterization of pair deviations in Lower equilibrium   It is easy to see that for every $i \leq s$, the pair of agents $(i, i + 1)$ (called *neighbors*) can always (weakly) gain as a coalition, by having agent $i + 1$ lowering her bid to b_{i+1}', so that $b_{i+1} > b_{i+1}' > b_{i+2}$.[5] In this case, agent $i + 1$ is not affected, but agent i gains the difference $x_i(b_{i+1} - b_{i+1}') > 0$. It is also clear that bidders ranked $s + 2$ or worse can never be part of a deviating pair. In terms of the stability score, this means that $s \leq \mathcal{D}_2(GSP, LE) \leq M_2 = \binom{s+1}{2}$.

Consider the pair of non-neighbors (k, j), where $k < j - 1 \leq s$. We want to derive a sufficient and necessary condition under which the pair (k, j) has a deviation. A simple observation is that given some Nash equilibrium, for an agent i to strictly gain by being allocated a new slot $i' \neq i$, the bid $b_{i'+1}$ must strictly decrease, since otherwise this would also be a deviation for i as a single agent (in contradiction to equilibrium). Therefore, either (1) k moves to a worse slot $k' = j - 1$, and $b_j' < b_j$; or (2) j moves to a better slot $j' = k$, k is pushed down to $k' = k + 1$, and $b_k' < b_k$.

---

[5]The assumption that CTRs are strictly decreasing is required here, as otherwise bidder $i + 1$ may not be able to lower her bid.

However, the utility of j in this case is at most the utility she would get by swapping slots with bidder k. Thus if j gains in case (2), then this means she is envy in bidder k under the current profile **b**. This is impossible, as we assumed **b** is an SNE. We conclude that the only deviation for non-neighbors is where $k' = j - 1; j' = j$. Further, this is a deviation only if $b_{j-1} > b'_k > b'_j \geq b_{j+1}$. Note that: (i) b'_k can get any value in this range without affecting the utility of k or j, (ii) the utility of j remains the same, and (iii) the most profitable deviation for k is one in which $b'_j = b_{j+1}$ (breaking the tie in favor of j).

The discussion above establishes a necessary condition for a pair deviation, and asserts that in every pair deviation of k, j only agent k can strictly gain, where $k < j$.

For the following results, we denote $a = x_{j-1} - x_j$ (for our fixed j), and $w_i = \frac{x_{i-1} - x_i}{x_j}$ for all $i \leq s+1$. We complete the characterization by establishing a sufficient condition for pair deviation.

Lemma 6.5. *Suppose that the pair k, j deviates from LE, by moving agent k to slot $k' = j - 1$. Let $u(k), u'(k)$ be the utility of agent k before and after the deviation, then*
$$u(k) - u'(k) \geq \sum_{t=k+1}^{j-1}(x_{t-1} - x_t)(v_k - v_t) - a \cdot v_j + a \sum_{i=j+1}^{s+1} w_i v_i.$$
Moreover, in the optimal deviation for agent k the last inequality holds with an equality.

Proof. Suppose agent j lowers her bid to $b'_j = b_{j+1} + \epsilon$ where $\epsilon \geq 0$ (so j keeps her slot). For any $\mathbf{x}, \mathbf{v}$ the utility of agent k changes as follows:

$$u(k) - u'(k) = (v_k - b_{k+1})x_k - (v_k - (b_{j+1} + \epsilon))x_{j-1}$$

$$= (x_k - x_{j-1})v_k - \sum_{t=k+1}^{s+1}(x_{t-1} - x_t)v_t + \sum_{i=j+1}^{s+1}\frac{x_{j-1}(x_{i-1} - x_i)}{x_j}v_i + \epsilon x_{j-1}$$

$$= \sum_{l=k+1}^{j-1}(x_{l-1} - x_l)v_k - \sum_{t=k+1}^{j}(x_{t-1} - x_t)v_t + \left(\frac{x_{j-1}}{x_j} - 1\right)\sum_{i=j+1}^{s+1}(x_{i-1} - x_i)v_i + \epsilon x_{j-1}$$

$$= \sum_{t=k+1}^{j-1}(x_{t-1} - x_t)(v_k - v_t) - (x_{j-1} - x_j)v_j + \frac{x_{j-1} - x_j}{x_j}\sum_{i=j+1}^{s+1}(x_{i-1} - x_i)v_i + \epsilon x_{j-1}$$

$$= \sum_{t=k+1}^{j-1}(x_{t-1} - x_t)(v_k - v_t) - a \cdot v_j + a \sum_{i=j+1}^{s+1} w_i v_i + \epsilon x_{j-1}.$$

The inequality follows since $\epsilon \geq 0$. In the optimal deviation $\epsilon = 0$ in which case we get an equality. Note that $\sum_{i=j+1}^{s+1} w_i v_i$ is a weighted average of valuations. In particular, it is always between v_{s+1} and v_{j+1}. $\square$

As a direct corollary from Lemma 6.5, we get that in LE the pair k, j (where $k < j - 1$), has a deviation *if and only if*

$$\sum_{t=k+1}^{j-1}(x_{t-1} - x_t)(v_k - v_t) < a \cdot v_j - a \sum_{i=j+1}^{s+1} w_i v_i. \tag{6.4}$$

Upper equilibrium It is easy to check that a similar characterization to Eq. (6.4) applies to the UE. However, the conditions differ with respect to bidders that are two positions apart (see Proposition D.2 in the appendix). This result holds under all valuation and CTR functions; hence $\mathcal{D}_2(GSP, UE) \geq 2s - 1$. This means that the UE may be slightly less stable than LE (whose stability is expressed in Theorem 6.6). Yet, it is not too difficult to show that the number of pair

| CTR / Valuations | ← Concave → | | ← Convex → |
	β-concave	Linear	β-convex
Concave 2-concave	All $\binom{s+1}{2}$	All $\binom{s+1}{2}$	-
Linear	$\Omega(s^2)$	$\Theta(s\sqrt{s})$	$O(s \cdot \log_\beta(s))$
Convex 2-convex	-	s	s

Table 6.1: The table summarizes the number of pairs that have a deviation, i.e., $\mathcal{D}_2(GSP, LE)$. When one function is strictly concave and the other is strictly convex, the score may depend on the exact structure of both functions.

deviations from UE and LE are asymptotically the same. Therefore, in the remainder of this section we focus on stability scores of LE.

Counting pair deviations   It turns out that the asymptotic number of pair deviations strongly depends on the shape of both the CTR function and the valuation function. In particular, convexity (as well as concavity and β-convexity) will play a major role in our results. Let $g_1, \ldots, g_m$ be a monotonically *nonincreasing* vector.

Similarly to the way defined convex cost functions in Section 6.3, we say that g is *convex* if it has a decreasing marginal loss; i.e., $g_i - g_{i+1} \geq g_j - g_{j+1}$ for every $i < j$. Similarly, if g has an *increasing* marginal loss then it is *concave*. Note that linear functions are both convex and concave. A special case of convexity (resp., concavity) is when the marginal loss decreases (resp., increases) exponentially fast:

Let $\beta > 1$. We say that g is β-*convex* if $g_{i-1} - g_i \geq \beta(g_i - g_{i+1})$ for every i. Similarly, g is said to be β-*concave* if $\beta(g_{i-1} - g_i) \leq g_i - g_{i+1}$ for every i. [6]

Intuitively, as either valuations or CTRs are "more" convex,[7] a bidder who deviates by moving to a lower (i.e., worse) slot faces a more significant drop in her utility. Thus we can hope that pairs that are sufficiently distant from one another will not be able to deviate jointly. This intuition is further formalized and quantified in the remainder of this section. For convenience, the results are summarized in Table 6.1.

The next proposition demonstrates that convexity induces greater stability.

Theorem 6.6. *Suppose that both CTR and valuation functions are* convex. *The number of pairs with deviations in the Lower equilibrium can be upper bounded as follows.*
(a) $\mathcal{D}_2(GSP, LE) = O(s\sqrt{s})$.
(b) if CTRs are β-convex then $\mathcal{D}_2(GSP, LE) = O(s \log_\beta s)$.
(c) if valuations are β-convex, for any $\beta \geq 2$, then $\mathcal{D}_2(GSP, LE) = s$ (i.e., only neighbor pairs).

We present the proof of the first statement, so as to demonstrate the proof technique.

Proof of 6.6a. Recall that $a = x_{j-1} - x_j > 0$. A crucial observation is that $\sum_{i=k+1}^{s+1} w_i v_i$ is in fact a weighted average of valuations, where the weight w_i is proportional to the difference $x_{i-1} - x_i$. Therefore this average is biased toward low values when CTR is convex, and toward high values when it is concave.

---

[6]Lucier *et al.* [2012] studied GSP auctions with *well-separated* CTR functions, which is a closely related term. In particular, a $\frac{1}{\beta}$-well separated function is also β-convex.

[7]When referring to convexity of CTR/valuation functions, we only consider the first $s + 1$ values.

Also, since CTRs are convex, we have that for all $i < j$, $x_{i-1} - x_i \geq a$. Thus by Lemma 6.5,

$$u(k) - u'(k) \geq a \sum_{t=k+1}^{j-1} (v_k - v_t) - a \cdot v_j + a \sum_{i=j+1}^{s+1} w_i v_i$$

$$= a \left(\sum_{t=k+1}^{j-1} (v_k - v_t) + \sum_{i=j+1}^{s+1} w_i v_i - v_j \right) \geq a \left(\sum_{t=k+1}^{j-1} (v_k - v_t) + \operatorname*{avg}_{s+1 \geq i \geq j+1} (v_i) - v_j \right).$$

$$(6.5)$$

Therefore, in order to prove that the pair j, k can deviate, it is necessary to show

$$\sum_{t=k+1}^{j-1} (v_k - v_t) < v_j - \operatorname*{avg}_{s+1 \geq i \geq j+1} v_i. \tag{6.6}$$

We note that under linear CTRs, all inequalities become equalities (in which case Equation (6.6) is also a sufficient condition). Observe that closer pairs are more likely to deviate. e.g., for pairs s.t. $j = k + 2$, it is sufficient that $v_k - v_{k+1} < v_{k+2} - \operatorname*{avg}_{s \geq t' \geq k+3} v_{t'}$ to have a deviation. Let $h = j - 1 - k \geq 1$, and $z = v_k - v_{j-1} = v_k - v_{k+h}$.

From convexity of $\mathbf{v}$ it holds that for all $h' < h$, $\frac{v_k - v_{k+h'}}{h'} \geq \frac{v_k - v_{k+h}}{h} = \frac{z}{h}$, thus for the LHS of Eq. (6.6),

$$\sum_{t=k+1}^{j-1} (v_k - v_t) \geq \sum_{t=k+1}^{j-1} z \frac{t-k}{h} = \frac{z}{h} \frac{h(h+1)}{2} = \frac{h+1}{2} z. \tag{6.7}$$

Bounding the RHS of Eq. (6.6), we have

$$v_j - \operatorname*{avg}_{s+1 \geq i \geq j+1} v_i \leq v_j - v_{\operatorname{avg}\{s+1 \geq i \geq j+1\}} v_j - v_{\lceil \frac{j}{2} + \frac{s}{2} \rceil} \qquad \text{(convexity of } \mathbf{v}\text{)}$$

$$= v_j - v_{\lceil j + \frac{s-j}{2} \rceil} \leq \sum_{i'=1}^{\lceil (s-j)/2h \rceil} (v_{j+(i'-1)h} - v_{j+i'h}) \leq \sum_{i'=1}^{\lceil (s-j)/2h \rceil} (v_k - v_{k+h}), \tag{6.8}$$

which is at most $\lceil \frac{s-j}{2h} \rceil z$. By using the bounds we showed on both sides of the equation, condition (6.6) implies $h + 1 < \lceil \frac{s-j}{h} \rceil$, which must be false whenever $h + 1 = j - k > \sqrt{s}$. Therefore each winner $k \leq s$ can deviate with at most $\sqrt{s}$ other bidders, and there can be at most $s\sqrt{s}$ such pairs. □

It is evident from Theorem 6.6, that convexity can guarantee some level of stability, and further, that "more" convexity can induce more stability. Our next result complements this observation, by showing that *concavity* of valuation and CTR functions affects stability in the opposite direction.

Theorem 6.7. *Suppose that both CTR and valuation functions are* concave. *The number of pairs with deviations in the Lower equilibrium can be lower bounded as follows.*
(a) $\mathcal{D}_2(GSP, LE) = \Omega(s\sqrt{s})$.
(b) if CTRs are β-concave for any $\beta > 1$, then $\mathcal{D}_2(GSP, LE) = \Omega(s^2)$ (i.e., a constant fraction of all pairs).
(c) if valuations are β-concave, for any $\beta \geq 2$, then $\mathcal{D}_2(GSP, LE) = \binom{s+1}{2} = M_2$ (i.e., all pairs).

A linear function is both convex and concave. Therefore, in the special case where both CTRs and valuations are linear, we obtain an asymptotically tight estimation of $\mathcal{D}_2(GSP, LE)$.

Deviations of more than two agents   We first characterize the structure of such deviations (compare with VCG in Section 6.4.2). Indeed, we claim that a coalition $R \subseteq N$ has a deviation if, and only if, R contains a pair of bidders that has a deviation.

In order to prove the characterization (see Lemma D.3 in the appendix), we must show that the bidder that is ranked last among the deviators is an *indifferent bidder*. Every deviating coalition R also contains a *free-rider*, which gains from the deviation but does not need to change his bid, and can therefore be removed (as long as some non-indifferent bidders remain). This crucial observation facilitates the computation of the number of deviations by coalitions of size r for any $r \geq 3$.

Recall that M_r denotes the number of coalitions of size r, and that under VCG auction all of these coalitions actually have a deviation. Clearly, $\mathcal{D}_r(GSP, LE) \leq M_r$. We next show how the accurate number of coalitions asymptotically depends on the size of the coalition r and on the number of slots s.

Proposition 6.8. *If both CTRs and valuations are convex, then* $\mathcal{D}_r(GSP, LE) \leq M_r \cdot O\left(\frac{r^2}{\sqrt{s}}\right)$. *In contrast, if both CTRs and valuations are concave, then for any positive constant $d < 1$,*

$$\mathcal{D}_r(GSP, LE) \geq M_r \cdot d \cdot \left(1 - \exp\left(-\Omega\left(\frac{r\sqrt{r}}{\sqrt{s}}\right)\right)\right).$$

Proposition 6.8 confirms that the GSP auction is far more stable than the VCG auction against collusions of relatively small coalitions (when CTR and valuations are convex). This result also establishes an almost sharp threshold for the case of linear CTRs and valuations: for every $r \gg \sqrt[3]{s}$, almost all coalitions of size r can deviate, while the proportion of coalitions of size $r \ll \sqrt[4]{s}$ that can deviate goes to 0 (when r is fixed and as s tends to infinity).

6.5   Plurality Voting

It is often useful to model voting systems as games where voters are strategic agents, and analyze them via game theoretic tools (see Chapter 5 and references therein). As we noted before, in most voting systems there are typically numerous Nash equilibria, and many of them do not make sense (e.g., when all voters vote for their most hated candidate). Thus the question of equilibrium selection is a highly important one, in order to give any valuable predictions or suggestions.

In a recent paper with Dvir Falik and Moshe Tennenholtz, we applied stability scores to the analysis of the Plurality voting system [Falik, Meir, and Tennenholtz, 2012]. In particular, we asked "what are the most stable outcomes?" from a coalitional stability perspective, and more importantly—who is the winner in these stable outcomes.

Somewhat surprisingly, it turns out that under a mild assumption on the profiles, the "most stable winner" under the Plurality system (i.e., the winner in the profile that has the lowest stability scores), is the *truthful winner* of a different voting system, known as Maximin.[8] In particular, the result in [Falik et al., 2012] generalizes an observation by Sertel and Sanver [2004], who showed that a candidate in Plurality can win in a strong equilibrium (i.e., has a stability score of 0 for every size of coalition), if and only if it is a Condorcet winner.

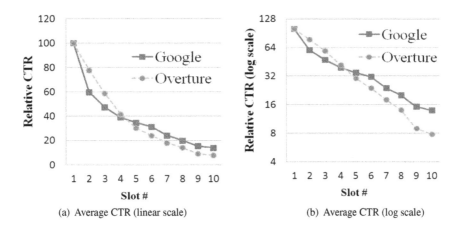

(a) Average CTR (linear scale)   (b) Average CTR (log scale)

Figure 6.1: The average click-through rate for ads positioned in any of the first ten slots are shown in Fig. 6.1(a) (numbers are normalized so that the CTR of slot 1 is 100). We can see that the shape of the CTR function is convex in both Google and Overture. In Fig. 6.1(b) we see the same data in log scale. Interestingly, the Overture CTR function is very close to exponential (with $\beta \cong 1.3$). Statistics are taken from Atlas Institute rank report [Brooks, 2004]. We present the data on the "click potential" attribute, which corresponds to the actual CTR in our model.

6.6 Conclusion

The main contribution in this chapter is the introduction of *stability scores*—a new stability measure for game equilibria. We demonstrated how stability scores can be used to compare equilibria in congestion games and to draw qualitative results regarding properties of the game and the profiles with high coalitional stability.

Other than comparing equilibria of a particular game, we demonstrated the usefulness of stability scores in comparing the stability of equilibria under mechanisms that are designed for similar settings—the setting of ad auctions in our case.

Auctions   Our results indicate that for a prominent class of CTR and valuation functions, GSP is far more stable than VCG. It is important to note that convex and even exponential CTRs are common in the real world, as can be seen in Figure 6.1. It is much harder to assess the shape of valuation functions, as it depends on private information that is not directly measurable.

In addition, we use the proposed score to compare different equilibria of the GSP mechanism; in particular we show that the *upper equilibrium* (UE) is somewhat less stable than the *lower equilibrium* (LE). As the UE generates a higher revenue, this result suggests a (small) tradeoff between revenue and stability.

It is known that the LE of GSP generates exactly the same revenue as VCG, and any other SNE of GSP generates an even higher revenue. This may suggest that GSP is better than VCG with respect to both revenue and stability. However, a relatively simple modification to the VCG mechanism (in particular, the introduction of a random reserve price, see Appendix D.3) induces a randomized mechanism that eliminates all coalitional deviations, thus turning it into a highly stable mechanism.

---

[8]Maximin is usually considered a better voting rule than Plurality, for example it is Condorcet consistent.

Part II

Welfare

Chapter 7

Mechanism Design without Money I

Facility Location Mechanisms

Abstract. In this chapter we consider mechanisms that place a single facility for public use (like a library or a swimming pool), based on the reported locations of multiple agents. We characterize strategyproof (SP) mechanisms and study the worst case approximation ratio that can be guaranteed by deterministic and randomized SP facility location mechanisms. In particular, we show that any deterministic SP mechanism on a large enough cycle must be close to dictatorial. When randomization is allowed, we describe a $3 - \frac{2}{n}$ approximation mechanism that works for every metric space even when agents are weighted.

7.1 Introduction

In the next two chapters we study *mechanisms without money* (see Section 1.1.3), whose goal is to incentivize agents to report truthfully information that required for solving an optimization problem. Mechanisms for the location of a public facility (which is a game-theoretic version of the Weber problem, see below) are the focus of this chapter.

The Weber problem In the classic *Weber problem* (also known as the Fermat-Weber problem), a set of points $\{a_i\}_{i \in N}$ in Euclidean space are given, each with a nonnegative weight w_i, and we should find the point x minimizing the sum of distances $\sum_{i \in N} w_i \|a_i - x\|_2$ [Weber, 1929]. The problem is an abstraction of situations where a public facility should be placed where it can optimally serve the people in the input locations.

We refer to the corresponding problem in metric spaces as the *metric Weber problem*, replacing the ℓ_2 norm with an arbitrary metric $d(a, x)$, for example distance on a city grid or on some other graph. The optimal solution for the metric Weber problem is known as the *Geometric median* or the *1-median*. In the *constrained [metric] Weber problem*, the facility x can only be placed in a predefined subset of the Euclidean [metric] space. Most of the literature regarding variants of the Weber problem deals with its algorithmic aspects, namely in how to efficiently compute the exact optimal location [Kuhn, 1973; Eckhardt, 1980; Hansen et al., 1982; Bajaj, 1986; Chandrasekaran and Tamir, 1990].

Facility location with private information The *facility location problem* is a variant of the metric Weber problem, where the locations of the agents are not publicly known. Rather, the location a_i is only known to agent i. Agents each report their location to a *facility location (FL) mechanism*, which consequently places the facility in one of the allowed locations, based on agents' reports. The objective of the mechanism designer is to locate the facility at a point that will minimize the average distance to the real locations of all agents.

The problem of false reports that bias the optimal location arise in many real-life scenarios. A similar problem arises also in virtual scenarios, such as deciding on the salary of a manager during a board meeting of a firm (see also next chapter).

When agents report their locations truthfully, the problem of finding the optimal location for the facility reduces to the constrained or unconstrained metric Weber problem. However, a naïve mechanism that computes and returns the optimal solution based on reported locations may fail if agents act strategically. For example, when considering whether to locate a bus station in one of both ends of a street, it is fairly easy to see that a mechanism that always picks the optimal end can be easily manipulated. In particular: an agent who lives closer to the non-selected end can report an even more extreme location. The false report may result in locating the station in the sub-optimal side.

Research objectives We look for mechanisms that are *strategyproof* (as presented in Section 2.1.1) and would thus discourage false reports by the agents. Since truthfulness is often at odds with optimality, we compare the outcome of each mechanism to the optimal outcome (the 1-median in the unconstrained case) to get the *approximation ratio*. Then, we seek the best possible approximation ratio that can be guaranteed using SP mechanisms, with and without using randomization.

7.1.1 Recent related work

Most work on facility location focused on *continuous* topologies, for example graphs where agents and facilities may be placed anywhere along the edges. Regarding deterministic mechanisms, the most relevant paper to our work is by Schummer and Vohra [2004], who characterized SP mechanisms on continuous intervals, cycles, and trees. While we focus on discrete graphs rather than continuous, our model is similar and adopts some of the standard definitions used by Schummer and Vohra.

The approximation approach to SP facility location was first formalized by Procaccia and Tennenholtz [2009]. Mechanisms for various continuous topologies have been subsequently suggested and studied by other researchers [Alon et al., 2010; Lu et al., 2010].

A randomized 3-approximation SP mechanism for general metric spaces was given in [Meir, 2008] (see also [Meir et al., 2009, 2012]).[1] In fact, this mechanism simply selects a dictator at random and places the facility in her preferred location. The same upper bound was later independently proved by Thang [2010], who also provided a lower bound of $2 - o(n)$.

Other variations of the SP facility location problem include for example the location of several facilities [Procaccia and Tennenholtz, 2009; Lu et al., 2009], the use of alternative optimization criteria [Alon et al., 2010], and the location of *obnoxious facilities* that agents prefer to place as far as possible [Cheng et al., 2011]. Such variations are outside the scope of this work.

---

[1] The problem studied in Meir *et al.* was a binary classification problem, but the proof was given for general metric spaces. See also next chapter.

7.1.2 Results in this chapter

For a deterministic setting, we provide a complete characterization of onto SP mechanisms for facility location on a discrete line. We then prove a discrete analog of a classic result by Schummer and Vohra [2004], showing that any deterministic onto SP FL mechanism on a cycle must be close to dictatorial (although every agent may have some small influence). One important corollary of this result is an alternative proof for the Schummer and Vohra's theorem, which is shorter, more structured, and also works in the discrete case. A second corollary will be applied in the next chapter to derive lower approximation bounds in other domains of AMDw/oM.

We then present a new mechanism for the facility location problem with weighted agents, with a guaranteed approximation ratio of $3 - \frac{2}{n}$, thereby improving the previously known upper bound from [Meir, 2008; Thang, 2010]. All bounds are summarized in Table 8.2 in the next chapter, where we can see that the $3 - \frac{2}{n}$ bound is tight.

7.2 Preliminaries

Consider a graph $G = \langle V, E \rangle$ with a set V of vertices and a set E of undirected edges. For ease of presentation, we assume edges are unweighted, although adding weights (i.e., lengths) would not change our results. The vertices $v \in V$ will be also referred to as *locations*. The distance between two vertices $v, v' \in V$, denoted $d(v, v')$, is the length of the minimum-length path between v and v', where the length of a path is defined as the number of edges in the path.[2] Note that d is a distance metric. We extend the notion of distance between vertices to distance between sets of vertices, where the distance between two sets of vertices $A, A' \subseteq V$, denoted $d(A, A')$ is defined as $d(A, A') = \min_{v \in A, v' \in A'} d(v, v')$. We will be especially interested in three classes of graphs, namely lines, cycles, and binary cubes (that will become important in Chapter 8). These classes are formally defined in the relevant sections.

In an instance of a facility location problem, there are n agents that are located on vertices of the graph, and a subset $V' \subseteq V$ of allowed locations for the facility. Let $N = \{1, \ldots, n\}$ be the set of agents, and $\mathbf{a} = (a_1, \ldots, a_n) \in V^n$ be a *location profile*, where a_j denotes the location of agent j for every $j \in N$. Instances where $V' = V$ are called *unconstrained*.[3]

Given an agent j's location $a_j \in V$ and a facility location $x \in V'$, agent j's cost is given by $d(a_j, x)$. It is assumed that agents prefer to minimize their cost; that is, an agent prefers having the facility located as close to her as possible (and is indifferent between locations of the same distance).

7.2.1 Mechanisms

A *facility location (FL) mechanism* for a graph $G = \langle V, E \rangle$ is a function $f_G : V^n \to V'$, specifying the chosen facility location for every location profile. An FL mechanism that operates on any graph is denoted by f.

A *randomized FL mechanism* f maps any location profile V^n to probability distribution p_f over V'. We denote by $p_f(v|\mathbf{a})$ the probability that mechanism f returns vertex $v \in V'$ given the profile

---

[2]If v, v' are not connected then $d(v, v') = \infty$, however we only consider connected graphs in this paper.

[3]Note that every instance where $a_i \in V'$ for all $i \in N$ is w.l.o.g. unconstrained, as we can eliminate all vertices of $V \subseteq V'$, and replace every path between $v, u \in V'$ with a single weighted edge.

a as input. For a randomized mechanism, we define the distance from the facility to agent i as the expected distance:

$$d(f(\mathbf{a}), a_i) = \mathbb{E}_{v \sim p_f} [d(v, a_i)] = \sum_{v \in V'} p_f(v|\mathbf{a}) d(v, a_i).$$

Mechanism properties   We start with several definitions of mechanism properties, which are independent of the graph topology. While some of these properties are standard in the literature, we provide their definitions for completeness.

Definition 7.1. *A mechanism f is* onto, *if for every $x \in V'$ there is $\mathbf{a} \in V^n$ s.t. $f(\mathbf{a}) = x$.*

This property is a very basic requirement (sometimes referred to as *society sovereignty*), and as such we will restrict our attention to mechanisms satisfying this condition. We are also interested in the following properties, which are stronger.

Definition 7.2. *A mechanism f is* unanimous *if for every $x \in V$, $f(x, x, \ldots, x) = x$.*

Definition 7.3. *A location $y \in V'$ is said to Pareto dominate a location $x \in V'$ under a given profile if all the agents strictly prefer y over x (i.e., $d(y, a_j) < d(x, a_j)$ for every $j \in N$). A mechanism f is Pareto if for all $\mathbf{a} \in V^n$, there is no location $y \in V'$ Pareto dominates $f(\mathbf{a})$ w.r.t. the profile $\mathbf{a}$.*

Note that this requirement is slightly weaker than the more common definition of Pareto, requiring that no other location can strictly benefit one of the agents without hurting any other agent. It is easy to verify that that either version of Pareto implies unanimity, which in turn implies onto.

A mechanism which returns the best location with respect to a location of a specific agent i (i.e., $f(\mathbf{a}) \in \operatorname{argmin}_{v \in V'} d(v, a_i)$) is called a *dictator mechanism*, and agent i is called a dictator. Note that on an unconstrained instance, a dictator mechanism returns a_i.

It is argued that dictatorial mechanisms are "unfair" in the sense that the agent's identity plays a major role in the decision of the facility location. Completely fair mechanisms that ignore agents' identities altogether are said to be anonymous.

Definition 7.4. *A mechanism f is* anonymous, *if for every profile $\mathbf{a}$ and every permutation of agents $\pi : N \to N$, it holds that $f(a_1, \ldots, a_n) = f(a_{\pi(1)}, \ldots, a_{\pi(n)})$.*

Our main interest is in *strategyproof* mechanisms, defined as follows.

Definition 7.5 (Strategyproof). *A mechanism f is said to be* strategyproof *(SP), if no agent can strictly benefit by misreporting her location; that is, for every profile $\mathbf{a} \in V^n$, every agent $j \in N$ and every alternative location $a'_j \in V$, it holds that*

$$d(a_j, f(a'_j, a_{-j})) \geq d(a_j, f(\mathbf{a})).$$

While for randomized mechanisms the definition above only concerns strategyproofness in expectation, the mechanisms we will discuss in this chapter have the stronger property of ex-post SP. That is, no agent would lie even if the outcome of the randomization is known in advance.

The following folk lemma gives a necessary condition for a mechanism to be onto and SP. For a proof see e.g., [Barberà and Peleg, 1990].

Lemma 7.1. *Every mechanism that is both onto and SP, is unanimous.*

The social cost   The *social cost* of a mechanism f on profile $\mathbf{a}$ is the (possibly weighted) sum of distances from all agents:

$$SC(f, \mathbf{a}) = \sum_{i \in N} w_i d(f(\mathbf{a}), a_i).$$

The optimal location for profile $\mathbf{a}$ is denoted by $\mathbf{opt}(\mathbf{a}) \in V'$ (i.e., $\mathbf{opt}(\mathbf{a}) \in \operatorname{argmin}_{x \in V'} SC(x, \mathbf{a})$), where we break ties consistently by some arbitrary order. The optimal social cost is denoted by $d^* = SC(\mathbf{opt}(\mathbf{a}), \mathbf{a})$. For a single agent i, $\mathbf{opt}(a_i)$ is simply the closest location to a_i in V'.

We measure the quality of the outcome of a mechanism using the standard notion of multiplicative *approximation*.

Definition 7.6. *A mechanism f provides an α-approximation if for every $\mathbf{a} \in V^n$, $SC(f(\mathbf{a}), \mathbf{a}) \leq \alpha \cdot d^*$.*

Note that randomized mechanisms are only required to attain approximation in expectation, and not necessarily with high probability.

There is an inherent tradeoff between strategyproofness and good approximation. A naïve mechanism which always returns $\mathbf{opt}(\mathbf{a})$), for example, is a 1-approximation mechanism, but may not be SP even in very simple instances. On the other hand, a mechanism that selects agent 1 as a *dictator*, and returns $\mathbf{opt}(a_1)$ is clearly SP but in general may give a very bad approximation (e.g., if all other agents are located in $a' \neq a_1$).

7.3   Deterministic Mechanisms on a Line

It is widely known that there are many SP facility location mechanisms on a line, including mechanisms that are optimal. In this section we characterize all SP and onto mechanisms on a discrete line.

Line graphs   A line graph with $k + 1$ vertices is denoted by $L_k = \{0, 1, \ldots, k\}$. We refer to an increase of the index as a movement in the *right* direction and similarly we refer to a decrease as a movement in the *left* direction. Clearly, in line graphs, every two vertices are connected by a single path. For $v' > v$, we denote by the closed interval $[v, v']$ the set of vertices $\{v, v+1, \ldots, v'-1, v'\}$, and by the open interval (v, v') the set of vertices $\{v + 1, \ldots, v' - 1\}$.

In this section (and also in the next one) we consider the unconstrained version of the facility location problem. That is, $V' = V = L_k$. Given a location $x \in L_k$, agent j's cost is $d(a_j, x) = |a_j - x|$. In the following definitions, a_j, b_j etc. are possible locations in L_k for agent j.

Definition 7.7. *A mechanism f on a line is* monotone *(MON) if for every $j \in N$ and every $b_j > a_j$, $f(a_{-j}, b_j) \geq f(a_{-j}, a_j)$.*

In other words, monotonicity of a mechanism means that if an agent moves in a certain direction, the facility cannot move in the other direction as an effect. The following two properties bound the effect of an agent's movement on the outcome of the mechanism.

Definition 7.8. *A mechanism f is m-step independent (m-SI) if the two following properties hold: (I) For every $j \in N, a_j' > a_j$, if $d([a_j, a_j'], f(\mathbf{a})) > m$, then $f(a_j', a_{-j}) = f(\mathbf{a})$. (II) For every $j \in N, a_j' \leq a_j$, if $d([a_j', a_j], f(\mathbf{a})) > m$, then $f(a_j', a_{-j}) = f(\mathbf{a})$.*

Definition 7.9. *A mechanism f is* disjoint independent *(DI) if for every $j \in N, a_j' \in L_k$, if $f(\mathbf{a}) = x \neq x' = f(a_j', a_{-j})$, then $|A \cap X| \geq 2$, where A is the segment defined by a_j and a_j' (i.e., $A = [\min(a_j, a_j'), \max(a_j, a_j')]$) and X is the segment defined by x, x'.*

Intuitively, m-SI means that if an agent moves inside an interval sufficiently far from the facility, it has no effect. The DI property means that an agent can affect the outcome of the mechanism only when its trajectory intersects the trajectory of the facility in at least two consecutive points.

A mechanism is said to be *strongly m-step independent* (m-SSI) if it is both m-SI and DI.

Consider for example the *median* mechanism, which returns the median location $f(\mathbf{a}) = a_{\lceil n/2 \rceil}$. The median mechanism (and in fact any order statistics mechanism) is strongly 0-SSI. Also note that the median is optimal: if we move right, then the facility becomes closer to at most $\lfloor n/2 \rfloor$ agents, and getting farther from at least $\lceil n/2 \rceil$ agents (at the same rate), thereby increasing the social cost.

Our primary result in this section characterizes all the mechanisms that satisfy the requirements of onto and SP on the line.

Theorem 7.2. *An onto mechanism f on the line is SP if and only if it is MON and 1-SSI.*

In the remainder of this section we sketch the proof of Theorem 7.2. Full proofs of all lemmas are deferred to Appendix E.1. An alternative characterization is given in the next chapter in Section 8.2.2, using the notations of the binary cube.

Lemma 7.3. *Every SP mechanism is monotone.*

Lemma 7.4. *A monotone mechanism f is Pareto iff it is unanimous.*

Notice that the Pareto property (Def. 7.3) has a simpler form on a line:

$$f(\mathbf{a}) \in [\min_{j \in N} a_j, \max_{j \in N} a_j].$$

The following lemma is the main building block in the proof of Theorem 7.2.

Lemma 7.5. *Every SP, unanimous mechanism for the line is 1-SI.*

A few remarks are in order. It is not hard to verify (see Lemma E.1 in the appendix) that every 0-SI monotone mechanism on the line is SP. This lemma can be seen as a particular case of Nehring and Puppe [2007] theorem. They show that for any subset of the binary cube (see Section 8.2.2), 0-SI (called IIA) and MON are sufficient and necessary conditions for being an SP mechanism, for a certain definition of SP that is stronger than ours. The following example shows that 0-SI is *not* a necessary condition under our definition: consider a setting with two agents and the following mechanism f on L_2: $f(a_1, a_2) = 2$ if $a_1 = 2$ or $a_2 = 2$, $f(a_1, a_2) = 1$ if $a_1 = a_2 = 1$, and $f(a_1, a_2) = 0$ otherwise. The reader can check that this is an SP, onto and unanimous mechanism; however, it is not 0-SI, since moving from the profile $(0, 1)$ to $(0, 2)$ changes the result from 0 to 2.

We now turn to sketch the proof of the main theorem of this section.

Proof sketch of Theorem 7.2 (the hard direction). Suppose f is an onto SP mechanism; then, by Lemmas 7.1 and 7.3, it is also monotone and unanimous, and therefore, by Lemma 7.5, it is 1-SI. Suppose that f does not satisfy 1-SSI; then, there is an agent i that violates DI (i.e., caused the violation). This means (by MON and 1-SI) that either the facility moved from $x = a_i - 1$ to a_i (which is a manipulation for i), or the facility moved from $x = a_i'$ to $x' = a_i' + 1$. In the latter case the movement $a_1' \to a_i$ is manipulation for i.   □

7.3.1 Descriptive and axiomatic characterizations

For continuous lines, the set of SP and onto mechanisms has been characterized as all *generalized median voting schemes* (g.m.v.s) [Border and Jordan, 1983; Schummer and Vohra, 2004]. This basically means that $f(\mathbf{a})$ is the median selection from some subset of agents. By slightly modifying our definitions above for continuous graphs (informally, by replacing the 1-SSI requirement with a 0-SI requirement), we get an alternative, axiomatic characterization that is similar to the one we give for the discrete case. While our definition of 0-SI seems very different from the definition of a g.m.v.s., the two definitions coincide by Theorem 7.2 (as both are equivalent to requiring onto and SP). Similarly, it is possible to give a descriptive characterization in the spirit of g.m.v.s. in the discrete case.

7.4 Deterministic Mechanisms on a Cycle

In this section we move forward from line graphs, where optimal SP mechanisms exist, to cycle graphs. As in the previous section, we consider the unconstrained version, where $V' = V = R_k$. After inspecting the main differences from the continuous case, we will continue to our main result, which puts a strong limitation on the possible SP mechanisms.

Recall that agent j is said to be a *dictator* in f if for every location profile $\mathbf{a} \in V^n$, it holds that $f(\mathbf{a}) = a_j$. We define the following relaxation of the dictatorship notion.

Definition 7.10. *An agent j is said to be an m-dictator in f, if for every $\mathbf{a} \in V^n$, it holds that $d(f(\mathbf{a}), a_j) \leq m$. A mechanism f is m-dictatorial if there exists an agent j that is an m-dictator in f.*

Note that a 0-dictator is just a dictator. Schummer and Vohra [2004] proved that any onto SP mechanism on the continuous cycle must be a dictatorship. However, this is not true for discrete cycles. Clearly, any dictator mechanism is both onto (and even unanimous) and SP, but the converse does not hold.

Consider some cycle R_k of even length k, with any number of agents. The following is an example of an SP mechanism: the cycle is partitioned to $k/2$ pairs of neighboring points. First, the pair in which agent 1 resides is chosen. The location within this pair of points is decided by a majority vote of all other $n - 1$ agents. This is not a dictatorial mechanism, and in fact every agent has some small effect on the outcome in some profiles. Moreover, if the cycle contains only few vertices, then there are even completely anonymous mechanisms (i.e., very far from dictatorships) that are SP. See Section 7.4.3 for detailed examples.

We still want to claim that when k is large enough, then any onto SP mechanism on the cycle R_k is "close" to a dictator. Note that even in the example above, the facility is always next to agent 1, which makes him a 1-dictator. The main result of this section shows that this is always the case (see formal statement in Theorem 7.15).

Main theorem . *For sufficiently large cycles, any onto SP mechanism is 1-dictatorial.*

In the next chapter we complete the characterization (for even k) by considering the embedding of the cycle in the binary cube. This will also enable us to derive a lower approximation bound for SP facility location and other problems.

As a proof outline of the main theorem, we go through the following steps: we first consider the case of two agents, proving that any SP mechanism must be Pareto and then that the facility must always be next to *one of the agents*. We then show that it is always the same agent, and thus a 1-dictator must exist. The next step is proving the same for three agents, using a reduction to the $n = 2$ case. Finally, we extend the result to any number of agents using an inductive argument close to the one used by Schummer and Vohra [2004] (and to similar ideas in [Kalai and Muller, 1977; Svensson, 1999]).

Before diving into the case of 2 agents, we need two general lemmas for onto SP mechanisms (a more formal statement is in Appendix E.2).

Lemma 7.6. *If agent 1 moves* toward x, *i.e. along the shorter arc between them, then* $x' = x$.

Lemma 7.7. *Suppose that agent 1 moves one step* away *from* x *(along the longer arc between them), Let y be the point on the longer arc s.t. $d(a', y) = d(a, x)$. Then either $x' = x$ (no change); or $d(x', y) \leq 1$.*

We also use a specific property of *cycle-Pareto*. For the exact definition see Def. E.1 in the appendix. However, for our proof sketch it is sufficient to note that cycle-Pareto is very similar to Def. 7.3 (in fact for even size cycles the definitions coincide).

We prove below that any SP mechanism for 2 agents on large enough cycles must satisfy cycle-Pareto. However, as Lemma E.3 in the appendix shows, this result is true for any number of agents.

7.4.1 Two agents on the cycle

Lemma 7.8. *If $a, b, f(a, b)$ are on the same semi-cycle,[4] then $f(a, b)$ is between a, b.*

Proof. Assume otherwise, w.l.o.g. $a \in (b, f(a, b))$. Then b can manipulate by reporting a, since $f(a, a)$ is closer to b than $f(a, b)$. □

Lemma 7.9. *Let $k \geq 13$, $n = 2$. If f is SP and onto on R_k, then f is cycle-Pareto.*

We give a simpler proof for large cycles. The full proof appears in Appendix E.2.1.

Proof sketch for $k \geq 100$. We start from some profile where $x = f(a, b)$ is violating cycle-Pareto. We use the notation $A \pm B$ as a shorthand for "in the range $[A - B, A + B]$". We show (Lemma E.4 in Appendix E.2.1) that cycle-Pareto can only be violated when the facility is at distance (exactly) 2 from some agent (w.l.o.g. $d(b, x) = 2$), and agents are almost antipodal.

(1) We set two locations for agent 1, as $a' = x + 20 = b + 22$ and $a'' = x + 30 = b + 32$. Observe that $f(a', b) = f(a'', b) = x$. For each of the profiles a', b and a'', b, we move agent 2 counterclockwise (away from x), and denote by b' [respectively, b''] the first step s.t. $f(a', b') \neq x$ [resp., $f(a'', b'') \neq x$]. Denote $x' = f(a', b'), x'' = f(a'', b'')$. See Figure 7.1 for an illustration.

(2) We show that b' must be roughly antipodal to a', as otherwise we get a violating profile that is contradicting (1). Then by Lemma 7.7, x' is a reflection of x along the axis $a' \leftrightarrow b'$. It follows that $|[x', x)| = |[x', b')| + |[b', x)| = 2|[b', x)| \pm 3 = k - 40 \pm 5$.

(3) From a similar argument, we get that $|[x'', x)| = k - 60 \pm 5$, which means $x' \neq x''$.

Finally, denote $z = f(a'', b')$. By Lemma 7.6, $z = f(a'', b'') = x''$, as agent 2 approaches x''. On the other hand, by the same argument $z = f(a', b') = x'$, as agent 1 approaches x'. Then we get a contradiction as $x' = z = x''$. □

---

[4]I.e., there is a segment of length at most $\frac{k}{2}$ that includes the three points.

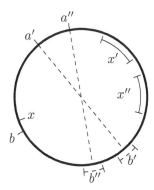

Figure 7.1: Agents' locations (a, b, etc.) appear outside the cycle, and facility locations (x, x', etc.) appear inside.

Lemma 7.10. *Let $k \geq 13$. For all $a, b \in R_k$, $x = f(a, b)$, $d(a, x) \leq 1$ or $d(b, x) \leq 1$.*

Proof. Assume that there is some violating profile, then w.l.o.g. it is $x = f(a, b)$, where $x = b+2$, and $a > x$. Also, by cycle-Pareto and Lemma 7.6, $a' = b + 5$ and $a'' = b + 7$ have the same outcome $x = f(a', b) = f(a'', b)$.

However, we show in the (full) proof of Lemma 7.9 that exactly this pair of profiles leads to a contradiction. □

We can now use the results above to prove the main result for two agents.

Theorem 7.11. *Assume $k \geq 13$, $n = 2$. Let f be an onto SP mechanism on R_k, then f is a 1-dictator.*

Proof. Take some profile a, b where $x = f(a, b)$, $d(x, b) > 1$. By Lemma 7.10, x is near a, i.e., $d(a, x) \leq 1$. We will show that agent 1 is a 1-dictator (in the symmetric case, agent 2 will be a 1-dictator). Assume, toward a contradiction, that there is some location b' for agent 2 s.t. $d(y, a) > 1$, where $y = f(a, b')$ (and by Lemma 7.10, $d(y, b') \leq 1$). We can gradually move agent 2 from b to b' until the change occurs, and thus w.l.o.g. $b' = b + 1$. By Lemma 7.6, moving agent 2 toward x cannot change the outcome, thus on the arc $[x, b']$ the order is $x < x + 1 < b < b'$.

We must have $d(b, x) \leq d(b, y)$, as otherwise there is a manipulation $b \to b'$. Thus $d(b, a) - 1 \leq d(b, b') + 1 = 2$, i.e., $d(a, b) \leq 3$. Also, $d(a, b) \geq 1$ since otherwise $d(y, a) = d(y, b) \leq 1$ in contradiction to our assumption. Thus there are three possible cases, and we will show that each leads a contradiction.

(I) If $d(a, b) = 1$, then since $d(x, b) > 1$ we have $x = a - 1$ (in contradiction to Lemma 7.8).

(II) If $d(a, b) = 2$, then $x = a$ (since $x = a - 1$ contradicts lemma 7.8). Thus $d(y, b) \geq d(x, b) = d(a, b) = 2$ which means $y = b' + 1 = b + 2$. This induces a manipulation for agent 1 $a \to b'$ (by unanimity).

(III) If $d(a, b) = 3$, then since $k > 8$, all of the points are on a semi-cycle and thus $x \in \{a, a + 1\}$, $y \in \{b', b' - 1\}$ (again, by lemma 7.8). However this clearly means that $d(y, b) \leq 1 < d(x, b)$, and there is a manipulation $b \to b'$ for agent 2. □

	$k \leq 12$	$k \in \{13, 14, 16\}$	$k = 15$ or $k \in [17, 21]$	$k \geq 22$
$n = 2$	**A** (Prop.7.16b)	**D** (Thm. 7.11)		
$n = 3$	**A** (Prop.7.16b)		**D** (Search)	**D** (Thm. 7.14)
$n > 3$	**ND** ($\Downarrow$ by Prop. 7.17)		**D** ($\Downarrow$ by Thm. 7.15)	

Table 7.1: Summary of results for SP mechanisms on R_k, with n agents. **D** means that every SP mechanism is 1-dictatorial. **ND** means there exists an SP non-1-dictatorial mechanism. **A** means there exists an SP anonymous mechanism.

7.4.2   Multiple agents on the cycle

Lemma 7.12. *Assume $k \geq 13$, $n = 3$. Let f be a unanimous SP mechanism on R_k. Then either f has a 1-dictator, or any pair is a 1-dictator. That is if there are two agents j, j' s.t. $a_j = a_{j'}$, then $d(f(\mathbf{a}), a_j) \leq 1$.*

Lemma 7.13. *Let f be an SP, unanimous rule for 3 agents on R_k for $k \geq 13$. For all $a, b, c \in R_k$, $x = f(a, b, c)$, $d(a, x) \leq 1$ or $d(b, x) \leq 1$ or $d(c, x) \leq 1$.*

The proof of Lemma 7.13 is using Lemma 7.12, which in turn requires the result for $n = 2$. Our next result for three agents relies on the previous lemmas.

Theorem 7.14. *Assume $k \geq 22$, $n = 3$. Let f be an onto SP mechanism on R_k, then f is a 1-dictator.*

Finally, we leverage the results of the previous sections to obtain a necessary condition for mechanisms on the discrete cycle for the general case of n agents.

Theorem 7.15. *Let f be an onto and SP mechanism on R_k, where $k \geq 22$, then f is 1-dictatorial.*

The last step of the proof is almost identical to the continuous case, as appears in [Schummer and Vohra, 2004]. For completeness, the proof is in the appendix.

7.4.3   Small cycles

A natural question is the critical size of a cycle, for which there still exist SP mechanisms that are not 1-dictatorial. The proofs above show that the critical size for $n = 2$ is at most 12, and for $n \geq 3$ it is at most 21. We next provide the exact numbers.

Proposition 7.16. *There are onto and anonymous SP mechanisms on R_k:*
(a) for $n = 2$, and all $k \leq 12$.
(b) for $n = 3$, and all $k \leq 14$ or $k = 16$.

For $k \leq 7$, the following "median-like" mechanism will work for $n = 3$: let $(a_3, a_1]$ be the longest clockwise arc between agents, then $f(\mathbf{a}) = a_2$. Break ties clockwise, if needed. For two agents we simply fix the location of one virtual agent (see proof in Appendix E.2.3). Note that like the median mechanism, this "median-like' mechanism is also optimal in terms of social cost.

For higher values of k the "median" mechanism is no longer SP, but we have been able to construct anonymous SP mechanisms using a computer search for all the specified values. A tabular description of these mechanisms is available online.[5]

---

[5]http://tinyurl.com/mrqjcbt

Proposition 7.16a settles the question of the maximal size for which non-1-dictatorial mechanisms for two agents exist. For three agents, we close the gap between Proposition 7.16b and Theorem 7.14 by performing an exhaustive search on all mechanisms with three agents for $k \in \{15, 17, 18, 19, 20, 21\}$.[6] Indeed, it turns out that every mechanism in this range must be 1-dictatorial. Thus we have a full characterization of the cycle sizes for which non-1-dictatorial SP mechanisms exist.

As a direct corollary from Proposition 7.16 we get the following result, by adding any number of agents from which the mechanism ignores.

Proposition 7.17. *For all $n \geq 3$, $k \leq 14$ and $k = 16$, there are onto SP mechanisms for n agents on R_k that treat the first 3 agents symmetrically. In particular, these mechanisms are not 1-dictatorial.*

Note however that the resulting mechanism is not an anonymous one. The exact sizes of cycles for which an anonymous/non-dictatorial mechanism exists appear on Table 7.1.

7.4.4 Implications of the main theorem

In this section we cover some strong implications of the result that any SP mechanism on a large cycle must be almost-dictatorial.

The social cost Recall that our initial goal was to prove upper and lower bounds on the approximation ratio of SP mechanisms. Dictatorial mechanisms typically have poor performance in terms of social welfare (or cost), and we will use this to prove a lower bound on the approximation ratio of facility location mechanisms (on a cycle, and thus on general graphs as well). While for a low number of agents a dictatorial facility location mechanism is not so bad (in fact, for $n = 2$ the dictator mechanism is optimal w.r.t. the social cost), for more agents the main theorem provides us with a lower bound that linearly increases with the number of agents (the corollary still holds for lower values of k, as appear on Table 7.1).

Proposition 7.18. *Every SP mechanism on R_k for $k \geq 22$ has an approximation ratio of at least $\frac{9}{10}n - 1$. The ratio converges to $n - 1$ as k tends to infinity.*

Cyclic graphs A second implication is that our result about cycles extends to a much larger class of graphs. A natural conjecture is that any SP (and onto) mechanism on any graph containing a cycle that matches the conditions of the theorem, must be 1-dictatorial on a subdomain. However, we need to be careful. In the continuous case studied by Schummer and Vohra [2004], *any cyclic graph* contains a continuous cycle and thus their negative result automatically applies.

In the discrete case, this is only guaranteed to be true if we add edges *outside* the cycle. We define a *minimal cycle* as a cycle that is not cut by any string. Equivalently, the shortest path between every two vertices on the cycle is going through the edges of the cycles. The extension of our main theorem is as follows.

Corollary 7.19. *Let $G = (V, E)$ be a graph that contains some minimal cycle $R \subseteq V$ that is sufficiently large (according to Table 7.1). Then any SP onto mechanism on G has a "cycle 1-dictator" $i \in N$. That is, if all agents lie on R then $d(f(\mathbf{a}), a_i) \leq 1$.*

---

[6]While the number of mechanisms for 3 agents and bounded k is finite, the size of the search space is huge ($k^{\Theta(k^n)}$). Thus any naïve search would be infeasible. However, by using the lemmas from Section 7.4 we can significantly reduce the search space so that the search completes in several minutes.

If we take a large cycle and add internal edges (so that it is no longer minimal), then there may be non-dictatorial mechanisms that are SP. As a simple example, the main theorem applies on R_{14} with $n = 2$. However if we add the edge $(0, 7)$, this forms two cycles of length 8. The following mechanism is SP and onto: if the two agents are on different cycles, then $f(\mathbf{a}) = 0$. If they are on the same cycle, then we apply the "median-like" mechanism for R_8 described in Appendix E.2.3, where the point 0 serves as the dummy agent for both cycles.

The continuous case   As we mentioned in Section 7.3.1 for continuous lines, one can repeat the steps of our proof, with some adjustments, when the underlying graph is continuous. This results in an alternative proof that every onto SP mechanism on a continuous cycle is *dictatorial*. In fact, some steps of our proof are greatly simplified in the continuous case, leaving us with a relatively short and intuitive proof for Theorem 2 in [Schummer and Vohra, 2004, p.22]. We do not include the full details here.

7.5   Randomized Mechanisms for Metric Spaces

A simple randomization has been demonstrated to break the lower bound given by Theorem 8.6, and to achieve a constant approximation ratio *with respect to any concept class*.

For the unconstrained version of the facility location problem, it is widely known that the "weighted random dictator" (**WRD**) mechanism (which selects each agent i as a dictator with probability w_i) is SP and guarantees 2-approximation. Meir, Procaccia, and Rosenschein [2009] showed that when applied to general instances, the approximation ratio of **WRD** is $3 - 2w_{\min}$ and this is tight.

When all agents have the same weight, we have that $w_{\min} = \frac{1}{n}$, in which case the approximation bound reduces to $3 - \frac{2}{n}$ (or $2 - \frac{2}{n}$ for unconstrained instances).

7.5.1   Improving the upper bound for weighted agents

As we will see later in Chapter 8, the $3 - \frac{2}{n}$ bound cannot be further improved for the constrained unweighted case, as any SP mechanism is essentially a random dictator mechanism. However we are still free to define the probabilities of selecting different agents, and we may take agents' weights into account. The **WRD** mechanism is an example of such a randomization, but we can design others.

A simple variant of the **WRD** mechanism is the *squared-weight mechanism* (**SRD**). That is, the mechanism would select every dictator $i \in N$ with probability proportional to w_i^2. In fact, for $n = 2$, the **SRD** guarantees 2-approximation, and cannot be further improved (for details see [Meir et al., 2011]).

Unfortunately, while **SRD** does attain some improvement over the **WRD** mechanism, it does not match the lower bound, even for $n = 3$. The approximation ratio of the **SRD** mechanism is at least 2.4 on some instances with three agents (i.e., strictly higher than $\left(3 - \frac{2}{n}\right) = 2\frac{1}{3}$). A similar counterexample exists for individually realizable datasets, where the approximation ratio of **SRD** is above 1.39 (i.e., strictly above $2 - \frac{2}{n}$ for $n = 3$). See Examples E.5 and E.6 in the appendix.

We therefore must take a somewhat different approach in the selection of the dictator. Consider the mechanisms **CRD** and **RRD**, where the latter is a small variation of the former.

The **CRD** and **RRD** mechanisms are clearly SP, as the probabilities are unaffected by the reported location.

Mechanism 2 The Convex-weight Random Dictator Mechanism (**CRD**)

for each $i \in N$, set $p_i' = \frac{w_i}{2-2w_i}$.
compute $\alpha_{\mathbf{w}} = \frac{1}{\sum_{i \in N} p_i'}$.
select agent i with probability $p_i = \alpha_{\mathbf{w}} p_i'$.
return opt(a_i).

Mechanism 3 The Realizable-weight Random Dictator Mechanism (**RRD**)

$h \leftarrow \text{argmax}_{i \in N} \, w_i$.
if $w_h > \frac{1}{2}$ **then**
    return opt(S_h).
end if
for each $i \in N$, set $p_i' = \frac{w_i}{1-2w_i}$.
compute $\beta_{\mathbf{w}} = \frac{1}{\sum_{i \in N} p_i'}$.
select agent i with probability $p_i = \beta_{\mathbf{w}} p_i'$.
return opt(a_i).

Theorem 7.20. *The following hold for Mechanism 2:*
(a) $\alpha_{\mathbf{w}} \leq 2 - \frac{2}{n}$.
(b) ***CRD*** *has an approximation ratio of* $1 + \alpha_{\mathbf{w}}$, *i.e., at most* $\mathbf{3 - \frac{2}{n}}$.
(c) *for unconstrained instances, the approximation ratio is* $\frac{\alpha_{\mathbf{w}}}{2} + 1$, *i.e., at most* $2 - \frac{1}{n}$.

Proof sketch of part (b). Denote $c_i = \mathbf{opt}(a_i); c^* = \mathbf{opt}(\mathbf{a})$. Note that for all i, $d(c_i, c^*) \leq 2d(a_i, c^*)$, since otherwise c^* is closer to a_i than c_i.

$$SC(\mathbf{CRD}(\mathbf{a}), \mathbf{a}) = \sum_{i \in N} p_i SC(c_i, \mathbf{a}) = \sum_{i \in N} p_i \sum_{j \in N} w_j d(c_i, a_j) = \sum_{i \in N} \left(p_i w_i d(c_i, a_i) + \sum_{j \neq i} p_i w_j d(c_i, a_j) \right)$$

$$\leq \sum_{i \in N} \left(p_i w_i d(c^*, a_i) + \sum_{j \neq i} p_i w_j (d(c_i, c^*) + d(c^*, a_j)) \right) \qquad \text{(by triangle ineq.)}$$

$$= \alpha_{\mathbf{w}} \sum_{i \in N} \frac{w_i}{2(1-w_i)} d(c_i, c^*)(1 - w_i) + \sum_{j \in N} w_j d(c^*, a_j) \sum_{i \in N} p_i \leq \alpha_{\mathbf{w}} \sum_{i \in N} \frac{w_i}{2} 2d(a_i, c^*) + \sum_{j \in N} w_j d(c^*, a_j)$$

$$= (\alpha_{\mathbf{w}} + 1) \sum_{j \in N} w_j d(c^*, a_j) = (\alpha_{\mathbf{w}} + 1) SC(c^*, \mathbf{a}) \leq \left(3 - \frac{2}{n} \right) d^*, \qquad \text{(from part (a))}$$

which shows the upper bound. □

By Theorem 8.7, no SP mechanism can do better on a general graph in the worst case, thus **CRD** is optimal. However, if the instance is unconstrained (i.e., it is known that $a_i \in V'$ for all $i \in N$), then **CRD** is suboptimal, and **RRD** is strictly better (in the worst case).

Theorem 7.21. *The following hold for Mechanism 3:*
(a) $\beta_{\mathbf{w}} \leq 1 - \frac{2}{n}$.
(b) ***RRD*** *has an approximation ratio of at most* 4, *and at least* 3 *(in the worst case).*
(c) *for unconstrained instances, the approximation ratio is* $1 + \beta_{\mathbf{w}}$, *i.e., at most* $\mathbf{2 - \frac{2}{n}}$.

Observe that for two agents, **RRD** simply selects the heavier dictator. Thus if the dataset is constrained, the approximation ratio can be as high as 3, which accounts for the lower bound in (b).

Implications   We conclude the results at the end of the next chapter. As we will show, the **CRD** mechanism matches the lower bound for *any* set of weighted agents, thereby showing that the uniform weight case is, in fact, the hardest. The situation with the **RRD** mechanism is similar—no randomization of dictators can do better. However, it is still an open question whether there are better, more sophisticated, randomized mechanisms for the unconstrained case (see Table 8.2). The natural conjecture would be that there are none, as we showed for deterministic mechanisms in Section 7.4. Note that when weights are uniform, then the **CRD**, **RRD**, **SRD** and **WRD** mechanisms all coincide, and all guarantee a $3 - \frac{2}{n}$ approximation ratio in the constrained case, and $2 - \frac{2}{n}$ in the unconstrained case.

Curiously, **RRD** is better than **CRD** when the input in *known* to be unconstrained, whereas in the general (i.e., constrained) case the converse is true. Therefore, a *different* mechanism should be used, depending on our assumptions on the world. However, the mechanism must be decided on *a-priori*—we cannot select between **CRD** and **RRD** after observing the reported locations, as this would not be strategyproof!

Chapter 8

Mechanism Design without Money II

From Binary Classification to a Unified Approach

Abstract. We consider facility location problems on graphs that are subsets of the binary cube. We show how we can embed line and cycle graphs in the cube in order to attain complete characterization of strategyproof (SP) mechanisms on these graphs. Then, we show that facility location on the cube is essentially equivalent to the strategyproof binary classification problem, as presented in [Meir, 2008] (and to other mechanism design problems), thereby deriving tight upper and lower bounds on the approximation ratio of SP mechanisms in both settings.

8.1 Introduction

While the results in the previous chapter were quite technical, the contribution of this chapter is more conceptual. We consider the strategyproof (SP) binary classification problem, as defined in [Meir, 2008; Meir et al., 2009], and show that it is equivalent to the strategyproof facility location problem where the underlying graph is a multi-dimensional binary cube. Other problems of mechanism design without money are also closely related.

Binary classification An essential part of the theory of machine learning deals with the *binary classification problem*: a setting where a decision maker must classify a set of input points with binary labels, while minimizing the expected error (for an overview, see for example [Devroye et al., 1997]). In contrast with the standard assumption in machine learning, SP classification is required in situations where the labels of the input points are reported by self-interested agents, rather than by a credible expert. Agents might lie in order to obtain a classifier that more closely matches their own opinion, thereby creating a bias in the data; this motivates the design of mechanisms that discourage false reports.

Judgment and partition aggregation Partition aggregation is just another name for aggregation of several binary classifiers, albeit not in the context of machine learning. In *judgment aggregation*, every judge reports her opinion over a set of issues which are logical expressions. These opinions are then aggregated into a single assignment that is consistent across all expressions (for example, if the issue "*X and Y*" is assigned a value of "true", then the issue "*X or Y*" must also get a value of "true").

8.1.1   Previous work

The study of SP classification mechanisms was initiated in Meir's M.Sc. thesis [2008] (see also [Meir et al., 2008, 2009, 2010]). These papers provided SP classification mechanisms for some special cases, and completed them with lower bounds on the worst-case approximation ratio attainable by SP mechanisms. In particular, it was shown that no *deterministic* SP mechanism can guarantee a constant approximation ratio. Similarly, no randomized SP mechanism can guarantee a ratio better than $3 - \frac{2}{n}$. However, many questions remained unanswered, in particular regarding randomized mechanisms in settings where agents are weighted.

Properties of mechanisms for judgment/partition aggregation have been discussed extensively in the literature since the 1970's [Wilson, 1975; Mirkin, 1975; Leclerc, 1984; Barthèlemy et al., 1986; Fishburn and Rubinstein, 1986]. A recent paper that deals explicitly with manipulations is by Dokow and Holzman [2010], which characterize strategyproof aggregation rules. *Approximation* in judgment aggregation are considered by Nehama [2011]. However, Nehama does not study social welfare, but rather approximate notions of consistency and independence.

Our current work differs in two important ways from the literature on judgment aggregation. First, we explicitly measure the quality of proposed mechanisms (in the spirit of AMDw/oM, see Section 1.1.3), which enables us to compare SP mechanisms to one another. Second, we study not only deterministic mechanisms, but also *randomized* ones. We believe that the notion of approximation, and the use of randomization (both a common practice in computer science) can also contribute to the study of more "standard" judgment aggregation settings.

8.1.2   Results in this Chapter

In this chapter we aim to provide a complete picture of the power and limitations of strategyproof mechanisms, closing most of the gaps left open by previous work in the field for both deterministic and randomized mechanisms.

A primary conceptual contribution is the observation that binary classification and facility location can be treated within a unified framework. More specifically we show how various structures can be naturally embedded in the multi-dimensional binary cube, which serves us for several purposes. First, by considering a natural embedding of the cycle R_k, we provide a full characterization of SP mechanisms on even-length cycles. Second, by embedding the line L_k we give an alternative characterization for facility location mechanisms on lines, using similar terms. Lastly, we show how every binary classification instance can be mapped to a subset of the binary cube, demonstrating that binary classification is a special case of the facility location problem.

As a consequence, many of the results on approximation ratios of facility location and binary classification mechanisms (from Chapter 7 and from the literature) hold in both domains. Since binary classification and judgment aggregation are essentially equivalent, results hold in the judgment aggregation domain as well. Our results, together with previous results that can be translated using the above mapping, are concentrated in Table 8.2.

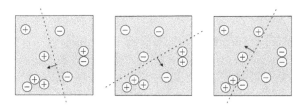

Figure 8.1: A dataset with labels. Here, $\mathcal{X} = \mathbb{R}^2$, $\mathcal{C}$ is the class of linear separators over $\mathbb{R}^2$, and $n = 3$. The data points X of all three agents are identical, but the labels, i.e., their types, are different. The best classifier from $\mathcal{C}$ with respect to each S_i is also shown (the arrow marks the positive halfspace of the separator). Only the rightmost dataset is realizable.

8.2 Preliminaries

8.2.1 Binary classification

Our definitions follow [Meir, 2008; Meir et al., 2009].

Let $\mathcal{X}$ be an input space, which we assume to be either a finite set, or a subset of $\mathbb{R}^d$. A *classifier* c is a function $c : \mathcal{X} \to \{+, -\}$ from the input space to the *labels* $\{+, -\}$. A *concept class* $\mathcal{C}$ is a set classifiers. For example, the class of linear separators over $\mathbb{R}^d$ is the set of classifiers that are defined by the parameters $\mathbf{q} \in \mathbb{R}^d$ s.t. $|\mathbf{q}| = 1$ and $b \in \mathbb{R}$, and map a point $\mathbf{x} \in \mathbb{R}^d$ to $+$ if and only if $\mathbf{q} \cdot \mathbf{x} + b \geq 0$.

Denote the set of *agents* by $N = \{1, \ldots, n\}$, $n \geq 2$. The agents are interested in a (finite) set of k data points $X \in \mathcal{X}^k$. We typically assume that X is *shared* among the agents, that is, all the agents are equally interested in each data point in X.[1] Naturally, the points in X are common knowledge.

Each agent has a private *type*: its labels for the points in X. Specifically, agent $i \in N$ holds a function $Y_i : X \to \{+, -\}$, which maps every point $x \in X$ to the label $Y_i(x)$ that i attributes to x. Each agent $i \in N$ is also assigned a *weight* w_i, which reflects its relative importance; by normalizing the weights we can assume that $\sum_{i \in N} w_i = 1$. Let $S_i = \{\langle x, Y_i(x) \rangle : x \in X\}$ be the partial *dataset* of agent i, and let $\mathbf{S} = \langle S_1, \ldots, S_n \rangle$ denote the complete *dataset*. S_i is said to be *realizable* w.r.t. a concept class $\mathcal{C}$ if there is $c \in \mathcal{C}$ which perfectly separates the positive samples from the negative ones. If S_i is realizable for all $i \in N$, then $\mathbf{S}$ is said to be *individually realizable*. Figure 8.1 shows an example of a dataset labeled by three agents.

We use the common 0-1 loss function to measure the error. The *risk*, or negative utility, of agent $i \in N$ with respect to a classifier c is simply the relative number of errors that c makes on its dataset. Formally,

$$\mathbf{R}_i(c, \mathbf{S}) = \frac{1}{k} \sum_{\langle x, y \rangle \in S_i} \llbracket c(x) \neq y \rrbracket = \frac{1}{k} \sum_{x \in X} \llbracket c(x) \neq Y_i(x) \rrbracket . \tag{8.1}$$

Note that S_i is realizable if and only if $\min_{c \in \mathcal{C}} \mathbf{R}_i(c, \mathbf{S}) = 0$. The *global risk* (which is the social cost) is defined as

$$\mathbf{R}_N(c, \mathbf{S}) = \sum_{i \in N} w_i \cdot \mathbf{R}_i(c, \mathbf{S}) = \frac{1}{k} \sum_{i \in N} \sum_{x \in X} w_i \cdot \llbracket c(x) \neq Y_i(x) \rrbracket . \tag{8.2}$$

---

[1] Some of our previous work relaxes this assumption [Meir et al., 2010].

8.2.2   The binary cube

A binary cube of dimension k is denoted by C_k. The set of vertices of C_k is the set of binary vectors of size k. Two vertices $v, v' \in C_k$ are *connected* if they differ in a single coordinate. Given a vertex v, we denote by $v[\ell] \in \{0, 1\}$ the ℓ'th coordinate of v. Therefore, $d(v, v') = |\{\ell : v[\ell] \neq v'[\ell]\}|$.

Suppose that V is some subset of C_k. Since every location can be thought of as having k coordinates (or attributes), the cube structure calls for some new definitions. We next define several properties of facility location mechanisms that operate on the binary cube C_k or on its subsets.

Definition 8.1. *A mechanism f is* Cube-monotone, *if changing coordinate ℓ of an agent can only change coordinate ℓ in the same direction. That is, if $a_j[\ell] \neq a'_j[\ell]$ and $f(\mathbf{a})[\ell] \neq f(a_{-j}, a'_j)[\ell]$, then $f(\mathbf{a})[\ell] = a_j[\ell]$.*

Another property often considered in a multi-attribute setting is *independence in irrelevant attributes (IIA)*. This means that coordinate ℓ of the facility is only determined by the values of coordinate ℓ of the agents' locations. While this property seems unnatural in the general case of aggregating agent location on a subset of the cube, it is reasonable in a lot of related aggregation problems. For example, in *preference aggregation*[2] the IIA property means pair-wise aggregation and is accepted as a desired property. We relax this notion as follows.

Definition 8.2. *A mechanism f is m-independent of irrelevant attributes (m-IIA) if $f(\mathbf{a})[\ell]$ is determined by coordinates $\ell - m, \ldots, \ell + m$ of the voters in $\mathbf{a}$.*

Note that the m-IIA property depends on coordinates order, and is not preserved under a permutation of coordinates' names. 0-IIA is just IIA. The following property is also quite natural.

Definition 8.3. *A mechanism f is* independent of disjoint attributes *(IDA), if the coordinates changed by the agent and the coordinates changed in the facility (if it moved) always intersect. Formally, if a_j, a'_j differ by coordinates $S \subseteq K$, and $f(a_j, a_{-j}), f(a'_j, a_{-j})$ differ by coordinates $T \subseteq K$, then either $T = \emptyset$ (i.e., no change in outcome) or $S \cap T \neq \emptyset$.*

A similar property was suggested by Dietrich [2007] as *independence in irrelevant information* (in our case a coordinate is relevant to its neighborhood, and irrelevant to all other coordinates).

Definition 8.4. *We say that a mechanism f is* Cube-Pareto, *if whenever all the agents agree on the same coordinate, then this is the aggregated coordinate as well. Formally, if $a_j[\ell] = 0$ for all $j \in N$, then $f(\mathbf{a})[\ell] = 0$, and likewise for 1.*

8.3   Embedding Line and Cycle Graphs in the Cube

8.3.1   Alternative characterization for SP mechanisms on lines

We give a natural embedding of L_k in C_k. Map every $x \in L_k = \{0, 1, \ldots, k\}$ to a vector $\varphi(x) \in \{0, 1\}^k$, whose first x entries are 1. Thus $\varphi(x)[i] = 1$ iff $i \leq x$. It is easy to verify that φ is distance-preserving, i.e., that $d(\varphi(x), \varphi(x')) = |x - x'| = d(x, x')$.

Every mechanism f on L_k induces a mechanism f_φ on the embedded space $\varphi(L_k) \subseteq C_k$. The following correspondences of properties follow directly from distance preserving of the mapping φ.

---

[2]Preference aggregation is similar to voting, only the outcome is a complete order over candidates rather than a winner. Dietrich and List [2007] show that preference aggregation can be seen as aggregation on the cube. Note that this means that all of our upper bounds apply to preference aggregation as well.

Lemma 8.1. *Let f be a mechanism on L_k.*

1. *f is monotone iff f_φ is Cube-monotone.*
2. *f is m-SI iff f_φ is m-IIA.*
3. *f is DI iff f_φ is IDA.*
4. *f is Pareto iff f_φ is Cube-Pareto.*

Corollary 8.2 (From Theorem 7.2). *An onto mechanism on $\varphi(L_k)$ (The line embedded in C_k) is SP if and only if it is 1-IIA, Cube-monotone, and IDA.*

8.3.2   Full characterization of SP mechanism on the cycle

Every cycle of even length can be thought of as "two lines attached in their ends". Indeed, R_{2k} can be embedded in the binary cube C_k in a very similar way to the embedding of the line. This is by mapping the first k points on the cycle (setting order and orientation on the cycle. We later show that these can be arbitrarily chosen) to vectors of the form $0^{k_1} 1^{k_2}$ (as with L_k), and the remaining k points to vectors of the form $1^{k_1} 0^{k_2}$. In particular, $\varphi(0) = 0^k$, and $\varphi(k) = 1^k$. As with L_k, it is not hard to verify that our mapping preserves distances, as

$$d(\varphi(x), \varphi(x')) = d(x, x') = |x - x'| \ (\mod 2k).$$

We can now turn to completing the characterization of SP mechanisms on the cycle, extending Theorem 7.15.

Theorem 8.3. *Let $2k \geq 18$ (or $2k \geq 14$ for $n = 2$). An onto mechanism on the cycle R_{2k} is SP if and only if it is 1-dictatorial, Cube-monotone, and IDA.*

Note that our characterizations for SP mechanisms on lines (Corollary 8.2) and on cycles (Theorem 8.3) use almost the same terms when formulated using the properties of the cube.

8.4   Binary Classification as Facility Location on a Cube

Consider a dataset labeled by several agents, and the binary cube whose dimensions correspond to the samples in the dataset. We argue that our classification model is equivalent to facility location on the binary cube, where the label vector of each agent corresponds directly to a specific vertex of this cube.

Lemma 8.4. *For any instance $\langle \mathbf{S}, \mathcal{C} \rangle$ of the classification problem, there is an equivalent instance of the facility location problem over C_k, where k is the number of samples.* Equivalent *means that any outcome in the original instance (a classifier), has a corresponding outcome in the location instance (a vertex), with the same quality, and vice versa.*

Proof. Consider the dataset $\mathbf{S} = \langle X, (Y_i)_{i \in N} \rangle = \langle S_1, \ldots, S_n \rangle$ in the classification domain. Set $k = |X|$, and translate $\mathbf{S}$ to the following facility location problem over C_k (one dimension per each data point $x_\ell \in X$). Every classifier $c : X \to \{-, +\}$ corresponds to a vertex q_c of the binary cube, where $q_c[\ell] = 1$ if and only if $c(x_\ell) = $ '$+$'. We extend the mapping q to sets in the natural way. In particular, the location of every agent $i \in N$ is the vertex $a_i \in \{0, 1\}^k$ corresponding to Y_i (that is, $a_i = q_{Y_i}$), and the concept class $\mathcal{C}$ corresponds to the set of allowed vertices $V' \subseteq \{0, 1\}^k$. See Figure 8.2.

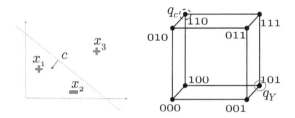

Figure 8.2: A dataset with labels $(x_i, Y(x_i))_{i=1}^3$, and a classifier c (left). Each of Y and c is translated to a vertex of the cube C_3 (right).

To see that the facility location instance $\langle \mathbf{a}, V' \rangle$ is completely equivalent to the original classification instance $\langle \mathbf{S}, \mathcal{C} \rangle$, observe that for any agent $i \in N$ and any classifier $c \in \mathcal{C}$, it holds that

$$\mathbf{R}_i(c, \mathbf{S}) = |\{x_\ell \in X : Y_i(x_\ell) \neq c(x_\ell)\}| = |\{\ell \leq k : q_{Y_i}[\ell] \neq q_c[\ell]\}| = d(a_i, q_c).$$

A similar mapping can be applied in the other direction, by mapping each vertex $a \in C_k$ (or $a \in V$) to a labeling function q_a^{-1}, where $q_a^{-1}(x_\ell) = {}'+'$ iff $a[\ell] = 1$. It then holds that for every agent $i \in N$ and every location $z \in V$, $d(a_i, z) = \mathbf{R}_i(q_z^{-1}, \mathbf{S})$, where $S_j = (X, q_{a_j}^{-1})$ for all $j \in N$. $\square$

The binary classification problem (and the judgment/partition aggregation problem) is thus a *special case* of the facility location problem. Other concepts can also be naturally mapped between the domains. It is easy to see that $\mathbf{S}$ is *individually realizable* if and only if $\mathbf{a}$ is *unconstrained* w.r.t. $G = \langle V, E \rangle$. That is, every agent has a perfect classifier iff every agent can have the facility located exactly at her location.[3]

Every general facility location mechanism f_{FL} in particular operates on binary cubes in arbitrary sizes, and thus induces a classification mechanism f_{BC}. In particular, if f_{FL} has an approximation ratio of α, then the induced classification mechanism f_{BC} also has α-approximation. Similarly, if f_{FL} is SP then so is f_{BC} (meaning that no agent can gain by misreporting her labels). We recall the following known results on SP binary classification.

8.4.1   Transferring upper bounds and lower bounds across domains

Upper bounds on approximation ratios of SP mechanisms translate immediately from the general case (facility location) to the special case (classification/judgment aggregation). Lower bounds go through in the other direction.

Corollary 8.5 (From Theorems 7.20 and 7.21). *There is a randomized SP $3 - \frac{2}{n}$ approximation mechanism (**CRD**) for the binary classification problem. For individually realizable instances, there is a $2 - \frac{2}{n}$ approximation mechanism (**RRD**).*

---

[3]To see why judgment aggregation coincides with binary classification, observe that we can map between every issue on the agenda and a single sample. Thus, a logical assignment to all issues corresponds to a classifier (an binary assignment to all samples). Similarly, every agenda corresponds to a concept class, which contains all assignments that are logically consistent with the agenda. The requirement that the opinion of every judge itself be consistent is thus equivalent to the individual rationalizability requirement. Other concepts could be similarly mapped onto one another.

As for lower bounds, we recall the following known results.

Theorem 8.6 (Meir *et al.* [2010; 2012]). *There exist concept classes for which any deterministic SP mechanism has an approximation ratio of at least $\Omega(n)$, even if all the weights are equal.*

The proof of the theorem uses a reduction from voting scenarios, and applies the Gibbard-Satterthwaite impossibility theorem (see Section 2.1.2). The proof is a variation of the proof of Theorem 3.1 in [Meir et al., 2010]. The details of the constructed scenario and the mapping to the corresponding voting problem are somewhat different and are given in Appendix F for completeness.

For general concept classes, the following lower bound is known.

Theorem 8.7 (Meir *et al.* [2011]). *There exist concept classes for which any randomized SP mechanism has an approximation ratio of at least $3 - \frac{2}{n}$, even if all weights are equal.*

Corollary 8.8. *No randomized facility location mechanism (on constrained instances) can guarantee an approximation ratio better than $3 - \frac{2}{n}$, even when agents are unweighted.*

Remark 8.1. The proof of Theorem 8.7, as appears in [Meir et al., 2011] has an unfortunate (but fixable) bug. The proof relies on a theorem by Gibbard [1977], stating that every randomized voting rule that is SP must be a mixture of duples and SP *unilateral* rules. The proof did not consider the possibility of unilateral rules other than the dictatorial rule. However, this problem can be easily fixed, by noticing that every unilateral rule other than dictatorial would have a poor performance in the case of unanimous vote (similarly to the way duples are handled in [Meir et al., 2011, Lemma 10]).

8.4.2 A lower bound for classification

Transferring bounds in the other direction is not so trivial, since in general facility location is *not* a special case of classification. Recall that in Chapter 7 we proved a lower bound of $\Omega(n)$ for (unconstrained) facility location mechanisms. In order to apply it to classification, we use the fact that the particular graph on which the bound was attained (i.e., the cycle graph) can be embedded in the binary cube, as shown in Section 8.3.2. Moreover, we will next observe that the embedded cycle corresponds to a very natural class of binary classifiers, known as *linear separators*.

The cycle R_{2k} (embedded in C_k) contains the $2k$ vectors $0^{k_1}1^{k_2}$ and $1^{k_1}0^{k_2}$, where $k_1+k_2 = k$. Note that these are exactly all the possibilities to classify (using a 1-dimensional linear separator) an arbitrary dataset of $k - 1$ points $\{x_1, x_2, \ldots, x_{k-1}\}$, where $x_\ell \in \mathbb{R}$. For example, the vector $1^{k_1}2^{k_2}$ corresponds to the separator defined by $\mathbf{q} = -1, b = x_{k_1}$.

We get that any SP mechanism for linear classification is in particular an SP facility location mechanism on the cycle R_{2k}. The following corollary then follows from Proposition 7.18. Note that this result in particular entails Theorem 8.6.

Corollary 8.9. *Every SP classification mechanism for linear classifiers in $\mathbb{R}^d$ (for any $d \geq 1$) has an approximation ratio of $\Omega(n)$, even when datasets are individually realizable.*

8.5 Conclusion

Tables 8.1 and 8.2 summarize the results of both Chapters 7 and 8. In particular, we provided the best possible (randomized) SP mechanism for weighted agents, and proved proved that the

	General datasets Constrained FL	Realizable datasets Unconstrained FL
Upper bound	$O(n)$ (#)	$\Rightarrow$ $O(n)$
Lower bound	$\Omega(n)$ (Th. 8.6)	$\Omega(n)$ (Cor. 8.9)

Table 8.1: Summary of results (deterministic mechanisms). The corresponding theorem for each result appears in parentheses. #—[Meir et al., 2009].

	General datasets / Constrained FL	Realizable datasets / Unconstrained FL
WRD	3 (#)	2 (#)
SRD	> 2.4 for $n = 3$ (Prop. E.5)	> 1.39 for $n = 3$ (Prop. E.6)
CRD	$3 - \frac{2}{n}$ (Thm.7.20)	$2 - \frac{1}{n}$ (Thm.7.20)
RRD	≥ 3 (Thm.7.21)	$2 - \frac{2}{n}$ (Thm.7.21)
Best upper bound	$3 - \frac{2}{n}$ (**CRD**)	$2 - \frac{2}{n}$ (**RRD**)
Lower bound	$3 - \frac{2}{n}$ (Thm.8.7 †)	1

Table 8.2: Summary of results (randomized mechanisms). We conjecture that the upper bound for realizable datasets is tight, but this remains an open question. #—[Meir et al., 2009], †—[Meir et al., 2011].

approximation ratio of any deterministic SP mechanism is linear in the number of agents—even in the unconstrained/realizable case. As we noted above, all results apply both for the more general problem of SP facility location in metric spaces, and to the special case of binary classification (or judgment aggregation, where realizability is known as *consistency*).

Interestingly, the techniques we used thus far seem insufficient for proving lower bounds on randomized mechanisms in unconstrained/realizable scenarios. Since realizability is common and sometimes necessary (e.g., in judgment aggregation), closing this gap is both important and interesting.

Chapter 9

Parking Allocation and Online Matching

Abstract. We study online bipartite matching settings inspired by parking allocation problems, where rational agents arrive sequentially and select their most preferred parking slot. Our focus is on natural and simple pricing mechanisms, in the form of posted prices. We construct optimal and approximately optimal pricing mechanisms under various informational and structural assumptions, and provide approximation upper bounds under the same assumptions.

9.1   Introduction

In recent years, smart parking systems are being deployed in an increasing number of cities. Such systems allow commuters and visitors to see in real time, using cellphone applications or other digital methods, all available parking slots and their prices.[1] At the same time, dynamic pricing becomes more popular in various domains [Lewis et al., 2010], including for example congestion tolls [Yildirim, 2001], smart grids [Roozbehani et al., 2011], and electric vehicle charging [Gerding et al., 2011; Stein et al., 2012].

Parking allocation as matching   We consider the problem of maximum online bipartite matching with dynamic posted prices, motivated by the real-world challenge of efficient parking allocation. As in the standard online matching setting, one side of the bipartite graph (representing the parking slots) is known in advance. The vertices of the other side (representing commuters) arrive sequentially and each demand a slot. However, in contrast to standard online matching setting where edges incident to each arriving vertex are revealed upon its arrival, the preferences of an agent over available slots are *private* and are only known to the driver. We focus on natural posted price mechanisms: drivers are assumed to be rational agents, and select a slot based on their private preferences and prices of available slots at the time of arrival.

While private preferences of agents and the restriction to posted price mechanisms impose additional challenges relative to standard online matching, in the parking allocation domain there are some natural structures on agent preferences that can be exploited to achieve more efficient

---

[1] San Francisco and other cities in California are already supporting such an application for some time now. Other cities are rapidly catching up [Richtel, 2011; Povich, 2012].

allocation. Specifically, we assume that every agent has a goal (e.g., her office building), and prefers parking slots closer to her goal, ceteris paribus. An agent's valuation of a parking slot thus depends on its distance to her goal. In this paper, we consider two natural single-parameter valuation schemes: MAXDISTANCE and LINEARCOST. In MAXDISTANCE, an agent is willing to accept any slot within a certain distance from her goal, while in LINEARCOST, an agent's valuation of a slot decreases linearly with the distance between the slot and her goal.

The objective of a system designer is to set up (dynamic) prices for available parking slots to prompt the most efficient allocation, in terms of social welfare. That is, the sole purpose of payments is to align the incentives of the agents with that of the society, rather than to make a profit. Note that our problem is two-fold: first, an optimal allocation may not be possible in the online setting *even if the agents were not strategic* (in contrast, for example, to the problems studied in Chapters 7, 8); second, the best *online algorithm* may not be implementable with fixed prices.

Although our problem is motivated by the application of parking allocation, the general setup is applicable to other domains with private preferences that have similar structural restrictions. An example is online procurement, where each agent has some ideal product or service in mind (the goal), but must select from a limited range of available options based on their similarity to her goal and current prices. However, in such domains, the system designer may arguably be more interested in maximizing revenue, whereas we focus on social welfare.

9.1.1 Related work

"Smart parking" has attracted much attention in urban planning. For example, Geng and Cassandras [2011] proposed a system asking each agent to report her maximum acceptable distance to her goal and maximum parking cost and leveraging integer programing to decide an allocation. Such systems do not consider the strategic nature of agents and have not yet provided theoretical guarantees on efficiency. Some related online allocation problems such as charging of electrical vehicles [Gerding et al., 2011; Stein et al., 2012] and WiFi bandwidth allocation [Friedman and Parkes, 2003] use auction-like mechanisms that are based on agents' reported type. The main difference in our approach is that it uses posted prices, which come with their pros and cons. The decision making of agents become very easy, but the mechanism may not get information that is required for a better allocation.

Matching   The parking allocation problem we study closely relates to maximum online matching in unweighted bipartite graphs, as defined by Karp *et al.* [1990].[2] In fact, one variant of our problem coincides with it exactly. In this case, we can easily implement their well-known RANKING algorithm, using random posted prices. Karp *et al.* proved that RANKING achieves an approximation ratio of $1 - 1/e$, and that no online algorithm (and thus no pricing mechanism) can do better.[3]

Some later work on online bipartite matching studied the best possible approximation ratio that can be guaranteed in several variants of the original problem, typically by varying the informational and distributional assumptions on arriving vertices [Mehta et al., 2007; Feldman et al., 2009; Karande et al., 2011]. The motivation behind some of these comes from the AdWords assignment problem (matching ads to search queries). A setting where all slots reside on a line was also studied, albeit with a focus on *minimum matching* [Koutsoupias and Nanavati, 2004].

---

[2]This is yet another difference from online allocation settings such as EV charging, where the underlying optimization problem does not always resemble matching.

[3]Note that in contrast to the two previous chapters where we tried to minimize the cost, in this chapter we are trying to maximize welfare, and thus higher approximation ratios (closer to 1) are better.

An extension of the matching problem to the case where every known node of the bipartite graph has a fixed *capacity* (as is often the case in parking assignments) is in [Kalyanasundaram and Pruhs, 2000]. The authors provide a deterministic online algorithm whose approximation ratio approaches $1 - 1/e$ as the capacity grows, and proved that no deterministic algorithm can do better.*

Weighted matching   While the general problem of online matching with weights is quite difficult (even in bipartite graphs), better algorithms exist if certain restrictions are made. Aggarwal *et al.* [2011] extended the result of Karp *et al.* [1990] to vertex-weighted matching, where every vertex on the *known* side (the parking slots in our case) has a weight. In one of our models, there are values (weights) attributed to the *unknown* vertices (the agents), in which case the approximation ratio may be unbounded. A different restriction on weights that has been considered—namely triangle inequality—has led to a $\frac{1}{3}$-approximation mechanism [Kalyanasundaram and Pruhs, 1991].[4]

Allocation with posted prices   Chawla *et al.* [2010] recently tackled a much more general challenge of resource allocation (not necessarily matching) using posted prices. They gave constant approximation bounds (between $\frac{1}{8}$ and $\frac{2}{3}$) for maximum revenue in a range of allocation problems.[5] Among other differences from our model, their model assumes that each arriving agent is sampled from some known distribution, whereas our results are distribution-free.

9.1.2   Results in this chapter

We study the parking allocation problem under MAXDISTANCE and LINEARCOST valuation schemes respectively and with various informational and structural assumptions.

For MAXDISTANCE, our contribution is two-fold. At the conceptual level, we isolate explicit structural and informational assumptions inspired by real-world parking allocation and establish connections to the well-studied online bipartite matching problem.

At the technical level, we provide several pricing mechanisms that are simple to implement. We show that when the population (but not the order of arrival) is known in advance, an optimal mechanism exists provided that we have access to each agent's goal. For other variants of the problem we provide approximation mechanisms and approximation upper bounds. Our results for the MAXDISTANCE valuation scheme are summarized in Table 9.1. In particular, when all slots reside on an interval between two goals, we show a pricing mechanism that attains an approximation ratio of $\frac{2}{3}$, which is better than the upper bound on the general case. In the most general setting without weights, when there is no restriction on the structure, the answers to most questions follow directly from [Karp et al., 1990]. We therefore focus on the weighted case, providing a constant approximation bound under the assumption that all types (but not the order of arrival) are known in advance.

For the more intricate LINEARCOST scheme, we focus on the case where both the population and the goals are known. By means of constructing a reduction to the *generalized second price* auction (see Section 6.4), we provide a pricing mechanism that guarantees the optimal social welfare.

---

*Meir, Chen and Feldman [2013, Theorem 18] supposedly show that a better approximation ratio is attainable in the capacitated problem. Soon after we learned about the paper by Kalyanasundaram and Pruhs [2000], which contradicts our results, we found an error in our paper (thanks to Yossi Azar and Niv Buchbinder). The erroneous theorem was not inserted into this chapter, which is based on [Meir, Chen, and Feldman, 2013].

[4]While distances between parking slots hold triangle inequality, the utility functions we define are not the distance (rather, they are decreasing as distance grows). Thus the weighted bipartite graph induced by parking allocation instances does not obey the triangle inequality constraint.

[5]Chawla *et al.* [2010] claimed that the same bounds hold for maximum social welfare.

9.2 Preliminaries

An instance of a parking allocation problem is a tuple $H = \langle \mathcal{S}, N, \pi \rangle$, consisting of a *structure*, a *population* and an arrival order. Specifically, the structure is given by a tuple $\mathcal{S} = \langle S, G, d \rangle$, where S is a finite set of parking slots, G is a finite set of goals, and d is a distance metric over $S \cup G$. We denote $m = |S|, k = |G|$. The population consists of a set of agents N with their preferences, where $n = |N|$. Finally, π is a permutation of $[n]$, indicating the order of arrival.

The preference of an agent $j \in N$ is given by (g_j, v_j), where $g_j \in G$ is the goal of agent j, and $v_j : S \to \mathbb{R}$ is a function specifying the valuation of agent j for being allocated some slot s. We assume that $v_j(s)$ is *distance based*, in the sense that it only depends on the distance between the allocated slot and j's goal. More specifically, $v_j(s) = \phi_j - C_j(s)$, where ϕ_j is a constant and $C_j(s)$ is some non-decreasing function of $d(g_j, s)$. ϕ_j can be interpreted as the cost of using a default option, in case the agent j is not allocated any slot, and is referred to as the agent's *type*. In the parking domain, such a default option might be a large parking lot that is always available, but is either expensive or inconveniently located. Throughout the paper we assume that agents with the same goal share the same type, i.e., $\phi_j = \phi_g$ whenever $g_j = g$. Note that agents of the same type can still have different utility functions. A special case is $\phi_j = \phi_g = \phi$ for all agents, for example, when there is a single default option available for all goals.

An allocation of slots S to agents N is a matching $\sigma : N \to S \cup \{\emptyset\}$, specifying for each agent her allocated slot (or in the case of $\emptyset$, no slot is allocated). Given any $i, j \in N$, the allocation satisfies $\sigma(i) \neq \sigma(j)$ unless $\sigma(i) = \sigma(j) = \emptyset$. That is, each slot can be allocated to at most one agent.

Mechanisms and pricing A mechanism M maps an instance of a parking allocation problem to an allocation. Let σ denote the allocation outputted by M for instance H. The *social welfare* achieved by mechanism M at instance H is defined as the sum of agent valuations at the allocation, i.e., $SW(M, H) = SW(\sigma) = \sum_{j \in N} v_j(\sigma(j))$. We emphasize that although the agent's decision is eventually based on the prices of slots, the social welfare is not influenced by monetary transfers.[6] For randomized mechanisms, we treat $SW(M, H)$ as the expected value over all realizations of prices and allocations.

We consider posted price mechanisms. Agents with private preferences arrive in sequence according to π and are presented with a posted price $p(s)$ for every available parking slot $s \in S$. The utility of an agent for selecting a slot s is quasi-linear, defined as $u_j(s) = v_j(s) - p(s)$. We emphasize that the price of a slot may change through the run. Also, the mechanism can block a slot, which is equivalent to setting the price to infinity (or just higher than any ϕ_i).

From a game theoretic perspective, posted price mechanisms are the most simple ones. Every agent is only affected by her own allocation, and the price each agent is facing does not depend on her actions or private information (the mechanism does not ask for this information). Thus the mechanism is *straight-forward* (see Section 2.1.1). As agents are assumed to be rational, they each follow their dominant strategy by selecting a slot to maximize their utility—or reject all slots and use the default option if none of the slots provides nonnegative utility.

The goal of the system designer is to design a posted price mechanism that maximizes social welfare. We emphasize that prices are just means to align incentives, and do not affect the social welfare.

---

[6]Equivalently, we can count payments in and sum over all agents and the parking authority in calculating the social welfare.

In the rest of this section, we define the criterion for evaluating pricing mechanisms, and various assumptions that can be made on agents' valuation functions, knowledge of the system designer, and structure of the parking space that our analysis will consider.

Approximation ratio We adapt the competitive model of Karp *et al.* [1990] to evaluate pricing mechanisms. The structure S is common knowledge among all agents and the system designer. We allow our mechanism to flip coins when setting prices. An adversary who knows the mechanism selects a set of agents N (i.e., their preferences) and an arrival order π.[7] The performance of the mechanism is compared to that of the optimal allocation, in the worst selected instance. Formally, the *approximation ratio*[8] of a pricing mechanism M over a structure S is $\min_N \min_\pi \frac{SW(M,\langle S,N,\pi\rangle)}{SW(\sigma^*(\langle S,N\rangle))}$, where $\sigma^*(\langle S,N\rangle)$ is the social welfare achieved by the optimal allocation for structure S and agents N. For convenience, denote $\mathbf{opt}(\langle S, N\rangle) = \sigma^*(\langle S, N\rangle)$ (or just $\mathbf{opt}$ when the context is clear). Note that the approximation ratio is at most 1, with equality if and only if the mechanism is optimal. Optimal allocations are w.l.o.g. deterministic.

Unless explicitly stated otherwise, we assume that the instances are "large enough". That is, the number of allocated slots in the optimal allocation, n and m are sufficiently large to ignore rounding issues.

Valuation Schemes We will consider two valuation schemes of agents in this paper. Each agent's preferences under each scheme can be characterized by a *single parameter* on top of her type.

MAXDISTANCE: In this scheme each agent j has a parameter m_j, specifying the maximum distance she is willing to walk. Thus if agent j is allocated slot $s_i \in S$, her valuation is $v_j(s_i) = \phi_j$ if $d(g_j, s_i) \leq m_j$, and 0 otherwise.

LINEARCOST: Each agent j incurs a cost c_j for walking a unit of distance. Thus, the valuation of a parking slot $s_i \in S$ for agent j is $v_j(s_i) = \phi_j - c_j d(g_j, s_i)$.

Informational assumptions In some cases, we make simplified assumptions on what the system designer knows.

Assumption KP (Known Population): the size of N and the distribution of agent preferences are public information. That is, the system designer knows how many agents exist for what preference, but does not know the preference of any arriving agent.

Assumption KG (Known Goal): g_j is public information. E.g., each commuter has a chip in her car to identify her employer.

Assumption UV (Uniform Values): $\phi_j = \phi$ for all j. We refer to UV as the *unweighted* case.

For the purpose of comparing our results with standard results on online matching algorithms, we also define Assumption PI (Public information), which means that the full preferences of each arriving agent is public information. Clearly PI entails KG.

Structural restrictions We will consider the following three classes of structures.
1. Structures with a single goal.
2. Structures with two goals, where all slots are scattered along an interval between them. That is, $d(s, g_1) = R - d(s, g_2)$ for all $s \in S$ and some constant R.
3. General structures.

---

[7]Following Karp *et al.*, this is a non-adaptive adversary.
[8]This ratio is sometimes referred to as *competitive ratio*.

9.3   General Observations

It is sometimes useful to decompose the allocation problem into two steps: find the right partition of space for the goals; and then optimally allocate space assigned to each goal to agents with that goal.

Observation 9.1. *Finding an optimal offline allocation is a special case of maximum weighted bipartite matching. Thus, under Assumption KP, the optimal allocation (and in particular an optimal partition of the space) can be found in polynomial time.*

To see this, suppose we define agents to be the vertices of the left side of the graph, and slots to be the vertices of the right side. We add an edge between every agent j and slot i, whose weight is the valuation of j for slot i. Then, an allocation is a matching and its social welfare is exactly the total weight of the matching. Maximum weighted matching can be found in polynomial time, e.g., by the Edmonds-Karp algorithm.

According to Observation 9.1, the MAXDISTANCE model under Assumption UV is a special case of maximum cardinality (unweighted) matching in bipartite graphs. Our next result shows that they are equivalent.

Lemma 9.2. *Let (I, S, E) be a bipartite graph with vertex sets I and S and edge set E. Then there is an instance of* MAXDISTANCE *where $d(s, g_i) \leq m_i$ if and only if $(i, s) \in E$.*

Proof. For every $i \in I$, denote by $\Gamma(i) \subseteq S$ the neighbors of i. Let $m = |S|$, and consider the $(m-1)$-dimensional regular simplex (with unit side length) over vertices S. Let d_k be the radius of a k-dimensional face in this simplex, then $d_k = \sqrt{\frac{k}{2(k+1)}}$. Note that $0 = d_0 < d_1 < \cdots < d_{m-1}$. Let $x_s \in \mathbb{R}^{m-1}$ denote the coordinates of slot s. For every agent $i \in I$ we define a single goal g_i, and place it in the middle of the face defined by $\Gamma(i)$. That is $x_{g_i} = \frac{1}{|\Gamma(i)|} \sum_{s \in \Gamma(i)} x_s$. Finally, we define the type of agent i as $(g_i, d_{|\Gamma(i)|})$. Thus $d(i, s) \leq m_i$ iff $s \in \Gamma(i)$. $\qquad \square$

Given the last lemma, we have the equivalence of the online problems under Assumptions PI+UV.

Corollary 9.3. *Under the* MAXDISTANCE *model with Assumptions PI+UV, the parking allocation problem is equivalent to the online maximum cardinality matching problem.*

This is simply because if the preference of an arriving agent is known, we have the same information as in online matching. We can allocate any desired slot s to this agent by setting the price of s to 0, and prices of other slots to infinity. It follows that any algorithm or approximation upper bound for online algorithms in one domain (bipartite matching/parking allocation) immediately applies to the other as well.

Our next observation is that given a partition of space to k goals, $P = (S_1, \ldots, S_k)$, the online allocation problem reduces to a single goal problem provided that we have access to agents' goals.

Observation 9.4. *Suppose we have a pricing mechanism that finds an optimal allocation for a single goal. Then under Assumption KG, we have a pricing mechanism that implements the optimal allocation for any given partition P.*

Upon the arrival of an agent with goal g, we block all slots of $S_{g'}, g' \neq g$, and price the slots of S_g as if this is the entire space. Since our pricing for every set S_g yields an optimal allocation of these slots, we get the best possible allocation for P.

Thus, under Assumption KG we have the following recipe:

1. Design an optimal online pricing mechanism for a single goal.
2. Based on prior information, find a good partition of slots to goals (either optimal or approximately optimal). For example, by Observation 9.1, an optimal offline partition can be found under Assumption KP.
3. Run the single goal mechanism for the appropriate goal whenever an agent arrives.

9.4 Parking at a Fixed Cost within the Maximal Distance

In this section, we assume the MAXDISTANCE scheme. We first note that by the equivalence to matching, even trivial mechanisms work reasonably well if all agents have the same type ϕ.

Observation 9.5. *Under Assumption UV, any maximal matching is a $\frac{1}{2}$-approximation. A maximal matching can be easily attained by setting prices of all slots to 0.*

A single goal We next consider a restricted setting, in which there is a single goal g, with value ϕ. In this case, we sort all slots according to non-decreasing distance from g. Thus $d(g, s_i) \leq d(g, s_{i'})$ for all $i < i'$. It is easy to see that if we take agents in an arbitrary order, and place j on the highest (i.e., most distant) slot s_i s.t. $d(g, s_i) \leq m_j$, then this allocation would be optimal. Indeed, if some m^* slots are allocated, then either all agents got slots; or all m^* slots closest to g are allocated, in which case there are no agents with $m_j > m^*$. The allocation in both cases is clearly optimal.

Proposition 9.6. *There is an optimal mechanism for a single goal.*

The mechanism is very simple: we sort slots according to nondecreasing distance from g, and set prices to $p_i = (m - i)\epsilon$ for all i, with some $\epsilon < \phi/m$. We refer to this mechanism as *monotone pricing scheme*. Under these prices, each agent prefers the most distant slot s.t. $d(g, s_i) \leq m_i$.

By Observations 9.1 and 9.4, monotone pricing can be easily extended to any number of goals in arbitrary spaces.

Corollary 9.7. *Under Assumptions KP+KG, there is an optimal pricing mechanism.*

In the remainder of this section, we study the best approximation ratio that can still be guaranteed when these assumptions are relaxed. For easy comparison, the results are summarized in Table 9.1. Throughout this section, we use the notation $\alpha = \frac{\max_g \phi_g}{\min_{g'} \phi_{g'}} \geq 1$.

9.4.1 Two goals on an interval

Our next setting involves two goals, residing on the two ends of an interval containing all slots. We sort all slots by non-decreasing distance from g_1, and this is also a non-increasing distance from g_2. We assume, w.l.o.g. $\phi_1 \geq \phi_2$, thus $\phi_1 = \alpha\phi_2$.

We say that $P_t = (S_1, S_2)$ is a *threshold partition* for threshold t if $s_i \in S_1$ for all $i \leq t$ and $s_i \in S_2$ for all $i > t$.

Lemma 9.8. *There is always an optimal threshold partition P_{t^*}. Moreover, w.l.o.g. t^* is exactly the maximal number of agents with goal g_1 that can be placed in the optimal allocation.*

Proof. If there is an agent with goal g_1 getting a higher slot than some agent with goal g_2, we could just switch them. Also, if there are gaps on both sides of the threshold, we could push down the threshold t^*. If we could assign a slot to one more agent from goal g_1 when $\alpha > 1$, this would shift the threshold up by one, which would displace at most one agent of goal g_2. Since $\phi_1 \geq \phi_2$, this would weakly increase welfare.   □

Lemma 9.9. *For any threshold partition P_t, we can implement with posted prices an allocation that is at least as good as P_t.*

Proof. The mechanism THRESHOLD is defined as follows. We need each agent to select the most distant slot s_i from her goal g, s.t. $d(g, s_i)$ is bounded by both m_j and the threshold t. In other words, the slot closest to t s.t. $d(g, s_i) \leq \min\{m_j, d(g, t)\}$.

On arrival, we price available slot s_i by ϵd_i, where d_i is the *number of the currently available slots* between s_i and t (not the distance); and ϵ is small enough such that, for all i, ϵd_i is less than ϕ_2 and if $\alpha > 1$ it is also less than $\phi_1 - \phi_2$. Moreover, if all slots in S_2 are full and $\alpha > 1$, we add ϕ_2 to the price of all slots in S_1.

Now, suppose that a type 1 agent with parameter m_j, denoted (g_1, m_j), arrives and selects s_i. There are three cases: (a) There is one cheapest slot closer than m_j, below t (i.e., on the "correct" side). Then this is the slot assigned to j by the optimal allocation anyway. (b) There are two cheapest slots, one on each side of t. Then one of these is the one from case (a), which is preferred by default since it is closer to g_1. (c) $s_i > t$ (but below m_j). This means that all slots $s < s_i$ are taken, and it cannot prevent future agents from being allocated slots above s_i. Thus, this new allocation is still optimal for the threshold t.

A similar argument works for agents with goal g_2, except that in case (c) all available slots belong to S_1 and thus cost more than ϕ_2. Therefore, agents with goal g_2 are never allocated slots $i \leq t$.   □

Given a threshold t, we can still implement an optimal allocation for t without knowing agents' goals. By Lemma 9.8, the optimal partition is indeed a threshold partition, we thus have the following.

Corollary 9.10. *Under Assumption KP, there is an optimal mechanism for two goals on an interval.*

We will later see that this no longer holds even in slightly more complex structures.

Unknown population   We next relax the strong assumption of KP, starting with an upper bound on the performance of online algorithms. Naturally, posted price mechanisms cannot do better.

Proposition 9.11. *(a) Every online algorithm under Assumption UV has a worst-case approximation ratio of at most $\frac{3}{4}$, even on an interval. (b) If we relax Assumption UV, then the bound is at most $\frac{1}{2}$.*

Proof sketch of (a). Consider the following two sequences of n agents, where $n = m$. The first $n/2$ agents (denoted N') are of type (g_1, n), with goal g_1 and maximum distance to walk n. They can be allocated any slot. Our two instances differ in the next $n/2$ agents (denoted N''). In H_1, we have $n/2$ agents of type $(g_2, \frac{1}{2}n)$. In H_2, we have $n/2$ agents of type $(g_1, \frac{1}{2}n)$. Note that $\textbf{opt}(H_1) = \textbf{opt}(H_2) = n$.

We look at both halves of the interval. After N' arrive, at least one of them is at least half empty (w.l.o.g. the half closer to g_1). Then in H_2 at least $m/4$ slots remain empty. Similarly if the half closer to g_2 is half empty, then the mechanism fails on H_2.   □

We present a mechanism called TWO-THRESHOLDS, which guarantees s $\frac{2}{3}$-approximation for unweighted instances when the goal is known. Denote by T_i the $m/3$ slots closest to g_i. Whenever an agent with goal i arrives, the mechanism sets infinite price on all slots in T_{-i}, and applies monotone pricing for the remaining slots.

Proposition 9.12. *Under Assumptions KG+UV, the TWO-THRESHOLDS mechanism guarantees an approximation ratio of $\frac{2}{3}$ on the interval.*

Proof. At the end of the sequence, if T_i is not full, then all agents of type i were allocated. If both T_1, T_2 are full or both are non-full, then the allocation must be optimal (either all slots are taken, or all agents are assigned). Thus suppose that exactly one of T_i (w.l.o.g. T_1) is full. Denote by T' the middle segment. If T' is full, then at least $\frac{2}{3}m$ slots are allocated and we are done. Let x_1, x_2 be the number of type 1 and type 2 agents in T', and let y be the number of un-allocated type 1 agents (that could be allocated in σ^*). There are no unallocated agents of type 1 with range above $\frac{2}{3}m$, as they would go the gaps in T'. However, every type 2 agent in T' prevents the allocation of at most one type 1 agent. Thus $y \leq x_2$.

Our mechanism allocated all of T_1, plus $x_1 + x_2$ slots from T', plus $z_1 + z_2$ slots from T_2 (to agents of types 1,2). That is $m/3 + x_1 + x_2 + z_1 + z_2$ in total. The optimal allocation would assign at most $x_2 + z_2$ slots to type 2 agents (as all were allocated), plus $m/3 + x_1 + y + z_1$ slots to type 1 agents. Thus the approximation ratio is at least

$$\frac{m/3 + x_1 + x_2 + z_1 + z_2}{m/3 + x_1 + y + z_1 + x_2 + z_2} \geq \frac{m/3 + x_2}{m/3 + x_2 + y} \geq \frac{m/3 + x_2}{m/3 + 2x_2} \geq \frac{m/3 + m/3}{m/3 + 2m/3} = \frac{2}{3}.$$

$\square$

To conclude the section, we present a mechanism that matches the upper bound on the interval in the weighted case. In fact, we use the THRESHOLD mechanism with a particular threshold.

Proposition 9.13. *The THRESHOLD mechanism with the threshold $\hat{t} = m/2$ provides us with a $\frac{1}{2}$-approximation for two goals on the interval.*

9.4.2 General structures

The RANKING algorithm by Karp *et al.* [1990] assigns a random priority over slots, and matches every arriving node to its highest-priority neighbor. They prove that the algorithm has an approximation ratio of $1 - 1/e \cong 0.632$ in expectation, and that no online algorithm can do better on general unweighted bipartite graphs. By Corollary 9.3, it follows that no better mechanism exists for the general parking allocation problem either.

The RANKING algorithm can easily be implemented with posted prices without any additional assumption (in the unweighted case), by assigning random prices to slots and keep these prices fixed.

In contrast, when ϕ_g's significantly differ, no constant approximation can be guaranteed even under Assumption PI.

Proposition 9.14. *No online algorithm can guarantee an approximation ratio better than $1/\alpha$.*

Proposition 9.15. *Setting fixed prices at 0 guarantees a $1/2\alpha$ approximation.*

Thus, the approximation ratio on general structures without further assumptions is $\Theta(1/\alpha)$. Another bound we can get is in terms of the number of goals. Consider the RANDOM-PARTITION mechanism, which generates a random partition of space $P = (S_1, ..., S_k)$ to the k goals. We know by Observation 9.4 that any partition including P can be optimally implemented with posted prices under Assumption KG.

Proposition 9.16. *Under Assumption KG, for any number of goals k, RANDOM-PARTITION is a $\frac{1}{k}$-approximation mechanism. Moreover, it can be derandomized.*

Proof sketch. A random partition allocates every goal roughly $1/k$ of the slots at every possible distance (in expectation). Further, with a deterministic queuing algorithm, we can make sure that *at least* $1/k$ of the slots at distance *at most* d are allocated to goal g - for every goal g and distance d.

Suppose that in the optimal allocation some set $N_i \subseteq N$ of goal g_i's agents are allocated slots. Then such a partition guarantees that at least $1/k$ of the agents in N_i can still be allocated. $\square$

Known population Our upper bounds thus far relied on the inherent difficulty of the online matching problem. When the population is known, the online matching problem (which is equivalent to parking allocation with Assumption PI) is trivial by Corollary 9.7, and thus this setting highlights the mechanism design challenge. That is, how does the fact that the allocation is done by a pricing mechanism affect the approximation ratio.

We next show that if agents' goals are unknown, then no pricing mechanism can implement the optimal allocation even if the population is initially known. Further, this holds even if the space is a mild variation of the interval setting from Section 9.4.1. We still use two goals on a one-dimensional line. However, there can be slots on either side of each goal.

Proposition 9.17. *For the structure of two goals on a line, under Assumption KP, there exists no pricing mechanism that implements the optimal allocation.*

Proof sketch. Consider a structure $\mathcal{S}$ over a line of size 8, $\{s_1, \ldots, s_8\}$, with two goals $g_1 = s_4, g_2 = s_7$, and four vacant slots $\{s_1, s_5, s_6, s_8\}$. All other slots are blocked. We set $\phi_1 = 2, \phi_2 = 1$. The population N has five agents: $(g_1, 1); (g_1, 8); (g_2, 1); (g_2, 1); (g_2, 8)$. Note that in the optimal solution we can place both type 1 agents and two other agents, thus $\mathbf{opt} = 2\phi_1 + 2\phi_2 = 6$. Our proof shows that for any *deterministic* mechanism M, $\min_\pi SW(M, \langle \mathcal{S}, N, \pi \rangle) \leq 5 = \frac{5}{6}\mathbf{opt}$. Since there is only a finite number of outcomes, it follows that the approximation of any randomized mechanism is also bounded away from 1. $\square$

While no optimal mechanism exists, the knowledge of the population can be exploited to achieve a constant approximation ratio. The mechanism computes an optimal offline allocation. Then it blocks low-value agents from getting slots that belong to high-value goals, by using appropriate pricing.

Proposition 9.18. *Under Assumption KP, the described mechanism has an approximation ratio of $\frac{1}{2}$.*

9.5 Parking at a Cost that is Linear in the Distance

We begin by characterizing the optimal offline allocation for a single goal under the LINEARCOST scheme. Suppose that we decide to allocate exactly $m' \leq m$ slots. Then it is clear that (a) these should be the m' slots closest to the goal; and (b) each of the m' agents with lowest cost c_j gets a slot. Assume slots are sorted by non-decreasing distance from g, and let $\sigma_{m'}$ be the optimal allocation of the cheapest m' agents. Then the social welfare is

$$SW(\sigma_{m'}) = \sum_{i \leq m'} (\phi - d(g, s_i) c_{\sigma^{-1}(i)}) = m' \cdot \phi - \sum_{i \leq m'} d(g, s_i) c_{\sigma^{-1}(i)}.$$

Uniform values for goals (UV)

Structure \ Assumptions	KP+KG	KP	PI or KG	none
Single goal		1 (Prop. 9.6)		
Interval (2 goals)	1 (Prop. 9.7)	1 (Prop. 9.10)	UB: $3/4$ (Prop. 9.11) LB: $2/3$ (Prop. 9.12)	$3/4$ LB: 0.632
Any		LB: 0.632	0.632 (#)	

Different values for goals

Structure		KP+KG	KP	PI or KG	none
Interval (2 goals)			1 (Prop. 9.10)	0.5 (Prop. 9.13,Prop. 9.11)	
Any	UB:	1 (Prop. 9.7)	< 1 (Prop. 9.17)	$O(1/\alpha)$ (Prop.9.14)	$O(1/\alpha)$
Any	LB:		0.5 (Prop. 9.18)	$1/k$ (Prop. 9.16)	$\Omega(1/\alpha)$ (Prop. 9.15)

Table 9.1: Summary of results for MAXDISTANCE. KP = Known Population, KG = Known Goal, PI = Public information. $\alpha = \frac{\max_g \phi_g}{\min_{g'} \phi_{g'}}$. Proposition numbers appear in brackets. Entries with no reference follow from other entries. #—[Karp et al., 1990].

Sort agents by cost c_j in non-decreasing order. In order to minimize $\sum_{i \leq m'} d(g, s_i) c_{\sigma^{-1}(i)}$ (and thus maximize welfare), we need to assign $s_{m'}$ (farthest occupied slot) to agent 1 who has the lowest cost c_1, assign $s_{m'-1}$ to agent 2 and so on. Thus to find the optimal allocation we can try all $m' \leq \min\{m, n\}$, and for each m' apply the optimal allocation of m' agents described above. Denote by $m^* = \text{argmax}_{m' \leq \min\{m,n\}} SW(\sigma_{m'})$ the optimal number of agents (and slots) to allocate. We will assume for the rest of this section that no slot is at distance 0.

9.5.1 Parking as a position auction

We will leverage results on generalized second price (GSP) auction [Varian, 2007] to set posted prices for our parking allocation problem under the LINEARCOST scheme and with Assumptions KP+KG.

Position auctions, and GSP in particular, were presented in Section 6.4.1. We follow similar notations here, except that we use s as a subscript for the slot (j is already used for agents). In a GSP auction, there are a set of slots with quality $(x_s)_{s \in S}$, and a set of agents with valuation $(v_i)_{i \in N}$. The utility that agent i extracts from slot s at price p_s is $U(i, s) = (v_i - p_s)x_s$. Agents each submit a bid $(b_i)_{i \in N}$. The GSP auction allocates the slot of the highest quality to the agent with the highest bid and so on. It then charges the agent assigned to slot s a price $p_s = b_{\sigma^{-1}(s+1)}$ per click. Hence, if $(x_s)_{s \leq m}$ and $(v_i)_{i \leq n}$ are non-increasing, then $U(i, s) = x_s(v_i - p_s) = x_s(v_i - b_{\sigma^{-1}(s+1)}) = x_s(v_i - b_{i+1})$.

The following table aligns the corresponding (not necessarily equivalent) concepts in both domains:

GSP:	CTR x_s	value per click v_i	bid b_i	price per click p_s	utility $U(i, s)$
Parking:	distance $d(g, s)$	cost per distance c_i	-	total price $p(s)$	utility $u_i(s)$

Varian [2007] characterized the Symmetric Nash Equilibria (SNE) of GSP auctions and provided closed-form expressions of agent's bid b_i at an SNE in terms of $(x_s)_{s \in S}$ and $(v_i)_{i \in N}$. The extreme solutions of this convex set are the *lower* and *upper equilibrium* (LE and UE), as they appear in Equations (6.2) and (6.3), respectively. Varian showed that these SNEs are *envy-free*. That is, for any two agents i and i' it holds that $U(i, \sigma(i)) \geq U(i, \sigma(i'))$. These results suggest that if we can calculate p_s (without engaging in the bidding process) and use them to derive posted prices for the parking slots, we can achieve the same allocation as the GSP auction at an SNE. Varian's expressions of b_i make it possible to remove the actual bidding process. Given $(x_s)_{s \in S}$ and $(v_i)_{i \in N}$, we can "simulate" bids at an SNE and then calculate the price for a parking slot, as $p(s) = p_s x_s = b_{\sigma^{-1}(s+1)} x_s$.

We now map a single-goal parking allocation instance to a GSP auction. Let $D = \max_s d(g, s)$, and set the quality (CTR) as $x_s = D - d(g, s)$. To determine the valuation of each agent, we set $v_i = c_i$.

The utility of agent i for getting a parking slot s is thus

$$u_i(s) = \phi - d(g, s)c_i - p(s) = \phi - (D - x_s)c_i - p_s x_s = \phi - Dc_i + x_s(v_i - p_s) = \mu_i + U(i, s).$$

That is, the utility of i in the parking allocation is exactly the utility of i in the induced ad-auction allocation, plus a constant $\mu_i = \phi - Dc_i$ that does not depend on the allocation.

For slots S and agents N, let $\mathbf{p} = \mathbf{p}(S, N)$ be a vector of SNE prices (there are usually more than one). As $u_i(s)$ is an affine transformation of $U(i, s)$, $\mathbf{p}$ induces an envy-free parking allocation.

Suppose we optimally assign the m' closest slots (ordered by non-decreasing distance) to the m' lowest-cost agents (ordered by non-increasing cost), that is $\sigma(i) = i$. Let $\mathbf{p} = (p_1, \ldots, p_{m'})$ be a vector of SNE prices for the first m' slots, based on the first m' agents (in the translated GSP instance).

Lemma 9.19. *By setting $p(s) = p_s x_s$ for all $s \leq m'$, the agents' utility is non-decreasing in index (and in the distance from g). That is, $u_j(j) \leq u_i(i)$ for all $j < i \leq m'$.*

We now define mechanism GSP-PARK for a single goal under Assumption KP.

Mechanism 4 GSP-PARK(S, N)

Extract $\sigma = \sigma^*$ and m^* by computing all optimal offline allocations $\sigma_1, \sigma_2, \ldots, \sigma_m$

Sort the cheapest m^* agents by *non-increasing* cost, and all slots by non-decreasing distance from g

    ▷ *Note that $\sigma(j) = j$ for all $j \leq m^*$*

Set $v_i \leftarrow c_i$ for each $i \leq m^*$, and $x_s \leftarrow D - d(g, s)$ for each $s \leq m^*$

Simulate some SNE bids $b_1, \ldots, b_{m^*}$ for these agents (in the induced GSP auction)

    ▷ *A particular SNE may be required, see proof*

Set the price of slot s_i to $p(i) \leftarrow p_i x_i = b_{i+1} x_i$ for all $i \leq m^*$

if $m^* \geq n$ **then return** prices $p(i)$ for all i

else

    Set $\gamma \leftarrow u_1(s_1, p(1)) - \epsilon$ (for some low ϵ)

return prices $p'(i) \leftarrow p(i) + \gamma$ for all i

end if

Theorem 9.20. *Under Assumption KP, GSP-PARK is optimal for a single goal.*

Proof sketch. Due to envy-freeness, we know that each agent $j \leq m^*$ prefers the slot allocated to her over any other slot at these prices. The translation γ prevents high-cost agents (those that are not allocated in the optimal allocation) from selecting a slot on arrival.

It remains to prove that the mechanism is individually rational (no negative utilities for agents), which follows from Lemma 9.19, after showing that no high-cost agent will want the first slot. □

An immediate corollary from Observations 9.1 and 9.4, is that under Assumptions KP+KG, there is an optimal pricing mechanism for LINEARCOST for any structure and number of goals.

9.6 Conclusion

In this chapter we established a firm link between online bipartite matching mechanisms and practical parking allocation problems. We then provided pricing mechanisms that can exploit the rising popularity of advanced city-wide parking systems in order to increase the social welfare of the population.

In the MAXDISTANCE scheme our main results were for the simple structure of an interval, where we showed a mechanism that slightly improves upon the upper bound of the general case (under the assumption that the goal is known). In particular this improves the lower bound of online bipartite matching (which is equivalent to Assumption PI) for this special structure. We conjecture that the upper bound of $3/4$ is tight, i.e., that better mechanisms exist—even without KG. Interestingly, when the population is not known in advance, same approximation ratios are attainable whether we reveal the full type on arrival or just the goal.

Our result for the LINEARCOST scheme reveals an interesting connection between parking allocation and ad auctions. While in this paper we showed how known results from GSP auctions can be applied to parking allocation, the other direction is interesting too: the multi-goal version of our problem can be interpreted as a generalization of the ad auction setting. That is, where the value of a slot to different advertisers may depend on different spatial attributes. As a concrete example, think of ads that are displayed across the screen. While advertisers in English value ads by their proximity to the left end of the screen, advertisers in languages that are written from right to left (like Hebrew and Arabic) value ads by their closeness to the right end. Interestingly, this motivating example exactly coincides with our interval structure from Section 9.4.1.

To conclude, while the assumption that the goals of agents are known is often realistic, the population itself is unlikely to be completely known in advance. Hence a realistic model of *partial knowledge* would be of great interest.

Chapter 10

Conclusions and Future Work

Throughout the thesis, I studied through a game-theoretic lense how self-interested agents interact, focusing on the *mechanisms* that regulate these interactions. I analyzed known and new mechanisms in a large range of domains, measured their stability in face of strategic behavior, and the level of welfare they guarantee to society. I see my main contribution in presenting new mechanism that improve the state-of-the-art, and in exposing the assumptions and conditions under which those mechanisms operate well.

In this final chapter, I tie together some of the results we have seen, and draw some general conclusions. I will also specify what else is required, in my opinion, to further promote research in the field of mechanism design.

Discussion and Lessons Learned

Towards a realistic picture of coalitional stability   In both Chapters 4 and 6, I showed how restricted cooperation can be used to achieve a higher degree of stability. In the first model the interaction structure was explicit, whereas in the latter we could not know which coalitions might deviate, and simply tried to minimize their number. A combined approach to coalitional stability would consider both known and unknown limitations on collusion, possibly attributing more importance to coalitions with a stronger incentive to deviate. This approach can both contribute to and gain from the ongoing efforts in game theory to combine the solution concepts of cooperative and non-cooperative games [Aumann, 1961]. Combined models would enable us to better predict realistic outcomes of games, and to improve the mechanisms we design. In future research, coalitional stability considerations should be taken into account, along with other goals such as welfare and fairness.

Welfare in voting   Despite the focus in Chapter 5 on showing stability of voting procedures, the ultimate goal of voting procedures is not stability, but rather to have a "good president", a worthy Oscar winner, etc. One of the major problems of the Plurality rule (other than its susceptibility to strategic voting), is that the truthful outcome can be quite unwelcome. There are multiple ways to qualitatively or quantitatively evaluate the welfare of a particular voting outcome (i.e., how good is the winner), and the *truthful* outcome of Plurality often turns out to be a poor choice under most of them [Xia et al., 2007]. For example, a Plurality winner may be ranked last by all but a small number of voters.

However, it is quite possible that *strategic behavior* under the Plurality rule or other voting methods is not just more stable, but also better for the society than voting truthfully (see Section 6.5). This line of thought is directly linked to the approach of *mechanism design without money*, as covered in Chapters 7 and 8. The iterative dynamics proposed in Chapter 5, and alternative dynamic behaviors [Reijngoud and Endriss, 2012; Gohar, 2012; Grandi et al., 2013] show that higher welfare is sometimes achieved by strategic voting, and further research is required to determine under what conditions they indeed converge to better outcomes.

While the quality of the outcome can be assessed via theoretical tools and simulations, behavioral experiments are required in order to determine how human voters really vote in iterative settings. I am currently performing initial experiments (along with Ya'akov Gal), in order to see whether any of the myopic behaviors offered thus far captures important aspects of human voting behavior.

Stability vs. welfare   In some of the domains covered in this dissertation, the tradeoff between stability and welfare is not an issue: in cooperative games (Chapters 3 and 4), outcomes with higher value are also easier to stabilize; also, in both of the domains that were studied in Chapter 6 (resource selection games and auctions), all of the equilibria we considered were optimal in terms of social welfare, and only differed in their level of stability. Conversely, in facility location and other mechanism design problems (Chapters 7 and 8), stability and welfare stand in sharp contrast. Therefore, the welfare criterion should be weighed against stability and other properties that I did not discuss, such as fairness (see a lucid survey by Budish [2012]).

In Chapter 9, the choice of using posted price mechanisms eliminates the need to deal with agents' incentives, and allows the designer to focus on welfare optimization. In other words, the inherent constraints of today's parking systems settle the tradeoff between stability and welfare. It is reasonable to assume that future applications will gather increasingly rich and detailed input on our preferences—whether for the purpose of parking allocation or other tasks—that can *in principle* lead to better outcomes, but may also cause stability to deteriorate as users are gaming the system. Good mechanisms should find the way to reconcile between the two.

One thing I made an effort to demonstrate in this dissertation is how concepts and methods originally developed in one domain often become useful in another. The concept of *treewidth*, which received much attention from AI researchers in the context of efficient computation, turns out to have strong economic implications (Chapter 4), and I am confident that this connection can lead to more breakthroughs. In Chapter 9 I showed how the concept of *envy-free* equilibrium in auctions can be exploited for the implementation of optimal posted prices mechanisms for parking allocation. The modeling of a voting scenario as a non-cooperative game in Chapter 5 can be used to give predictions about the outcome—and in the other direction, a reduction to voting scenarios is used to prove lower approximation bounds in other games, as explained in Chapter 8. These connections and many others vividly illustrate that mechanism design is inter-disciplinary in its essence, and that tighter integration of fields will boost the development of valuable mechanisms in all of them.

Is Mechanism Design "Useful"?

It is often argued that game-theory is not practical in the real world (see for example [Rubinstein, 1991]). While game theory can be studied purely from a mathematical perspective, much of its appeal is derived from the perception that it does help us to understand and predict human behavior in situations of conflict. This is particularly true for mechanism design, whose motivation clearly comes from actual problems in the real world.

In order to make mechanisms "practical", we need to make sure that the underlying assumptions (which typically follow standard game theoretic assumptions) will be as close as possible to the actual state of affairs. While this statement is true for most engineering problems, making "real" assumptions when it comes to human behavior is much harder than, say, making the right assumptions about file sizes in a database. As a result, the theory of mechanism design has only been successfully applied in a handful of domains. In several specific domains like *ad auctions*, players (who are typically *firms* rather than individuals) do try to maximize their expected profit as game theory assumes. Other mechanisms that are having groundbreaking success (for example in *kidney exchange* [Roth et al., 2004] and in *school assignments* [Abdulkadiroğlu et al., 2005]) keep decision making as simple as possible, even when there is non-trivial theory "under the hood".

More than its theoretical guarantees, the *simplicity* of a mechanism might determine whether people will use it successfully (or at all). Indeed, most mechanisms studied in this dissertation (random dictators, posted prices, etc.) are relatively simple, make minimal assumptions, and require inductive rather than deductive reasoning (see Section 5.6). I believe that this makes them practical, an hope that practitioners will find them useful as well.

Behavioral mechanism design What can we do when good, simple mechanisms are not at hand, and we have no particular reason to assume that players are more rational than the average person? The relatively recent agendas of *behavioral economics* and *behavioral game theory* provide us with a partial answer [Mullainathan and Thaler, 2000; Camerer, 2003]. By integrating empirical data with economic and cognitive theories (e.g., prospect theory by Kahneman and Tversky [1979]), corrected assumptions on human behavior in games can be made; by validating assumptions through experiments (as I mentioned earlier in the context of voting), and by constantly comparing predictions versus true results, unfit models can be discarded and the prominent ones can continue to improve. Needless to say, improved game theoretic models will enable the design of more practical and valuable mechanisms.

In the future, I intend to adopt more insights from behavioral game theory into my own work on mechanism design. For a computer scientist this has a sense of closure, as similar ideas to those guiding behavioral game theory have long been advocated within the AI community under the title of *bounded rationality* [Simon, 1957]. A new agenda of *behavioral mechanism design* will hopefully have much to contribute.

In conclusion, the occasional wrongs of the market's *invisible hand* can often be righted by the confident hands of a skilled designer. I sincerely hope that the models and results presented in this dissertation will promote further research in the field, and will lead to the design of mechanisms that are stable, optimal, and practical. Such mechanisms, in turn, will gradually make our world *better for everyone*.

—Jerusalem, May 2013

Part III

Appendices

Appendix A

Proofs for Chapter 3

A.1 Proofs for Section 3.3

A technical lemma that is crucial in the proof of the upper bound of $\sqrt{n}$, and that we will also use, is the following.

Lemma A.1 (Bachrach et al. [2009b]). *Let $G = \langle N, v \rangle$ be a superadditive profit-sharing game. Then there exists a solution $\{\delta_S\}_{S \subseteq N}$ to $\overline{G}$ such that for every $R, T \subseteq N$ with $\delta_R \neq 0$, $\delta_T \neq 0$ we have $R \cap T \neq \emptyset$.*

(See [Bachrach et al., 2009b, top of p. 7])

Theorem 3.7. *Let $G = \langle N, v \rangle$ be a superadditive profit-sharing game. Then for any positive integer $k < |N|$ we have $\mathrm{RSR}(G|_k) \leq k$. In the other direction, for any n and any $k \leq \sqrt{n}$, there exists a game G with $\mathrm{RSR}(G|_k) > k(1 - o(1))$.*

Proof. If $k \geq \sqrt{n}$ then by Theorem 3.4 we are done. Thus, we can assume that $k < \sqrt{n}$. Let $\{\delta_S\}_{S \subseteq N}$ be a solution to $\overline{G}|_k$ that satisfies the conditions of Lemma A.1. If $\delta_N = 1$, then we have $\delta_S = 0$ for $S \neq N, \emptyset$ and hence Equation (3.5) implies $\mathrm{RSR}(G|_k) = 1$. Now, suppose that $\delta_N < 1$. We claim that in this case $\delta_T > 0$ for some coalition T with $|T| \leq k$. Indeed, otherwise all terms in Equation (3.5) except possibly for $\delta_N v|_k(N)$ would be equal to 0 and we would get $\mathrm{RSR}(G|_k) = \frac{1}{v|_k(N)} \delta_N v|_k(N) = \delta_N < 1$, a contradiction.

Now, consider a coalition T with $|T| \leq k$, $\delta_T > 0$. We have

$$
\begin{aligned}
\mathrm{RSR}(G|_k) &= \frac{1}{v|_k(N)} \sum_{S \subseteq N} \delta_S v|_k(S) \leq \frac{1}{v|_k(N)} \sum_{i \in T} \sum_{S \subseteq N : i \in S} \delta_S v|_k(S) \\
&\leq \sum_{i \in T} \sum_{S \subseteq N : i \in S} \delta_S = \sum_{i \in T} 1 = |T| \leq k,
\end{aligned}
$$

which completes the proof of the upper bound.

To see that this bound is asymptotically tight, let q be the largest prime number strictly below k. Note that $q > k - O(\ln k) = k(1 - o(1))$. Consider the game $G_q^* = \langle N^*, v^* \rangle$ with n^* agents described in Example 3.2. Note that $n^* = q^2 + q + 1 < (q + 1)^2 \leq k^2$. We now embed G_q^* into a larger game $G_q = \langle N, v \rangle$. Specifically, we set $N = N^* \cup N'$ for an arbitrary set N' of size

$n - n^*$, and let $v(S) = v^*(S \cap N^*)$ for every $S \subseteq N'$. It is immediate that G_q is superadditive. Further, it is easy to see that any payoff vector $\mathbf{p}$ in the core of $\overline{G_q|_k}$ satisfies $p_i = 0$ for $i \notin N^*$, and hence there is a natural one-to-one correspondence between the core of $\overline{G_q|_k}$ and that of $\overline{G_q^*}$. Consequently, we have

$$\mathrm{RSR}(G_q|_k) = \mathrm{RSR}(G_q^*) > \sqrt{q^2 + q + 1} > q \geq k(1 - o(1)).$$

$\square$

Proposition A.2 (Observation 3.8). *Set cover games are subadditive. Furthermore, every subadditive expense-sharing game can be described as a set cover game.*

Proof. Fix a set cover game G given by a tuple $\langle N, \mathcal{F}, w \rangle$. For every pair of subsets $S, T \subseteq N$ we have $S \cup T \subseteq \mathcal{F}^*(S) \cup \mathcal{F}^*(T)$. Therefore, $c(S \cup T) \leq c(S) + c(T)$, i.e., G is subadditive.

Conversely, given a subadditive expense-sharing game $G = \langle N, c \rangle$, we construct a set cover game by setting $\mathcal{F} = 2^N$, $w(F) = c(F)$ for every $F \in \mathcal{F}$. We will now argue that the resulting game $G' = \langle N, c' \rangle$ is equivalent to G. Indeed, consider a set S and its cheapest cover $\mathcal{F}^*(S)$. We have $c'(S) = \sum_{F \in \mathcal{F}^*(S)} c(F)$. Since G is monotone, we can assume that the sets in $\mathcal{F}^*(S)$ are pairwise disjoint: if we have $F_1 \cap F_2 \neq \emptyset$ for some $F_1, F_2 \in \mathcal{F}^*(S)$, we can replace F_2 with $F_2 \setminus F_1$ without increasing the overall cost. Now, set $F' = \cup_{F \in \mathcal{F}^*(S)} F$. The superadditivity of G implies that $c(F') \leq \sum_{F \in \mathcal{F}^*(S)} c(F) = c'(S)$. Further, since S is a subset of F', we have $c(S) \leq c(F')$ and hence $c(S) \leq c'(S)$. On the other hand, $\{S\}$ is a cover of S, so we have $c'(S) \leq c(S)$. Thus, $c'(S) = c(S)$. Since this holds for every set $S \subseteq N$, the games G and G' are equivalent. $\square$

Theorem 3.9. *Let G be a set cover game. Then $\mathrm{CRR}(G) = 1/\mathrm{IG}(G)$.*

Proof. Consider a set cover game $G = \langle N, \mathcal{F}, w \rangle$, whose integral solution is $ILP(G, N) = c(N)$. The dual to the (relaxed) linear program $\mathcal{LP}(G, N)$ is the following linear program $\mathcal{LP}_{\mathrm{dual}}(G, N)$ over the set of variables $\{p_i\}_{i \in N}$:

$$\max \sum_{i \in N} p_i \qquad \text{subject to:}$$

$$\sum_{i \in F_j} p_i \ \leq \ w(F_j) \text{ for each } F_j \in \mathcal{F} \qquad\qquad (\mathrm{A.1})$$

$$p_i \ \geq \ 0 \text{ for each } i \in N.$$

We can see that $\mathcal{LP}_{\mathrm{dual}}(G, N)$ is very similar to $\mathcal{LP}'$ (which defines the $\mathrm{addCoS}(G)$). In fact, it is the same program only with fewer constraints. Thus, let $\mathbf{p}$ be a stable sub-imputation for G. Since $\mathbf{p}$ is not blocked by any coalition, it satisfies all constraints of $\mathcal{LP}_{\mathrm{dual}}(G, N)$ and therefore $\sum_{i \in N} p_i \leq \mathrm{LP}(G, N)$, and $\mathrm{CRR}(G) \leq \frac{p^*(N)}{c(N)} \leq \frac{\mathrm{LP}(G,N)}{\mathrm{ILP}(G,N)}$.

In the other direction, let $\mathbf{p}$ be a feasible solution of $\mathcal{LP}_{\mathrm{dual}}(G, N)$. Consider a coalition S with cost $c(S)$. By definition of the cost function, the set S can be covered by a collection of subsets $\mathcal{F}^*(S) = \{F_1, \ldots, F_k\}$ of cost $c(S) = \sum_{\ell=1}^{k} w(F_\ell)$. Note that

$$\sum_{i \in S} p_i \leq \sum_{\ell=1}^{k} \sum_{i \in F_\ell} p_i \leq \sum_{\ell=1}^{k} w(F_\ell) = c(S).$$

That is, the payoff vector $\mathbf{p}$ is not blocked by any coalition.

Now, let $\mathbf{p}^*$ be an optimal solution to the LP (A.1). By strong LP duality, we have $\sum_{i\in N} p_i^* = \mathrm{LP}_{\mathrm{dual}}(G,N) = \mathrm{LP}(G,N)$ and hence $\mathrm{CRR}(G) \geq \frac{p^*(N)}{c(N)} = \frac{\mathrm{LP}(G,N)}{\mathrm{ILP}(G,N)}$ and the proof is complete. $\qquad\square$

Lemma 3.11. *Let $G = \langle N, c\rangle$ be an anonymous expense-sharing game. Then*

$$\mathrm{CRR}(G) = \frac{n}{c_n}\cdot\min_{k\leq n}\frac{c_k}{k}.$$

Proof. Pick $k^* \in \arg\min_{k\leq n} c_k/k$, and let $\mathbf{p}$ be a sub-imputation given by $p_i = c_{k^*}/k^*$ for all $i \in N$. Clearly, $\mathbf{p}$ is stable: for every $S \subseteq N$ we have $p(S) = |S|c_{k^*}/k^* \leq c(S)$ by our choice of k^*.

Now, suppose that there is a stable sub-imputation $\mathbf{q}$ with $q(N) > p(N)$. Consider a coalition S with $|S| = k^*$ that satisfies $q(S) \geq q(S')$ for all coalitions S' of size k^*. We have

$$q(S) \geq \frac{k^*}{n}q(N) > \frac{k^*}{n}p(N) = c_{k^*},$$

which means that $\mathbf{q}$ is not stable. Hence,

$$\mathrm{CRR}(G) = \frac{p(N)}{c(N)} = \frac{n}{c_n}\cdot\frac{c_{k^*}}{k^*},$$

which completes the proof. A symmetric argument proves Lemma 3.6. $\qquad\square$

Theorem 3.12. *Let $G = \langle N, c\rangle$ be an anonymous subadditive expense-sharing game. Then $\mathrm{CRR}(G) \geq 1/2 + \frac{1}{2n-2}$, and this bound is tight.*

Proof. For $n \leq 2$ the theorem is trivial. Thus assume $n \geq 3$. $c_n = c_{\frac{n}{k}\cdot k} \leq \lceil\frac{n}{k}\rceil c_k$, which means that $n\frac{c_k}{k} \geq \frac{n}{k}\frac{1}{\lceil\frac{n}{k}\rceil}c_n$ for any k, and in particular for $k^* = \arg\min\frac{c_k}{k}$.

We denote $\frac{n}{k^*}$ by a. Note that $a \geq \frac{n}{n-1} > 1$, thus $\lceil a\rceil \geq 2$. We first look at the case $\lceil a\rceil \geq 3$. This means that $a > 2$, and thus (for $n \geq 4$)

$$\frac{a}{\lceil a\rceil} \geq \frac{a}{a+1} \geq \frac{2}{3} \geq \frac{n}{2n-2}\ .$$

The alternative case is $\lceil a\rceil = 2$. Here, $a = \frac{n}{n-1}$ minimizes the expression $\frac{a}{\lceil a\rceil}$ (since the denominator is fixed), and we get that $\frac{a}{\lceil a\rceil} \geq \frac{n/(n-1)}{2} = \frac{n}{2n-2}$. Note that for $n = 3$ we are either in the second case, or $k^* = 1$, and thus $\frac{a}{\lceil a\rceil} = \frac{3}{3} = 1 > \frac{n}{2n-2}$ also holds.

We showed that in any case $\frac{a}{\lceil a\rceil} \geq \frac{n}{2n-2}$, thus, by Lemma 3.11 :

$$\mathrm{CRR}(G) = \frac{n}{c_n}\frac{c_{k^*}}{k^*} \geq \frac{n}{k^*}\frac{1}{\lceil\frac{n}{k^*}\rceil} = \frac{a}{\lceil a\rceil}$$

$$\geq \frac{n}{2n-2} = \frac{n-1+1}{2n-2} = 1/2 + \frac{1}{2n-2}.$$

For tightness, consider a game where $c_n = 2$, and $c_k = 1$ for any $k < n$. In this game $k^* = n - 1$, and by using Lemma 3.11,

$$\mathrm{CRR}(G) = \frac{n}{c_n} \frac{c_{k^*}}{k^*} = \frac{n}{2(n-1)} = \nicefrac{1}{2} + \frac{1}{2n - 2}.$$

$\square$

A.2   Proofs for Section 3.4

Proposition 3.13. *Let $G = \langle N, v \rangle$ be a profit-sharing game. Then $\mathrm{addCoS}(G) \leq n\epsilon_{\mathbf{S}}(G)$, and this bound is tight.*

Proof. If $\epsilon_{\mathbf{S}}(G) = 0$, we have $\mathrm{addCoS}(G) = 0$. Now, assume $\epsilon_{\mathbf{S}}(G) > 0$. Let $\mathbf{p}$ be a payoff vector in the strong least core of G. For every $S \subseteq N$ we have $p(S) \geq v(S) - \epsilon_{\mathbf{S}}(G)$. Consider the payoff vector $\mathbf{p}^*$ given by $p_i^* = p_i + \epsilon_{\mathbf{S}}(G)$ for all $i \in N$. Clearly, we have $p^*(S) \geq v(S)$ for every $S \subseteq N$, i.e., $\mathbf{p}^*$ is stable. Furthermore, it is easy to see that $p^*(N) = v(N) + n \cdot \epsilon_{\mathbf{S}}(G)$, so $\mathrm{addCoS}(G) \leq \mathrm{addCoS}(\mathbf{p}^*, G) \leq n\epsilon_{\mathbf{S}}(G)$.

To see that this bound is tight, consider the game $G = \langle N, v \rangle$ with $v(S) = 1$ for all $S \neq \emptyset$. It is easy to see that $\epsilon_{\mathbf{S}}(G) = (n-1)/n$. On the other hand, $\mathrm{addCoS}(G) = n - 1 = n \cdot \epsilon_{\mathbf{S}}(G)$. $\square$

Theorem 3.14. *Let $G = \langle N, v \rangle$ be a superadditive profit-sharing game, Then $\mathrm{addCoS}(G) \leq \sqrt{n} \cdot \epsilon_{\mathbf{S}}(G)$, and this bound is tight up to a small additive constant.*

Proof. By Lemma A.1 there exists a solution $(\delta_S)_{S \in \mathcal{D}}$ to $\overline{G}$ such that every two sets S and T with $\delta_S \neq 0$ and $\delta_T \neq 0$ have a non-empty intersection.

Since $(\delta_S)_{S \in \mathcal{D}}$ is a balancing weight vector for 2^N, applying the Bondareva–Shapley theorem to the game G_ϵ (which has a non-empty core), we obtain

$$\sum_{S \subseteq N} \delta_S(v(S) - \epsilon) = \sum_{S \subseteq N} \delta_S v_\epsilon(S) \leq v_\epsilon(N) = v(N).$$

Together with the fact that $\sum_{S \subseteq N} \delta_S \leq \sqrt{n}$ (cf. the proof of Theorem 3.4), this implies

$$\mathrm{addCoS}(G) = \sum_{S \subseteq N} \delta_S v(S) - v(N) \leq \sum_{S \subseteq N} \delta_S v(S) - \sum_{S \subseteq N} \delta_S(v(S) - \epsilon)$$

$$= \epsilon \sum_{S \subseteq N} \delta_S \leq \sqrt{n}\epsilon = \sqrt{n}\epsilon_{\mathbf{S}}(G),$$

which completes the proof of the upper bound.

To see that this bound is tight, consider the game G_q (see Example 3.2). Since G_q is a simple game, we have $\epsilon_{\mathbf{S}}(G_q) \leq 1$. Moreover, consider the payoff vector $\mathbf{p}$ given by $p_i = \nicefrac{1}{n}$ for all $i \in N$. If S is a winning coalition in G_q, then $|S| \geq q + 1$ and thus $p(S) \geq (q+1)/n \geq 1/\sqrt{n}$. Therefore $\epsilon_{\mathbf{S}}(G_q) \leq 1 - 1/\sqrt{n}$, and hence $\sqrt{n} \cdot \epsilon_{\mathbf{S}}(G) \leq \sqrt{n} - 1$. On the other hand, we have seen that $\mathrm{RSR}(G_q) > \sqrt{n} - 1$. Since G_q is a simple game, this implies

$$\mathrm{addCoS}(G_q) = \mathrm{RSR}(G_q) - 1 > (\sqrt{n} - 1) - 1 \geq \sqrt{n} \cdot \epsilon_{\mathbf{S}}(G) - 1.$$

$\square$

Theorem 3.15. *Let $G = \langle N, v \rangle$ be a profit-sharing game. Then* $\mathrm{addCoS}(G) \geq \frac{n}{n-1} \epsilon_{\mathbf{S}}(G)$, *and this bound is tight.*

Proof. If the core of G is non-empty, the inequality holds trivially. Thus, let us assume that G has an empty core. Let $\epsilon = \epsilon_{\mathbf{S}}(G)$.

Consider the game G_ϵ. An argument similar to the one used in Section 3.2.2 shows that there exists a minimal balanced collection of subsets $\mathcal{D} \neq \{N\}$ and a balancing weight vector $\{\delta_S\}_{S \in \mathcal{D}}$ for $\mathcal{D}$ for which the inequality in the statement of the Bondareva–Shapley theorem (applied to G_ϵ) holds with equality, i.e.,

$$\sum_{S \in \mathcal{D}} \delta_S v_\epsilon(S) = v(N). \tag{A.2}$$

Note that by minimality of $\mathcal{D}$ we have $N \notin \mathcal{D}$, as otherwise we would have $\mathcal{D} = \{N\}$. For each $i \in N$ we have $\sum_{S \in \mathcal{D}: i \in S} \delta_S = 1$. Summing over $i \in N$, we obtain

$$n = \sum_{i \in N} \sum_{S \in \mathcal{D}: i \in S} \delta_S = \sum_{S \in \mathcal{D}} \sum_{i \in S} \delta_S = \sum_{S \in \mathcal{D}} |S| \delta_S \leq (n-1) \sum_{S \in \mathcal{D}} \delta_S,$$

and hence

$$\sum_{S \in \mathcal{D}} \delta_S \geq \frac{n}{n-1}. \tag{A.3}$$

By definition, $v_\epsilon(S) = v(S) - \epsilon$ for every $S \subsetneq N$, so from (A.3) we obtain

$$v(N) = \sum_{S \in \mathcal{D}} \delta_S v_\epsilon(S) = \sum_{S \in \mathcal{D}} \delta_S (v(S) - \epsilon)$$

$$= \sum_{S \in \mathcal{D}} \delta_S v(S) - \epsilon \sum_{S \in \mathcal{D}} \delta_S \leq \sum_{S \in \mathcal{D}} \delta_S v(S) - \epsilon \frac{n}{n-1}.$$

By (3.5), this implies

$$\mathrm{addCoS}(G) \geq \sum_{S \in \mathcal{D}} \delta_S v(S) - v(N) \geq \epsilon \frac{n}{n-1},$$

which completes the proof of the lower bound.

To see that this bound is tight, consider the game $G = \langle N, v \rangle$, where $v(S) = 1$ if $|S| \geq n-1$ and $v(S) = 0$ otherwise. Clearly, we have $\mathrm{addCoS}(G) = 1/(n-1)$ and $\epsilon_{\mathbf{S}}(G) = 1/n$. $\qquad\square$

Proposition A.3. *For every profit-sharing game G with an empty core and 3 players, we have* $\mathbb{SLC}(G) \subseteq \mathbb{EC}(G)$.

Proof. Let $\mathcal{D}$ be a minimal balanced collection that is tight for the least core. That is, s.t. for every $S \in \mathcal{D}$ and $\mathbf{p} \in \mathbb{SLC}(G)$, $p(S) = v_\epsilon(S) = v(S) - \epsilon_{\mathbf{S}}$.

For $n = 3$ there are only five minimal balanced collection not including $\{N\}$, as in the following table.

We divide in cases, and explain how $\mathbf{p}$ can be extended to a stable payoff vector in each case. Suppose first that $\mathcal{D} = \{\{1\}, \{2\}, \{3\}\}$, and all coefficients $\delta_S = 1$. Then we simply set $p_i' = p_i + \epsilon$ for all $i \in \{1, 2, 3\}$. This clearly stabilizes the game, and $\mathrm{addCoS}(\mathbf{p}, G) \leq 3\epsilon$. On the other hand,

Sets	Coefficients
$\{1\}, \{2\}, \{3\}$	$(1, 1, 1)$
$\{1, 2\}, \{3\}$	$(1, 1)$
$\{1\}, \{2, 3\}$	$(1, 1)$
$\{2\}, \{1, 3\}$	$(1, 1)$
$\{1, 2\}, \{2, 3\}, \{1, 3\}$	$(\tfrac{1}{2}, \tfrac{1}{2}, \tfrac{1}{2})$

in the game G every stable payoff vector $\mathbf{q}$ holds that $q(N) \geq \sum_{S \in \mathcal{D}} \delta_S v(S)$, and in particular for the collection at hand.

$$\text{addCoS}(G) = \min_{\mathbf{q} \in \mathbb{S}(G)} q(N) - v(N) \geq \sum_{i=1}^{n} v(i) - p(N) = \sum_{i=1}^{3} (p_i + \epsilon) - p(N) = 3\epsilon.$$

Thus $\text{addCoS}(\mathbf{p}, G) \leq \text{addCoS}(G)$ (in fact equal), and $\mathbf{p} \in \mathbb{EC}(G)$.

The three next collections have the same structure, of a singleton and a pair, both with coefficients 1. W.l.o.g. $S_1 = \{1\}, S_2 = \{2, 3\}$. We set $p'_1 = p_1 + \epsilon = v(1)$. This clearly stabilizes any coalition containing agent 1. Now, if $v(2) < p_2$, we keep $p'_2 = p_2$, and set $p'_3 = v(2, 3) - p_2 = p_3 + \epsilon$. The equality is since $p_2 + p_3 = v(2, 3) - \epsilon$. By construction, $p'(2, 3) = v(2, 3)$ so it remains to show that $p'_3 \geq v(3)$. Indeed, since $\mathbf{p} \in \mathbb{SLC}(G)$, $p_3 \geq v_\epsilon(3) = v(3) - \epsilon$ which shows that $\mathbf{p}'$ is stable in this case.

If $v(2) \geq p_2$, we set $p'_2 = v(2)$ and $p'_3 = \max\{v(2, 3) - v(2), v(3)\}$. Clearly no coalition is blocking $\mathbf{p}'$.

It remains to show that no stable payoff has lower sum. In both cases we have either $p'(N) = v(1) + v(2, 3)$, or $p'(N) = v(1) + v(2) + v(3)$. Since both are balanced collections, they are upper bounded by $q(N)$ for any stable payoff vector $\mathbf{q}$.

The final case is when $\mathcal{D}$ contains the three pairs of agents, each with $\delta_S = \frac{1}{2}$. This means that $p(i, j) = v(i, j) - \epsilon$ for every pair. In this case $\mathbb{SLC}(G)$ contains exactly one vector $\mathbf{p}$, where $p_i = \frac{1}{2}(v(i, j) + v(i, k) - v(j, k) - \epsilon)$. By setting $p^*_i = p_i + \epsilon/2$ for every $i \in N$, it holds that all pairs are stabilized. If all singletons are also stabilized then we are done, since for any stable payoff vector $\mathbf{q}$:

$$2q(N) = 2(q_1 + q_2 + q_3) \geq v(1, 2) + v(2, 3) + v(1, 3) = 2p(N) + 3\epsilon,$$

i.e. $q(N) \geq p(N) + 1.5\epsilon = p^*(N)$.

Otherwise there is some agent (w.l.o.g. agent 1) s.t. $v(1) > p_1 + \epsilon/2$. This means that there is some minimally stable payoff vector $\mathbf{q}^*$ (i.e. in the core of $\overline{G}$), where $q^*_1 = v(1)$.[1]

Let $\mathbf{q}$ be any vector in $\mathbb{C}(\overline{G})$. Suppose that there is some $i \leq 3$ s.t. $p_i \leq v(i)$ (w.l.o.g. $i = 1$). Set $p'_1 = v(1); p'_2 = \max\{v(2), v(1, 2) - v(1)\}$. Note that

$$p_2 = v(1, 2) - p_1 - \epsilon \leq v(1, 2) - (v(1) - \epsilon)\epsilon = v(1, 2) - v(1),$$

thus $p'_2 \geq p_2$ (as required). If $p'_2 = v(2)$, set $p'_3 = \max\{v(3), v(2, 3) - v(2), v(1, 3) - v(1)\}$. This clearly stabilizes all coalitions. For all three cases where $p'_2 = v(2)$, we have that $p'(N)$ equals the sum of some balanced collection and thus $p'(N) \leq q(N)$.

---

[1] Consider $(v(1), p^*_2, p^*_3)$. It stabilizes every coalition that contains agent 1, and thus we never need to increase the first entry to get a stable vector.

If $p_2' = v(1,2) - v(1)$, then $p'(1,2) = v(1,2) \le q(1,2)$. Set $p_3' = \max\{v(3), v(2,3) - p'(2), v(1,3) - p'(1)\}$ (which stabilizes all coalitions). Thus in the first two cases, either

$$p'(N) = v(1,2) + v(3) \le q(1,2) + q(3) = q(N),$$

or

$$p'(N) = p'(1) + p'(2) + v(2,3) - p'(2) = p'(1) + v(2,3) = v(1) + v(2,3) \le q(N).$$

For the last case, consider the vector $\mathbf{q}^*$.

$$p'(N) = p'(1) + p'(2) + v(1,3) - p'(1) = v(1,2) - v(1) + v(1,3) = v(1,2) + v(1,3) - q_1^*$$
$$= q^*(1,2) + q^*(1,3) - q_1^* = 2q_1^* + q_2^* + q_3^* - q_1^* = q_1^* + q_2^* + q_3^* = q^*(N).$$

It thus holds that in all cases $\mathbf{p}$ can be extended to a stable vector $\mathbf{p}'$, and $p'(N) \le q(N)$ for any stable payoff vector $\mathbf{q}$. Therefore $\mathbf{p} \in \mathbb{EC}(G)$. □

A.3   Proofs for Section 3.5

Proposition 3.18. *Let $G = \langle N, g \rangle$ be a coalitional game, and let $G^* = \langle N, g^* \rangle$ be its s-additive cover. Then $\mathrm{addCoS_{cs}}(G) = \mathrm{addCoS}(G^*)$ and $\mathrm{multCoS_{cs}}(G) = \mathrm{multCoS}(G^*)$.*

Proof. We will prove this claim for the case when $G = \langle N, v \rangle$ is a profit-sharing game; for expense-sharing games the argument is similar.

Let $\widehat{CS} = \{S^1, \ldots, S^m\}$ be a coalition structure with the maximum social welfare. Set $\Delta = \mathrm{addCoS_{cs}}(G)$; by our choice of $\widehat{CS}$ we have $\Delta = \mathrm{addCoS}(G, \widehat{CS})$. Thus, there exists a subsidy vector $\mathbf{\Delta} \in \Phi(\widehat{CS}, \Delta)$ and a payoff vector $\mathbf{p}$ such that $(\widehat{CS}, \mathbf{p}) \in \mathbb{CSC}(G(\mathbf{\Delta}))$. We have $p(N) = v(\widehat{CS}) + \Delta = v^*(N) + \Delta$. Hence, $\mathbf{p} \in \mathbb{I}(G^*(\Delta))$. Moreover, under the payoff vector $\mathbf{p}$ no coalition has an incentive to deviate. Hence, $\mathbf{p} \in \mathbb{C}(G^*(\Delta))$ and therefore $\mathrm{addCoS}(G^*) \le \mathrm{addCoS_{cs}}(G)$.

Conversely, let $\mu = \mathrm{addCoS}(G^*)$, and let $\mathbf{q}$ be an arbitrary payoff vector in the core of $G^*(\mu)$. For $j = 1, \ldots, m$, set $\mu^j = q(S^j) - v(S^j)$. Note that $\mu^j \ge 0$, since otherwise coalition S^j would have an incentive to deviate under $\mathbf{q}$. We have

$$\sum_{j=1}^{m} \mu^j = q(N) - v(\widehat{CS}) = \mu.$$

Further, under the payoff vector $\mathbf{q}$ no coalition of has an incentive to deviate. Thus, the vector $(\mu^1, \ldots, \mu^m)$ stabilizes $\widehat{CS}$ and hence $\mathrm{addCoS_{cs}}(G) \le \mu = \mathrm{addCoS}(G^*)$.

We conclude that $\mathrm{addCoS_{cs}}(G) = \mathrm{addCoS}(G^*)$. Further, since $v(\widehat{CS}) = v^*(N)$, we also have $\mathrm{multCoS_{cs}}(G) = \mathrm{multCoS}(G^*)$. □

Appendix B

Proofs for Chapter 4

Proposition 4.1. *For any $k \in \mathbb{N}$, there is a simple superadditive game with* $\mathrm{RSR}(G) \geq k$ *over an interaction network H with $d(H) = 6$.*

Proof. We show that *any* superadditive simple game can be embedded in a 3-dimensional grid network $H = \langle N', E \rangle$, if N' is sufficiently large.

For this, consider first a 3-dimensional grid drawing W of the complete graph K_n. This is an embedding of n vertices in a grid, s.t. every edge (i, j) is replaced by a path, and paths—if drawn as straight lines—do not intersect. Such a drawing always exists using a grid of $O(n) \times O(n) \times O(n)$ (see e.g., [Cohen et al., 1997]). However, W itself is not a grid graph, but just another representation of K_n.

The graph $H' = \langle N', E' \rangle$ that we will use is a 3-dimensional grid that is attained by replacing every vertex in the grid underlying W, with a grid of $2n \times 2n \times 2n$ (thus $|N'| = O(n^6)$). In particular, every original vertex $i \in N$ is replaced with a cube $A_i \subseteq N'$ of n^3 vertices (and A_i is padded inside a larger cube of $8n^3$ vertices). Next, for every $(i, j) \in E$ (assume $i < j$), we identify a path $P(i, j) \subseteq N'$, s.t. $P(i, j)$ connects A_i and A_j; and no two paths intersect. Since the projection of W on H' is extremely sparse, it is very easy to refrain from path intersections. For example, define $Q(i, j)$ as the set of vertices whose convex hull completely contains the straight line between the centers of A_i, A_j. The sets $Q(i, j)$ themselves will hardly intersect, and we can take $P(i, j)$ to be almost any path inside $Q(i, j)$.

We next use G to define the embedded game $G' = \langle N', v' \rangle$, with the following winning coalitions. For every winning coalition $S \subseteq N$ of G, we set $v'(S') = 1$, where $S' = \bigcup_{i \in S} A_i \cup \bigcup_{i,j \in S} P(i, j)$. Since S is connected in K_n, then S' is connected in H'. Moreover, since G is superadditive, every two winning coalitions S_1, S_2 intersect at some $i \in N$. Thus S'_1, S'_2 also intersect (in all vertices of A_i), which entails that G' is also superadditive.

Finally, we argue that $\mathrm{RSR}(G'|_{H'}) = \mathrm{RSR}(G') \geq \mathrm{RSR}(G)$. Indeed, since every winning S' is connected, the first equality applies. Then, assume that there is some payoff vector $\mathbf{x}' \in \mathcal{S}(G')$ that stabilizes G'. We define a payoff vector $\mathbf{x}$ for G, where $x_i = x'(A_i) + \sum_{j \in N} x'(P(i, j))$. Clearly $x(N) \leq x'(N') = \mathrm{RSR}(G')$. Moreover, for every winning $S \subseteq N$, $x(S) = x'(S') \geq v'(S') = 1$, thus $\mathbf{x}$ stabilizes G.

For any k, there is a simple superadditive game G_k whose RSR is at least k (e.g., the game defined by the projective plane of order k. See Example 3.2. As shown above, G_k can be embedded (like any other game) in a grid H' of degree 6. $\qquad\square$

B.1 Proofs for Section 4.3

Theorem 4.4. *For every $k \geq 2$ there is a simple superadditive game $G = \langle N, v \rangle$ and an interaction network H over N such that $tw(H) = k$ and $\mathrm{RSR}(G|_H) = k + 1$.*

Proof. Instead of defining H directly, we will describe its tree decomposition $\mathcal{T}$. There is one central node $A = \{z_1, \ldots, z_{k+1}\}$. Further, for every unordered pair $I = \{i, j\}$, where $i, j \in \{1, \ldots, k+1\}$ and $i \neq j$, we define a set D_I that consists of 7 agents and set $N = A \cup \bigcup_{i \neq j \in \{1, \ldots, k+1\}} D_{\{i,j\}}$.

The tree $\mathcal{T}$ is a star, where leaves are all sets of the form $\{z_i, z_j, d\}$, where $d \in D_{\{i,j\}}$. That is, there are $7 \cdot \binom{k+1}{2}$ leaves, each of size 3. Since the maximal node of $\mathcal{T}$ is of size $k+1$, it corresponds to some network whose treewidth is at most k. We set $\mathcal{D}_i = \bigcup_{j \neq i} D_{\{i,j\}}$; observe that for any two agents $z_i, z_j \in A$ we have $\mathcal{D}_i \cap \mathcal{D}_j = D_{\{i,j\}}$. Given $\mathcal{T}$, it is now easy to construct the underlying interaction network H: there is an edge between z_i and every $d \in D_{\{i,j\}}$ for every $j \neq i$; see Figure 4.2 for more details.

For every unordered pair $I = \{i, j\} \subseteq \{1, \ldots, k+1\}$, let $\mathcal{Q}_I$ denote the projective plane of dimension 3 (a.k.a. the Fano plane) over D_I. That is, $\mathcal{Q}_I$ contains seven triplets of elements from D_I, so that every two triplets intersect, and every element $d \in D_I$ is contained in exactly 3 triplets in $\mathcal{Q}_I$. Winning sets are defined as follows. For every $i = 1, \ldots, k+1$ and every selection $\{Q_{\{i,j\}} \in \mathcal{Q}_{\{i,j\}}\}_{j \neq i}$ the set $\{z_i\} \cup \bigcup_{j \neq i} Q_{\{i,j\}}$ is winning. Thus for every z_i there are 7^k winning coalitions containing z_i, each of size $1 + 3k$. Let us denote by $\mathcal{W}_i$ the set of winning coalitions that contain z_i; observe that for every $d \notin A$, d appears in exactly $3 \cdot 7^{k-1}$ winning coalitions in $\mathcal{W}_i$: d belongs to some $D_{\{i,j\}}$, and is selected to be in a winning coalition with z_i if a triplet $Q_{\{i,j\}}$ containing d is joined to z_i. There are 3 triplets in $\mathcal{Q}_{\{i,j\}}$ that contain d, and there are 7^{k-1} ways to choose the other triplets (seven choices from every one of the other $k - 1$ sets).

We first argue that all winning coalitions intersect. Indeed, let C_i, C_j be winning coalitions such that $z_i \in C_i, z_j \in C_j$. Then both C_i and C_j contain some triplet from $\mathcal{Q}_{\{i,j\}}$. Suppose $Q_{\{i,j\}} \subseteq C_i, Q'_{\{i,j\}} \subseteq C_j$. Since $Q_{\{i,j\}}, Q'_{\{i,j\}} \in \mathcal{Q}_{\{i,j\}}$, they must intersect, and thus C_i and C_j must also intersect. This implies that the simple game induced by these winning coalitions is indeed superadditive and has an optimal value of 1. Note that if we pay 1 to each $z_i \in A$, then the resulting super-imputation is stable, since every winning coalition intersects A. To conclude the proof, we must show that any stable super-imputation must pay at least $k + 1$ to the agents.

Given a stable super-imputation $\mathbf{x}$, we know that $x(C_i) \geq 1$ for every $C_i \in \mathcal{W}_i$. Thus, $\sum_{C_i \in \mathcal{W}_i} x(C_i) \geq 7^k$. We can write $\sum_{C_i \in \mathcal{W}_i} x(C_i)$ as

$$
\begin{aligned}
\sum_{C_i \in \mathcal{W}_i} x(C_i) &= \sum_{C_i \in \mathcal{W}_i} \left(x_{z_i} + \sum_{d \neq z_i | d \in C_i} x_d \right) = 7^k x_{z_i} + \sum_{C_i \in \mathcal{W}_i} \sum_{d \neq z_i | d \in C_i} x_d \\
&= 7^k x_{z_i} + \sum_{d \in \mathcal{D}_i} 1 \sum_{C_i \in \mathcal{W}_i | d \in C_i} x_d = 7^k x_{z_i} + \sum_{d \in \mathcal{D}_i} 3 \cdot 7^{k-1} x_d \\
&= 7^k x_{z_i} + 3 \cdot 7^{k-1} x(\mathcal{D}_i).
\end{aligned}
$$

This immediately implies that $x_{z_i} \geq 1 - \frac{3}{7} x(\mathcal{D}_i)$. Observe that $\sum_{z_i \in A} x(\mathcal{D}_i) = 2 \sum_{i < j} x(D_{\{i,j\}})$, as each $D_{\{i,j\}}$ appears exactly twice in the summation: once in $\mathcal{D}_i$ and once in $\mathcal{D}_j$. Also, observe

---

Mechanism 5 STABLE-PW($G = \langle N, v \rangle, H, k, \mathcal{T}$)

Set $\mathcal{T} = (A_1, \ldots, A_m)$ $\mathbf{x} \leftarrow 0^n$ $I \leftarrow \{i \in N \mid v(\{i\}) = 1\}$
for $i \in I$ **do**
    $x_i \leftarrow 1$
end for
$N_1 \leftarrow N \setminus I$
for $j = 1$ to m **do**
    if there is some $S \subseteq N(\mathcal{T}_{A_j}) \cap N_j$ such that $v(S) = 1$ **then**
        for $i \in A_j \cap N_j$ **do**
            if $i \in N(\mathcal{T}_{A_j}) \setminus A_j$ **then**
                $x_i \leftarrow 1$
            end if
        end for
        $N_{j+1} \leftarrow N_j \setminus N(\mathcal{T}_{A_j})$
    else
        $N_{j+1} \leftarrow N_j$
    end if
end for **return** $\mathbf{x} = (x_1, \ldots, x_n)$

---

that $\sum_{i<j} x(D_{\{i,j\}}) = x(N \setminus A)$, so $\sum_{i=1}^{k+1} x(\mathcal{D}_i) = 2x(N \setminus A)$. Finally,

$$
\begin{aligned}
x(N) &= x(A) + x(N \setminus A) = \sum_{i=1}^{k+1} x_{z_i} + x(N \setminus A) \\
&\geq \sum_{i=1}^{k+1} \left(1 - \frac{3}{7}x(\mathcal{D}_i)\right) + x(N \setminus A) = \sum_{i=1}^{k+1} 1 - \frac{3}{7}2x(N \setminus A) + x(N \setminus A) \\
&= k + 1 + (1 - \frac{6}{7})x(N \setminus A) \geq k + 1
\end{aligned}
$$

Thus, the relative cost of stability in our game is at least $k + 1$. $\qquad\square$

B.2 Proofs for Section 4.4

Theorem 4.5. *For every TU game $G = \langle v, N \rangle$ and every interaction network H over N it holds that $\mathrm{RSR}(G|_H) \leq pw(H)$, and this bound is tight.*

Proof. Note first that it suffices to show that our bound holds for simple games; we can then use the reduction described in the proof of Theorem 4.3. For simple games, our proof is very similar to the proof of Theorem 4.2; however, here we will show that in every node A_j that satisfies the **if** condition of Algorithm 5 we can identify an agent that we do not need to pay.

Our algorithm first deals with winning coalitions of size 1. This step can be justified as follows. Suppose we remove all agents in $I = \{i \in N \mid v(\{i\}) = 1\}$ and construct a stable super-imputation $\mathbf{x}'$ for the game $G'|_H$, where $G' = \langle N', v' \rangle$, $N' = N \setminus I$, and $v'(S) = v(S)$ for each $S \subseteq N \setminus I$, so that $x'(N') \leq pw(H)$. Now, consider a super-imputation $\mathbf{x}$ for G given by $x_i = 1$ for $i \in I$,

$x_i = x'_i$ for $i \in N'$. We have $x(N) = x'(N') + |I|$, and, furthermore, $x(S) \geq v|_H(S)$ for every $S \subseteq N$, i.e., $\mathbf{x}$ is a stable super-imputation for $G|_H$. On the other hand, it is not hard to check that $\mathbf{OPT}(G|_H) = \mathbf{OPT}(G'|_H) + |I|$. Hence, we obtain

$$\frac{x(N)}{\mathbf{OPT}(G|_H)} = \frac{x'(N') + |I|}{\mathbf{OPT}(G'|_H) + |I|} < \frac{x'(N')}{\mathbf{OPT}(G'|_H)} \leq pw(H),$$

i.e., $\mathbf{x}$ witnesses that $\mathrm{RSR}(G|_H) \leq pw(H)$. Thus, we begin Algorithm 5 by paying all winning singletons 1 and ignoring them (and any winning coalitions that contain them) for the rest of the execution; note, however, that we *do not* remove the winning singletons from H, i.e., we do not modify our path decomposition or its width.

Next we show stability. Given a node A_j, we must make sure that each winning coalition in $N(\mathcal{T}_{A_j})$ is paid at least 1. By the proof of Theorem 4.2, paying all agents in A_j is sufficient. Note, however, that there is no need to pay an agent i that is not in $N(\mathcal{T}_{A_j}) \setminus A_j$: since we removed all winning singletons, every winning coalition in $N(\mathcal{T}_{A_j})$ that contains i (and that is not yet stabilized) must also contain another agent from A_j.

Finally, we must show that in every paid node A_j, $j \geq 2$, there is at least one agent that is not paid. Note that A_j has a unique child A_{j-1}. If $A_j \subseteq A_{j-1}$, then no agent in A_j is being paid (as they had already been paid when processing A_{j-1}). Otherwise, there is some agent $i \in A_j \setminus A_{j-1}$. Since $\mathcal{T}$ is a path and all nodes containing i must be connected, we have $i \notin N(A_j) \setminus A_j$. Thus i is not paid. Note that in Algorithm 5 the agents in A_1 are not paid in the first iteration of the algorithm.

To show tightness, we use a slight modification of the construction from Section 4.3.3. For any $k \geq 3$:

- Take the tree-width example for $k - 1$, remove all edges from the (star) tree.

- Add the central node (of size k) to all leaf nodes. Thus we get $O(k^2)$ nodes of size $k + 1$.

- Connect all nodes by an arbitrary path.

Then the path-width is $(k + 1) - 1 = k$, whereas the RSR is exactly as before (k) since we have the same set of winning coalitions. A cycle graph with $n \to \infty$ can be used for the case of $k = 2$. See [Meir et al., 2011] for details. $\square$

B.3   Computational Complexity

We define the decision problem OPTCS as follows: it receives as input a game $G = \langle N, v \rangle$, an interaction network H and some value $\alpha \in \mathbb{R}$; it outputs yes if and only if there is some partition $S_1, \ldots, S_k$ of N such that $\sum_{j=1}^{k} v|_H(S_j) \geq \alpha$. We assume oracle access to v.

It is known that if H is a tree and G is a simple monotone game then there is a simple polynomial algorithm for OPTCS . This is by selecting an arbitrary root and iteratively isolate winning coalitions from the leafs upwards (similarly to the procedure of Algorithm 1). However if we relax either of these three requirements, and the tree structure in particular, the problem becomes computationally hard.

The next three propositions prove the three parts of Proposition 4.6.

Proposition B.1. OPTCS *(G, H) is NP-hard even if G is simple and* $tw(H) = pw(H) = 2$.

Proof. Our reduction is from an instance of the SET-COVER [Garey and Johnson, 1979] problem. Recall that an instance of SET-COVER is given by a finite set C, list of sets $\mathcal{S} = (S_1, \ldots, S_n)$ and an integer M; it is a "yes" instance if and only if there is a subset $\mathcal{S}' \subseteq \mathcal{S}$ such that $\mathcal{S}'$ *covers* C, i.e. $\bigcup_{S \in \mathcal{S}'} S = C$, and $|\mathcal{S}'| \leq M$. Given an instance of SET-COVER $(C, \mathcal{S}, M)$, as described above, we define the player set to be $\{1, \ldots, n, x, y\}$. We define the characteristic function as follows: for any $S \subseteq \{1, \ldots, n\}$, $v(S \cup \{x\}) = 1$ if and only if the set $\{S_i\}_{i \in S}$ covers C; $v(S \cup \{y\}) = 1$ if and only if $|S| \geq n - M$. Our interaction network H over the player set is defined as follows: there are edges (i, x) and (i, y) for all $1 \leq i \leq n$; observe that $tw(H) = 2$. One can easily verify that an optimal coalition structure over $G|_H$ has a value of 2 if and only if $(C, \mathcal{S}, M)$ is a "yes" instance of SET-COVER. $\qquad \square$

Limiting our attention to monotone simple games seems to be somewhat restrictive. However, both monotonicity and bi-values are required for tractability. Note that in both cases we show that it is hard even to distinct between the cases where $v(CS^*(G|_T)) = 1$ and $v(CS^*(G|_T)) = 0$. Thus there is no efficient approximation algorithm either.

Proposition B.2. OPTCS (G, T) *is NP-complete if we allow inputs with a non-monotone G, even if we assume that the interaction network T is a tree and G is simple.*

Proof. Our reduction is from SUBSET-SUM [Garey and Johnson, 1979]; recall that an instance of SUBSET-SUM is given by a list of integer weights $w_1, \ldots, w_n$ and some quota q. It is a "yes" instance if and only if there is some subset of weights whose total weight is exactly q. Given an instance of SUBSET-SUM $\langle w_1, \ldots, w_n; q \rangle$, we construct the following game on $n + 1$ players: player i is assigned a weight w_i, while player $n + 1$ has a weight of 0. The value of $v(S)$ is 1 if and only if $\sum_{i \in S} w_i = q$ (and otherwise 0). The communication network H is a star centered in player $n + 1$, with the other n players as leaves. Observe that in this game, at most one coalition containing more than one member of $\{1, \ldots, n\}$ can form. To conclude, assuming that $w_i < q$ for all i, the optimal coalition structure in $G|_H$ has value of at most 1, and is 1 if and only we have a "yes" instance of SUBSET-SUM. $\qquad \square$

Finally, OPTCS is NP-complete for monotone non-simple games as well.

Proposition B.3. OPTCS (G, T) *is NP-complete, even if the interaction network T is a tree, G is monotone, and v is allowed only three different values.*

Proof. Our reduction is from the SET-COVER problem [Garey and Johnson, 1979]. Recall that an instance of SET-COVER is given by a finite set of elements M, a set $\mathcal{F} = \{S_1, \ldots, S_m\} \subseteq 2^M$ and a parameter k. It is a "yes" instance if and only if there is some subset $\mathcal{F}' \subseteq \mathcal{F}$ of size $\leq k$ such that $\bigcup_{S \in \mathcal{F}'} S = M$. We define a game with $n = m + 1$ agents. The characteristic function is as follows: there is an agent j corresponding to each $S_j \in \mathcal{F}$, plus one dummy agent d. The value of a coalition $C \subset N$ is 0 if it is empty, $2m$ if $\{S_j\}_{j \in C}$ cover M, and 1 otherwise. Our interaction network H is a star with d in the center, and with all $j \leq m$ as leaves. Thus, only one coalition that covers M may form. Clearly, in an optimal coalition structure a coalition C^* that covers M will form, with the addition of as many singletons as possible. The value of the optimal coalition structure is at least $2m + (m - k) = 3m - k$ if and only if $|C^*| \leq k$, which concludes the proof. $\qquad \square$

Appendix C

Proofs for Chapter 5

Lemma 5.1. *For any utility function u which is consistent with preference order $\succ_i$, the following holds:*

1. $a \succ_i b \Rightarrow \forall W \subseteq C \setminus \{a, b\}, \ u(\{a\} \cup W) > u(\{b\} \cup W)$;
2. $\forall b \in W, a \succ_i b \Rightarrow u(a) > u(\{a\} \cup W) > u(W)$.

Proof. Let $a, b \in C$ and $W \subseteq C \setminus \{a, b\}$.

$$u(\{a\} \cup W) = \frac{1}{|W| + 1}\left(u(a) + \sum_{c \in W} u(c)\right) > \frac{1}{|W| + 1}\left(u(b) + \sum_{c \in W} u(c)\right) = u(\{b\} \cup W).$$

Let $a \in C, W \subseteq C$ s.t. $\forall b \in W, a \succ_i b$. Then

$$u(a) = \frac{1}{|W| + 1}\left(u(a) + \sum_{b \in W} u(a)\right) > \frac{1}{|W| + 1}\left(u(a) + \sum_{b \in W} u(b)\right) = u(\{a\} \cup W)$$

$$> \frac{1}{|W| + 1}\left(u(W) + \sum_{b \in W} u(a)\right) = \frac{1}{|W| + 1}u(W) + \frac{|W|}{|W| + 1}u(W) = u(W).$$

$\square$

Proposition 5.5. *There is a counterexample with four candidates and three weighted agents that start from the truthful state and use best replies.*

Example 5.5. The initial score of candidates $\{a, b, c, d\}$ is $\hat{s} = (0, 1, 2, 3)$. The weight of each voter $i \in \{1, 2, 3\}$ is i. The preference profile is as follows. $c \succ_1 d \succ_1 b \succ_1 a$, $b \succ_2 c \succ_2 a \succ_2 d$, and $a \succ_3 b \succ_3 c \succ_3 d$.

The truthful profile is thus $\mathbf{a} = (c, b, a)$, which results in the score vector $(3, 3, 3, 3)$ where a is the winner.

$$
\begin{array}{ccccc}
\text{votes:} & (c, b, a) & \rightarrow & (d, b, a) & \rightarrow & (d, c, a) \\
\text{scores:} & (3, 3, 3, 3)\{a\} & & (3, 3, 2, 4)\{d\} & & (3, 1, 4, 4)\{c\} \\
& \uparrow & & & & \downarrow \\
& (c, b, b) & \leftarrow & (c, c, b) & \leftarrow & (d, c, b) \\
& (0, 6, 3, 3)\{b\} & & (0, 4, 5, 3)\{c\} & & (0, 4, 4, 4)\{b\}
\end{array}
$$

$\Diamond$

Theorem 5.6. *Let G_D be a Plurality game with deterministic tie-breaking. If $k = 2$ and both agents (a) use best replies **or** (b) start from the truthful state, a NE will be reached.*

Proof of 5.6a. Assume there is a cycle, and consider the winners in the first steps: $\{x\} \xrightarrow{1} \{y\} \xrightarrow{2} \{z\}$. Suppose that after step 1 both agents vote for different candidates ($a_{1,2} \neq a_{1,1} = y$). This holds for any later step, as an agent has no reason to vote for the current winner. An agent can never make a step of type 3 (after the first step), since at every step the winner is the candidate that the other agent is voting for. If the first step brings the agents to the same candidate, then in the second step they split again ($a_{2,1} \neq a_{2,2} = z$), and we are back in the previous case. $\square$

Proof of 5.6b. We show that the score of the winner can only increase. This clearly holds in the first step, which must be of type 1. Once again, we have that the two agents always vote for different candidates, and thus only steps that increase the score can change the identity of the winner. $\square$

Proposition 5.9. *If agents start from an arbitrary profile, there is a weak counterexample with 3 agents of weight 1, even if they use best replies.*

Example 5.9. There are 4 candidates $\{a, b, c, x\}$ and 3 agents with utilities $u_1 = (5, 4, 0, 3)$, $u_2 = (0, 5, 4, 3)$ and $u_3 = (4, 0, 5, 3)$. In particular, $a \succ_1 \{a, b\} \succ_1 x \succ_1 \{a, c\}$; $b \succ_2 \{b, c\} \succ_2 x \succ_2 \{a, b\}$; and $c \succ_3 \{a, c\} \succ_3 x \succ_3 \{b, c\}$. From the state $\mathbf{a}_0 = (a, b, x)$ with $\mathbf{s}(\mathbf{a}_0) = (1, 1, 0, 1)$ and the outcome $\{a, b, x\}$, the following cycle occurs:

$$(1, 1, 0, 1)\{a, b, x\} \xrightarrow{2} (1, 0, 0, 2)\{x\} \xrightarrow{3} (1, 0, 1, 1)\{a, x, c\} \xrightarrow{1} (0, 0, 1, 2)\{x\} \xrightarrow{2}$$

$$(0, 1, 1, 1)\{x, b, c\} \xrightarrow{3} (0, 1, 0, 2)\{x\} \xrightarrow{1} (1, 1, 0, 1)\{a, b, x\}.$$

$\Diamond$

Proposition 5.10. *(a) If agents use arbitrary better replies, then there is a strong counterexample with 3 agents of weight 1. Moreover, (b) there is a weak counterexample with 2 agents of weight 1, even if they start from the truthful state.*

Example 5.10a. $C = \{a, b, c\}$ with initial score $\hat{\mathbf{s}} = (0, 1, 0)$. The initial state is $\mathbf{a}_0 = (a, a, b)$— that is, $\mathbf{s}(\mathbf{a}_0) = (2, 2, 0)$ and the outcome is the winner set $\{a, b\}$. Consider the following cyclic sequence (we write the score vector and the outcome in each step): $(2, 2, 0)\{a, b\} \xrightarrow{2} (1, 2, 1)\{b\} \xrightarrow{1} (0, 2, 2)\{b, c\} \xrightarrow{3} (1, 1, 2)\{c\} \xrightarrow{2} (2, 1, 1)\{a\} \xrightarrow{3} (1, 2, 1)\{b\} \xrightarrow{1} (2, 2, 0)\{a, b\}$. If the preferences are $a \succ_1 c \succ_1 b$, $b \succ_2 a \succ_2 c$ and $c \succ_3 b \succ_3 a$, then each step is indeed an improvement step for the agent whose index is on top of the arrow. $\Diamond$

Example 5.10b. We use 5 candidates with initial score $(1, 1, 2, 0, 0)$, and 2 agents with utilities $u_1 = (5, 3, 2, 8, 0)$ and $u_2 = (4, 2, 5, 0, 8)$. In particular, $\{b, c\} \succ_1 c$, $\{a, c\} \succ_1 \{a, b, c\}$, and $\{a, b, c\} \succ_2 \{b, c\}$, $c \succ_2 \{a, c\}$, and the following cycle occurs:

$$(1, 1, 2, 1, 1)\{c\} \xrightarrow{1} (1, 2, 2, 0, 1)\{b, c\} \xrightarrow{2} (2, 2, 2, 0, 0)\{a, b, c\} \xrightarrow{1}$$

$$(2, 1, 2, 1, 0)\{a, c\} \xrightarrow{2} (1, 1, 2, 1, 1)\{c\}.$$

$\Diamond$

Proposition C.1. *There are strong counterexamples for (a) deterministic tie-breaking, and (b) randomized tie-breaking. This holds even with two non-weighted truth-biased agents that use best reply dynamics and start from the truthful state.*

Example C.1a. We use 4 candidates with no initial score. The preferences are defined as $c \succ_1 a \succ_1 b \succ_1 d$ and $d \succ_2 b \succ_2 a \succ_2 c$. The reader can easily verify that in the resulting 4×4 game there are no NE states. $\diamond$

Example C.1b. There are 4 candidates with initial scores $(0, 0, 1, 2)$. The preference profile is given by $a \succ_1 c \succ_1 d \succ_1 b$, $b \succ_2 d \succ_2 c \succ_2 a$. Consider the following cycle, beginning with the truthful state: $(1, 1, 1, 2) \xrightarrow{1} (0, 1, 2, 2) \xrightarrow{2} (0, 0, 2, 3) \xrightarrow{1} (1, 0, 1, 3) \xrightarrow{2} (1, 1, 1, 2)$. $\diamond$

Appendix D

Proofs for Chapter 6

D.1   Proofs for Section 6.3

Proposition 6.1. $\mathcal{D}_2(G, \hat{a}) = \Theta\left(\frac{qn^2}{m^2}\right).$

Proof. The first observation is that any NE profile must be almost-balanced, in the sense that every resource has $\lfloor n/m \rfloor$ agents (vacant) or $\lceil n/m \rceil$ agents (full). Note that there are exactly q full resources in each iteration.

The second observation is that a pair has a strict deviation if and only if they share a full resource in both iterations. Then one agent can switch to a vacant resource in the first iteration, and the other can do the same in the second iteration. In each iteration one of them strictly gains and the other is unharmed.

It follows that in $\hat{a}$ agents play the same partition in both iterations, and every pair that is in a full resource can deviate. Since there are q full resources, there are $q\binom{\lceil n/m \rceil}{2} = \Theta\left(\frac{qn^2}{m^2}\right).$ $\square$

Proposition 6.2.

(a) $\mathcal{D}_2(G, \mathbf{a}^*) = O\left(\frac{n^2}{m^2}\right).$

(b) if $n < m^2$ then $\mathcal{D}_2(G, \mathbf{a}^*) = 0$, i.e. $\mathbf{a}^*$ is 2-SE.

(c) if $q \leq m/2$, then $\mathcal{D}_2(G, \mathbf{a}^*) = 0.$

Proof. If $n < m^2$, then we show that $\mathbf{a}^*$ is a 2-SE profile. Let $\mathbf{A} = (A_1, A_2, \ldots, A_m)$ be any almost-balanced partition in the first iteration. That is, A_i contains the ($\lceil n/m \rceil$ or $\lfloor n/m \rfloor$) agents that select resource i in the first iteration. Assume each A_i is ordered as a vector (arbitrarily). Let $\overline{A}$ be vector of size n, created by concatenating the vectors $A_1, \ldots, A_m$. We construct the partition in the second iteration $\mathbf{B}$, by adding each agent $\overline{A}(j)$ to resource ($j \mod m$). Since every $|A_i| \leq m$, all agents in A_i end up in different resources in the second iteration. Thus $\mathcal{D}_2(G, \mathbf{a}^*) = 0.$

If $n > m^2$ and $q > m/2$, then there is at least one resource with $\geq m+1$ agents. By pigeon hole, at least two of these agents share a resource in the second iteration, thus $\mathcal{D}_2(G, \mathbf{a}^*) \geq 1.$

However we can still upper bound the stability score of $\mathbf{a}^*$. Indeed, take any vector A_i, and divide it to subvectors $A_{i1}, A_{i2}, \ldots$, each of size m. We now create the partition $\mathbf{B}$ as described in the previous paragraph. As $|A_i|$ may be more than m, it is possible that two agents from A_i now share a resource in $\mathbf{B}$. However if two agents belong to the same *subvector* $A_{i,t}$, they must be in distinct resources in $\mathbf{B}$, and thus cannot deviate. Also, every $j \in A_{i,t}$ shares a resource in $\mathbf{B}$ with at most 1 other agent from each other subvector $A_{i,t'}$. Thus the number of pairs in A_i shat share a resource in $\mathbf{B}$ is at most $\binom{\lceil |A_i|/m \rceil}{2}$ (for example, B_1 contains the first agent from each set $A_{1,t}$, one agent from each $A_{2,t}$, etc.). However, not all of these pair can deviate. It is necessary that the resource shared in the first step is full (i.e. $|A_i| = \lceil n/m \rceil$), and also the shared resource in the second step. Thus, only a fraction of q/m of the pairs end up in a full resource in $\mathbf{B}$. Thus for every full resource i, we have at most $\lceil |A_i|/m \rceil$ agents sharing a resource in $\mathbf{B}$. Summing the pairs from A_i over the q full resources of $\mathbf{B}$, we have (at most)

$$q\binom{\lceil |A_i|/m \rceil}{2} = \Theta\left(q\left(\frac{n}{m^2}\right)^2\right)$$

deviating pairs, and the total number of deviating pairs in all q full resources of $\mathbf{A}$ is

$$\mathcal{D}_2(G, \mathbf{a}^*) \leq q \cdot \Theta\left(q\left(\frac{n}{m^2}\right)^2\right) = \Theta\left(\frac{q^2 n^2}{m^4}\right) = \Theta\left(\frac{n^2}{m^2}\right).$$

For the last case, suppose that $q < m/2$. We take one agent from each full resource in $\mathbf{A}$, and move it to a (distinct) empty resource to create $\mathbf{B}$. Thus there is no resource that is full in both iterations. Hence the only agents that belong to a full resource (and thus may have an opportunity to gain) in both iterations are the ones we moved. None of these agents shares a resource with any other agent twice, and therefore no pair deviation is possible. $\square$

Proposition 6.3. *Let G be an SRSG with k steps, and $\mathbf{a}$ be a random NE in G. Denote $r = \frac{q(k-1)}{m^2}$, then $\mathcal{D}_2(G, \mathbf{a}) \cong \binom{n}{2}(1 - (1+r)e^{-r})$.*

Proof. Let $(1, 2)$ be a random pair of agents. In each iteration, they share a resource w.p. of $\frac{1}{m}$. Also, if they do share a resource, this resource is full w.p. of $\frac{q}{m}$, thus they have a probability of $\alpha = \frac{q}{m^2}$ to share a full resource. $(1, 2)$ can deviate iff they share at least two full resources. Equivalently, they do not have one iff they share exactly 0 or 1 full resource, which occurs at probability of

$$\begin{aligned}
\beta &= (1-\alpha)^k + k \cdot \alpha(1-\alpha)^{k-1} \\
&= (1-\alpha)^{k-1}(1-\alpha+k\alpha) \cong e^{-\alpha(k-1)}(1+\alpha(k-1)) \\
&= e^{-r}(1+r). \qquad\qquad\qquad\qquad (\text{as } r = \frac{q(k-1)}{m^2} = \alpha(k-1))
\end{aligned}$$

Since every pair *does not* have a deviation w.p. β, the expected number of pair deviations is $\binom{n}{2}(1 - \beta) = \binom{n}{2}(1 - (1+r)e^{-r})$. $\square$

D.2 Proofs for Section 6.4

D.2.1 Characterizing pair deviations

Lemma D.1. *The following condition is both necessary and sufficient for the pair $k < j - 1$ to have a deviation in UE:*

$$\sum_{t=k+1}^{j-1} (x_{t-1} - x_t)(v_k - v_{t-1}) < a \left(v_{j-1} - \sum_{r=j+1}^{s+1} w_r v_{r-1} \right),$$

where according to our notations $a = x_{j-1} - x_j$, and $w_r = \frac{x_{r-1} - x_r}{x_j}$.

Proof. The proof is very similar to that of Lemma 6.5. Let $u(k), u'(k)$ be the utility of agent k before and after the deviation. Recall that the best thing that the pair $k < j - 1$ can do, is that j reports $b'_j = b_{j+1}$, and k reports $b'_k = b_j$ (i.e. takes slot $j - 1$). The new utility of k in this case is $u'(k) = (v_k - b_{j+1})x_{j-1}$. For any $\mathbf{x}, \mathbf{v}$ the utility of k changes as follows:

$$u(k) - u'(k) = (v_k - b_{k+1}^U)x_k - (v_k - b_{j+1}^U)x_{j-1}$$

$$= (x_k - x_{j-1})v_k - \sum_{t=k+1}^{s+1} (x_{t-1} - x_t)v_{t-1} + \frac{x_{j-1}}{x_j} \sum_{r=j+1}^{s+1} (x_{r-1} - x_r)v_{r-1}$$

$$= \sum_{l=k+1}^{j-1} (x_{l-1} - x_l)v_k - \sum_{t=k+1}^{j} (x_{t-1} - x_t)v_{t-1} + (\frac{x_{j-1}}{x_j} - 1) \sum_{r=j+1}^{s+1} (x_{r-1} - x_r)v_{r-1}$$

$$= \sum_{t=k+1}^{j-1} (x_{t-1} - x_t)(v_k - v_{t-1}) - (x_{j-1} - x_j)v_{j-1} + \frac{x_{j-1} - x_j}{x_j} \sum_{r=j+1}^{s+1} (x_{r-1} - x_r)v_{r-1}$$

$$= \sum_{t=k+2}^{j-1} (x_{t-1} - x_t)(v_k - v_{t-1}) - a \cdot v_{j-1} + a \sum_{r=j+1}^{s+1} w_r v_{r-1}$$

$\square$

From Lemma D.1 we can derive bounds on stability scores that are asymptotically equal to the ones we derived for LE.

Proposition D.2. *Given a UE, the pair of agents $i, i + 2$ has a deviation for every $i < s$.*

Proof. We take Lemma D.1, and substitute j with $k + 2$. Then

$$u(k) - u'(k) = \sum_{t=k+1}^{k+1} (x_{t-1} - x_t)(v_k - v_{t-1}) - a \cdot v_{k+1} + a \sum_{r=k+2}^{s} w_{r+1} v_r$$

$$= (x_k - x_{k+1})(v_k - v_k) + a \sum_{r=k+2}^{s} w_{r+1} v_r - a \cdot v_{k+1} \le 0 + a(v_{k+2} - v_{k+1}) < 0.$$

$$\text{(since } a > 0\text{)}$$

Thus $u'(k) > u(k)$ and agent k strictly gains by deviating with $j = k + 2$. $\square$

D.2.2 Counting pair deviations

Theorem 6.6. *Suppose that both CTR and valuation functions are convex. The number of pairs with deviations in the Lower equilibrium can be upper bounded as follows.*

(a) $\mathcal{D}_2(GSP, LE) = O(s\sqrt{s})$.

(b) if CTRs are β-convex then $\mathcal{D}_2(GSP, LE) = O(s \log_\beta s)$.

(c) if valuations are β-convex for any $\beta \geq 2$, then only neighbor pairs can deviate. That is, $\mathcal{D}_2(GSP, LE) = s$.

Theorem 6.6a is proved in the main text.

Proof of 6.6b. W.l.o.g. $x_s = 1$. As in the previous proof, we denote $a = x_{j-1} - x_j \geq \beta^{s-j}(x_{s-1} - x_s) = \beta^{s-j}(\beta - 1)$. We can now rewrite differences between CTRs as $x_{i-1} - x_i \geq \beta^{j-i}a$ for all $i < j$. Continuing from Lemma 6.5,

$$u(k) - u'(k) \geq \sum_{t=k+1}^{j-1} \beta^{j-t}a(v_k - v_t) - a \cdot v_j + \frac{a}{x_j} \sum_{r=j+1}^{s+1} (x_{r-1} - x_r)v_r$$

$$\geq a\left(\sum_{t=k+1}^{j-1} \beta^{j-t}(v_k - v_t) - v_j + \operatorname*{avg}_{s+1 \geq r \geq j+1} v_r \right), \tag{D.1}$$

where the inequality follows from the convexity of **x**. Thus we replace condition (6.6) from the linear CTR case with

$$\sum_{t=k+1}^{j-1} \beta^{j-t}(v_k - v_t) \geq v_j - \operatorname*{avg}_{s+1 \geq r \geq j+1} v_r, \tag{D.2}$$

and make a similar analysis. Let h, z as in the linear case, then

$$\sum_{t=k+1}^{j-1} \beta^{j-t}(v_k - v_t) \geq \sum_{t=k+1}^{j-1} \beta^{j-t}z\frac{t-k}{h} \tag{as in (6.7)}$$

$$= \sum_{t=1}^{h} \beta^{h+1-t}z\frac{t}{h} = \frac{z}{h}\beta^{h+1} \sum_{t=1}^{h} \beta^{-t}t > \frac{z}{h}\beta^{h+1}\beta^{-1} = \frac{z}{h}\beta^h, \tag{D.3}$$

Suppose now that $h > \log_\beta \frac{s-j}{2}$, then from Eq. (6.8)

$$\sum_{t=k+1}^{j-1} \beta^{j-t}(v_k - v_t) \geq \frac{z(s-j)}{2h} \geq v_j - \operatorname*{avg}_{s+1 \geq r \geq j+1} v_r,$$

which means no agent gains from the deviation.

Thus each bidder can find at most $O(\log_\beta s)$ other bidders to collaborate with, or $O(s \log_\beta s)$ pairs in total.

For tightness, assume that valuations are linear. In this case, all inequalities except (D.3) become equalities. Now take any pair such that $j < s/2$; $2h < \log_\beta \frac{s-j}{2}$. Then we have

$$h < \log_\beta \frac{s-j}{2} - h < \log_\beta \frac{s-j}{2} - \log_\beta h = \log_\beta \frac{s-j}{2h} \qquad \Rightarrow$$

$$\sum_{t=k+1}^{j-1} \beta^{j-t}(v_k - v_t) = \sum_{t=1}^{h} \beta^{h+1-t} z\frac{t}{h} = \frac{z}{h}\beta^{h+1}\sum_{t=1}^{h}\beta^{-t}t$$

$$< \frac{z}{h}\beta^{h+1}h\beta^{-1} = z\beta^h < z\frac{s-j}{2h} = v_j - \operatorname*{avg}_{s+1 \geq r \geq j+1} v_r,$$

and k strictly gains by manipulating with j. Moreover, there are at least $\frac{s}{2}\frac{\log_\beta \frac{s}{4}}{2} = \Omega(s\log_\beta s)$ such pairs, thus our bound is tight. $\qquad\square$

Proof of 6.6c. Let any k, j such that $j \geq k + 2$.

$$\sum_{t=k+1}^{j-1}(v_k - v_t) \geq v_k - v_{k+1} \geq 4(v_j - v_{j+1}) \geq 2v_j \geq v_j - \operatorname*{avg}_{s \geq t' \geq j+1} v_{t'}.$$

Then by condition(6.6), the pair k, j cannot deviate. $\qquad\square$

Theorem 6.7. *Suppose that both CTR and valuation functions are* concave. *The number of pairs with deviations in the Lower equilibrium can be lower bounded as follows.*

(a) $\mathcal{D}_2(GSP, LE) = \Omega(s\sqrt{s})$.

(b) *if CTRs are β-concave for any $\beta > 1$, then* $\mathcal{D}_2(GSP, LE) = \Omega(s^2)$.

(c) *if valuations are β-concave, for any $\beta \geq 2$, then* all *pairs can deviate. I.e.,* $\mathcal{D}_2(GSP, LE) = \binom{s+1}{2} = M_2$.

Proof of 6.7a. Consider the proof of Theorem 6.6a. All the weak inequalities in the proof follow directly either from the convexity of $\mathbf{x}$, or from the convexity of $\mathbf{r}$. If both functions are concave, all weak inequalities are reversed (rounding expressions down rather than up). Therefore, a pair $k, j = k + h + 1$ can deviate whenever

$$h + 1 < \left\lfloor \frac{s-j}{h} \right\rfloor.$$

To see that there are $\Omega(s\sqrt{s})$ such pairs, consider for example all pairs where $j < s/2; h < \sqrt{s}/4$. $\qquad\square$

Proof of 6.7b. Consider Equation (D.2) in the proof of Theorem 6.6b. As $\mathbf{x}$ is now concave, rather than convex, we have $x_{t-1} - x_t \leq \beta^{t-j}(x_{j-1} - x_j)$ for all $t < j$, and we should reverse the inequalities (D.1) and (D.2). We get the following condition:

$$\sum_{t=k+1}^{j-1}\beta^{t-j}(v_k - v_t) < v_j - \operatorname*{avg}_{s+1 \geq r \geq j+1} v_r. \qquad (D.4)$$

Whenever condition (D.4) holds, deviation of k, j is guaranteed to succeed. Now, let $h = j - k - 1$ as in previous sections. We show that each of the top $(1 - \frac{1}{\beta})\frac{1}{4}s$ bidders can deviate with any bidder above her (note that this means that there is a constant fraction of the total number of pairs that can deviate). We first upper bound the LHS:

$$\sum_{t=k+1}^{j-1} \beta^{t-j}(v_k - v_t) \le (v_k - v_{j-1}) \sum_{t=k+1}^{j-1} \beta^{t-j} = (v_k - v_{j-1}) \sum_{t=1}^{j-k-1} \beta^t$$

$$< (v_k - v_{j-1}) \sum_{t=0}^{\infty} \beta^{-t} \le (v_k - v_{j-1})\frac{1}{1 - \frac{1}{\beta}} \le a \cdot h \frac{1}{1 - \frac{1}{\beta}}$$

$$\le a\left((1 - \frac{1}{\beta})\frac{1}{4}s\right)\frac{1}{1 - \frac{1}{\beta}} = \frac{1}{4} \cdot s \cdot a$$

For the RHS, we have

$$v_j - \operatorname*{avg}_{s+1 \ge r \ge j+1} v_r \ge v_j - v_{\frac{j+s+1}{2}} \ge v_j - v_{s/2} \ge a\left(\frac{s}{2} - j\right) \ge a\left(\frac{s}{2} - \frac{1}{4}\beta s\right) \ge \frac{1}{4} \cdot s \cdot a.$$

$$(\mathbf{v} \text{ is concave})$$

We therefore have that for all $k < j < (1 - \frac{1}{\beta})\frac{1}{4}s$, condition (D.4) holds. Since $\beta > 1$ then $(1 - \frac{1}{\beta}) > 0$, and therefore there are $\Omega(s^2)$ such pairs, where the constant depends on β. For example, for $\beta = 2$, there are at least $\binom{\lfloor \frac{1}{8}s \rfloor}{2} > \frac{1}{100}s^2$ deviating pairs.   □

Proof of 6.7c. By Equation (6.6), the pair j, k can deviate if

$$\sum_{t=k+1}^{j-1} (v_k - v_t) < v_j - \operatorname*{avg}_{s+1 \ge r \ge j+1} v_r.$$

Since $v_{i+1} - v_{i+2} > 2(v_i - v_{i+1})$ for every i, for every $t > k$ it holds that

$$v_k - v_t < \frac{v_t - v_{t+1}}{2^{t-k}}.$$

We get

$$\sum_{t=k+1}^{j-1} (v_k - v_t) = (v_k - v_{k+1})(j - k - 1) + (v_{k+1} - v_{k+2})(j - k - 2) + \cdots + (v_{j-2} - v_{j-1})$$

$$< \frac{v_{j-2} - v_{j-1}}{2^{j-k-2}}(j - k - 1) + \frac{v_{j-2} - v_{j-1}}{2^{j-k-3}}(j - k - 2) + \cdots + \frac{v_{j-2} - v_{j-1}}{2} + (v_{j-2} - v_{j-1})$$

$$= (v_{j-2} - v_{j-1}) \sum_{t=0}^{j-k-2} \frac{t+1}{2^t} < (v_{j-2} - v_{j-1})\left(\sum_{t=0}^{j-k-2} \frac{t}{2^t} + \sum_{t=0}^{j-k-2} \frac{1}{2^t}\right) < (v_{j-2} - v_{j-1})(2 + 2)$$

$$< v_j - v_{j+1} < v_j - \operatorname*{avg}_{s+1 \ge r \ge j+1} v_r.$$

This establishes the statement of the proposition.   □

D.2.3 Counting deviations of large coalitions

Lemma D.3. *Suppose that $R \subseteq N$ is a coalition that gains by a deviation, and let b_j, b'_j denote the bids of $j \in R$ before and after the deviation. Then the following hold:*

(a) *There is at least one bidder $i^* \in R$ that does not gain anything from the deviation (an indifferent bidder). Moreover, the slot allocated to i^* is not affected.*

(b) *There is at least one bidder $f \in R$ that does not contribute anything to the deviation (a "free rider"). That is, the utility of all bidders in $R \setminus \{f\}$ does not decrease if f bids her equilibrium bid, and at least one $j \in R \setminus \{f\}$ still gains.*

(c) *For all $j \in R$, either $b'_j < b_j$, or the utilities of all agents in R (including j) are unaffected by the bid of j.*

Proof. We prove each property separately.

Indifferent bidder First consider the bidder $i^* \in R$ that is ranked last after the deviation, and let i' be the new slot allocated to i^*. Clearly $b_{i'+1}$ did not change, and thus if i^* gains she would also gain by deviating unilaterally to $b'_{i^*} = b_{i'+1} + \epsilon$. Therefore i^* is indifferent. Note that by our assumption that the game is generic, $i' = i^*$, or otherwise bidder i^* would strictly lose.

Lowering bids Suppose that $k \in R$ strictly gains by bidding b'_k and moving to some slot i. Let k^* be the bidder such that $b_{k^*} < b'_k$, and maximal in that condition (i.e. the bidder located directly below the new slot of k). Then either: (i) $k^* \in R$ and $b'_{k^*} < b_{k^*}$; or (ii) there is some bidder $t \in R$ such that $t < k$ (i.e. $b_t > b_k$), but after the deviation $b'_t < b'_k$. Let t^* be the bidder t with the lowest b'_t. If neither of (i),(ii) holds, then k is allocated the same slot or worse, and pays at least as before.

Assume that $b'_k > b_k$. If case (ii) holds, then t^* strictly loses, or otherwise she would weakly gain by bidding b'_{t^*} in a single deviation. Otherwise, note that k itself does not gain, and consider some $j \in R$. Either $j < k$, j remains above k, or $j > k$ and remains below k. In both cases j is unaffected, unless $b'_j < b_k$ and maximal in that condition, in which case j strictly loses by the move of k.

Free rider If R contains a pair of neighbors, this pair has a deviation regardless of the actions of all other bidders, and we can clearly remove any bidder that is not a part of this pair. Assume therefore that R do not contain a pair of neighbors.

Consider the bidder $f \in R$ that is ranked first among all bidders of R (after the deviation), and denote her new slot by f'. Clearly f does not contribute do any other bidder in R. $R \setminus \{f\}$ still has a deviation (i.e. do exactly what they did when f was part of the coalition), unless f is the only bidder that strictly gains by the deviation of R. Suppose we are in the latter case. According to our generic games assumption, bidders that do not gain must keep their slots, and by the previous paragraph, for all $k \in R \setminus \{f\}$, $b_k \geq b'_k \geq b_{k+1}$. Consider $t \in R$, s.t. $t \neq f' + 1$ (there must be such t, as $|R| \geq 3$). If $t = 1$ bidder t is a free rider and we are done, thus assume $t > 1$.

Since R contains no neighbors, the bidder in slot $t - 1$ is not in R, and therefore the coalition $R \setminus \{t\}$ still has a deviation. $\qquad\square$

Proposition 6.8. *If both CTRs and valuations are convex, then*

$$\mathcal{D}_r(GSP, LE) \leq M_r \cdot O\left(\frac{r^2}{\sqrt{s}}\right).$$

In contrast, if both CTRs and valuations are concave, then

$$\mathcal{D}_r(GSP, LE) \geq M_r \cdot d \cdot \left(1 - \exp\left(-\Omega\left(\frac{r\sqrt{r}}{\sqrt{s}}\right)\right)\right)$$

for any positive constant $d < 1$.

Proof of Proposition 6.8, upper bound. Recall that we only consider the top $s+r-1$ bidders. The crucial observation is that a coalition R can deviate iff it contains a pair that can deviate. This follows directly from Lemma D.3, as we show in Section 6.4.3.

For the upper bound, we take a coalition R that is sampled uniformly from all M_r possible coalitions, and bound the probability that it contains a deviating pair. Recall that from the proof of Theorem 6.6a, a pair k, j can deviate only if they are at most $\sqrt{s-j} \leq \sqrt{s}$ slots apart.

A coalition of size r contains $\binom{r}{2} = O(r^2)$ pairs, and each such pair has a probability of at most $\frac{2\sqrt{s}}{s} = O\left(\frac{1}{\sqrt{s+r}}\right) = O\left(\frac{1}{\sqrt{s}}\right)$. From the union bound we get that the probability that a random coalition R contains *any* deviating pair is at most $O\left(\frac{r^2}{\sqrt{s}}\right)$. $\qquad\square$

Proof of Proposition 6.8, lower bound. If $r \geq s/2$, then R contains a pair of neighbors and therefore surely has a deviation. Similarly, if $r = \omega(\sqrt{s})$, then R contains a neighbor pair with high probability. Assume therefore that r is relatively small w.r.t. s, say $r < s^{2/3}$. Note that for all $t \leq r$, $\binom{s}{t} = \binom{s}{t-1}\frac{s-t}{t} \geq \binom{s}{t-1}s^{1/3}$. By induction, $\binom{s}{r} \geq \binom{s}{t}s^{1/3\cdot(r-t)}$.

Let $c < 1$ be a constant, $d = \sqrt{c}$.

Lemma D.4. *For a sufficiently large s, $\binom{s}{r} > d \cdot M_r$.*

Proof. Consider the sum $M_{r-1} = \sum_{t=1}^{r} - 1\binom{s}{t}$. It holds that

$$M_{r-1} \leq \sum_{t=1}^{r-1}\binom{s}{r}s^{1/3(t-r)} = \binom{s}{r}\sum_{t=1}^{r-1}(s^{1/3})^{-t} \leq 2s^{-1/3}\binom{s}{r}.$$

In particular, for a sufficiently large s, we have that $2s^{-1/3} < 1 - d$, and thus $M_{r-1} < (1-d)M_r$. Recall that $M_r = M_{r-1} + \binom{s}{r}$, thus

$$\binom{s}{r} = M_r - M_{r-1} > M_r - (1-d)M_r = d \cdot M_r.$$

$\qquad\square$

As we perform an asymptotic analysis, we indeed assume that s is as large as required.

Let $q = d^{2/r}$. We consider coalitions of size r in slots $1, 2, \ldots, qs$ (i.e. coalitions of the first type only). We show that there is only a small fraction of the $\binom{qs}{r}$ coalitions *do not* have a deviation.

Lemma D.5. $\binom{qs}{r} \geq d \cdot \binom{s}{r}$.

Proof.

$$q = d^{2/r} = e^{2\ln(d)/r} > \left(1 + \frac{2\ln d}{r}\right) \tag{D.5}$$

$$\frac{\binom{qs}{r}}{\binom{s}{r}} = \frac{(qs)!(s-r)!}{s!(qs-r)!} = \prod_{t=1}^{r} \frac{qs-t}{s-t} \geq \left(\frac{qs-r}{s-r}\right)^r > \left(\frac{s + \frac{2\ln d}{r}s - r}{s-r}\right)^r \tag{from (D.5)}$$

$$= \left(1 + \frac{2s\ln d}{r(s-r)}\right)^r > \left(1 + \frac{\ln d}{r-1}\right)^r \geq \exp\left(\frac{\ln(d)r}{r}\right) = \exp(\ln d) = d.$$

$\square$

Also, from Equation (D.5),

$$\sqrt{1-q} \geq \sqrt{1 - \left(1 + \frac{2\ln d}{r}\right)} = \sqrt{\frac{-2\ln(d)}{r}} > d'\frac{1}{\sqrt{r}}, \tag{D.6}$$

where $d' > 0$ is some constant independent of r and s.

We construct our coalition iteratively, lower bounding in every iteration the probability that a deviating pair is formed. Since all bidders are in slots $\leq qs$, it is sufficient for the first pair k, j to deviate if they are at most $\sqrt{s-j} \geq \sqrt{s-qs} = \sqrt{s(1-q)}$ slots apart. If the first pair are too far between, the third selected bidder has a double chance to deviate (with at least one of them). If this fails, the fourth bidder can be in the proximity of either of the first three, and so on.

Denote by E_t the event that the bidder selected in iteration t has a deviation with one of the previous bidders. Suppose that none of the $t-1$ previous bidders has a deviation. The new bidder t has $qs - (t-1)$ available slots. There are *at least* $(t-1)\sqrt{s(1-q)}$ slot that are in the proximity of previous bidders, since there is a "dangerous" interval of size (at least) $\sqrt{s(1-q)}$ around each bidder, and these intervals are distinct (otherwise there is a deviating pair). Formally, this can be written as

$$Pr(E_t | \forall t' < t, \neg E_{t'}) \geq \frac{(t-1)\sqrt{s(1-q)}}{qs-t+1}. \tag{D.7}$$

We have that for a random coalition R drawn from $1, 2, \ldots, qs$, the probability that R does *not* contain a deviating pair, is

$$Pr(\neg E_t \text{ for all } t = 2, 3, \ldots, r) = Pr(\neg E_2)Pr(\neg E_3 | \neg E_2) \cdots Pr(\neg E_r | \forall t' < r, \neg E_{t'})$$

$$\leq \left(1 - \frac{2\sqrt{s(1-q)}}{qs-1}\right) \cdots \left(1 - \frac{(r-1)\sqrt{s(1-q)}}{qs-r+1}\right) \tag{from (D.7)}$$

$$< \prod_{t=1}^{r-1}\left(1 - \frac{t\sqrt{s(1-q)}}{s}\right) \leq \prod_{t=\lfloor r/2 \rfloor}^{r-1}\left(1 - \frac{t\sqrt{s(1-q)}}{s}\right)$$

$$\leq \prod_{t=\lfloor r/2 \rfloor}^{r-1}\left(1 - \left\lfloor \frac{r}{2} \right\rfloor \frac{\sqrt{s(1-q)}}{s}\right) \leq \left(1 - \left\lfloor \frac{r}{2} \right\rfloor \frac{\sqrt{(1-q)}}{s}\right)^{\lceil \frac{r}{2} \rceil - 1}$$

$$\leq \left(1 - \frac{(r-1)\sqrt{1-q}}{2\sqrt{s}}\right)^{\frac{r-2}{2}} \leq \left(1 - d'\frac{r-1}{2\sqrt{s}\sqrt{r}}\right)^{\frac{r-2}{2}} \tag{from (D.6)}$$

$$\leq \exp\left(-d'\frac{(r-1)(r-2)}{4\sqrt{s}\sqrt{r}}\right) = \exp\left(-\Omega\left(\frac{r\sqrt{r}}{\sqrt{s}}\right)\right)$$

Thus there are at least $\binom{qs}{r}\left(1 - \exp\left(-\Omega\left(\frac{r\sqrt{r}}{\sqrt{s}}\right)\right)\right)$ coalitions of size r with deviations. Finally, we get from Lemmas D.5 and D.4 that $\binom{qs}{r} \geq d\binom{s}{r} \geq d^2 M_r = cM_r$, thus

$$\mathcal{D}_r(GSP, LE) \geq c \cdot M_r \cdot \left(1 - \exp\left(-\Omega\left(\frac{r\sqrt{r}}{\sqrt{s}}\right)\right)\right)$$

as required.   □

D.3   Eliminating Group Deviations

D.3.1   VCG with a reserve price

Consider a variant of the VCG mechanism that adds a fixed reserve price c. That is, only bidders that reports a value of c or higher get a slot, and payments are computed ignoring the other bidders (i.e. replacing their values with c).

This definitions may seem different than than the "standard" definition of VCG with reserve price c, which is typically defined as follows: remove bidders whose value is below c. Now run VCG on remaining bidders.

Lemma D.6. *The two definitions are equivalent.*

Proof. Let p_i denote the original payment of agent i in VCG *without* a reserve price. p'_i is the payment with reserve price according to the first definition, and p''_i is the payment according to the second definition. That is, $p''_i = \max(c, p_i)$ if $v_i \geq c$ and 0 otherwise.

Let $\alpha_i = \frac{x_i}{x_{i-1}}$. According to Varian [2007], $p_i = b_{i+1}$, where b_i is recursively defined as follows. $b_{s+1} = v_{s+1}$, and

$$p_{i-1} = b_i = \alpha_i v_i + (1 - \alpha_i)b_{i+1}.$$

Let j be the index of the lowest surviving bidder. Clearly if $j \geq s + 1$ then both auctions coincide with the original VCG auction, as the reserve price is not used at all. Therefore suppose $j \leq s$.

We now turn to compute p'_i in the same way. Suppose we add a positive term δ to all valuations. Then clearly all payments will also increase by δ.

Since all values (after removing the low bidders) are above c, we can decrease all v_i by c, to $v'_i = v_i - c$, and add c to the final payment. That is, $\mathbf{p}' = \mathbf{p}^* + c$, where $\mathbf{p}^*$ are the VCG payments for valuations $\mathbf{v}'$. We claim that $p^*_i = p_i - c$. The base case of the induction is $p^*_j = b^*_{j+1} = 0$ (since there are at most s bidders). The next bidder pays $p^*_{j-1} = b^*_j = \alpha_j v'_j = \alpha_j(v_j - c)$.   □

It is easy to verify that truth-telling remains a dominant strategy, and that Proposition 6.4 remains valid if the values of all bidders are strictly above c. However, a bidder whose value is exactly c will not join any coalition: by lowering her reported value she will lose her current slot for sure, whereas previously she enjoyed a positive utility.

Now, consider a VCG mechanism that chooses a reserve price as follows. With probability q, the reserve price is chosen randomly from a sufficiently large interval, and with probability $1 - q$, it is set to 0. Crucially, the probability distribution of the reserve price is common knowledge, but agents submit their reports before its realization is revealed. Let us denote the proposed mechanism by VCG*. While the proposed adjustment seems small, it results in a dramatic increase of stability.

Theorem D.7. *If $s \geq n$, then truth-telling is a SSE in VCG^*.*

Proof. First observe that VCG^* is a lottery over strategyproof mechanisms, thus no agent has an incentive to deviate unilaterally. Suppose by way of contradiction that there exists a deviating coalition, and let R be such a coalition of minimal size. Since R is minimal, the indifferent agent $i^* \in R$ (as defined in Prop. 6.4) must lower her reported value, otherwise the coalition $R \setminus \{i^*\}$ can also deviate. Assume, therefore, that $v'_{i*} = v_{i*} - \epsilon$ for some $\epsilon > 0$. It is easy to verify that i^* cannot gain in any outcome of the mechanism. In contrast, there is a non-zero probability that c is chosen in the range (v'_{i*}, v_{i*}), in which case the utility of i^* becomes 0, compared to $(v_{i*} - c)x_{i*} > 0$ under truth-telling. Therefore, agent i^* loses in expectation, contradicting the existence of a coalition R. □

By the last theorem, VCG^* guarantees stability whenever $n \leq s$.[1] However, if $s < n$ the bidder ranked $s + 1$ can serve as the indifferent bidder of any coalition. Consequently, VCG^* does not posses a SSE. That is, since the utility of agent $s + 1$ is always 0, she will not be discouraged by the random reserve price, even when her reported value falls below the reserve price.

In order to deal with the lack of slots (i.e., the case in which $s \leq n$), we introduce a modified VCG^* mechanism, which always induces truth-telling as a SSE.

Consider the following modification to VCG^*, termed VCG^*_λ. Let $0 < \lambda < \frac{1}{n}$. Given some slot $j \leq s$ with a CTR of $x_j > 0$, it is allocated to the bidder that is ranked j with probability $1 - \lambda$, and is allocated to the bidder that is ranked $s + 1$ with probability λ. This modification effectively creates a new slot $s + 1$, whose expected CTR is λx_j, whereas the new (expected) CTR of slot j becomes $(1-\lambda)x_j$. This procedure can be applied to the desired additional $n-s$ slots. In particular, a possible instantiation is where the new expected CTR of position s will be $(1 - (n - s)\lambda)x_s$, and there will be $n - s$ new slots with an expected CTR of λx_s. Since the new auction has n slots, the mechanism VCG^* can be performed to eliminate all coalitional deviations.

The careful reader will notice that by changing the CTRs, the equilibrium in the new auction may change. However, as long as the order of the slots is preserved, the equilibrium allocation is not affected, and this is ensured by satisfying $\lambda < \frac{1}{n}$. Moreover, the new payment differs from the original payment by at most $v_1 \cdot n \cdot \lambda$; thus for a sufficiently small λ the difference is negligible. As a result, we get the following corollary.

Corollary D.8. *Truth-telling is a SSE in mechanism VCG^*_λ for every $0 < \lambda < \frac{1}{n}$. Moreover, the payments and revenue of VCG^*_λ can be arbitrarily close to the payments and revenue of VCG.*

D.3.2 GSP with a reserve price

As evident from the results in the last section, stability of the VCG mechanism is significantly increased by augmenting the mechanism with a random reserve price and additional subtle randomization. It might be tempting to apply the same technique to the GSP mechanism, in an attempt to increase its stability, while maintaining the possibility to achieve a higher revenue than VCG. Unfortunately, this approach fails since (in contrast to VCG) adding a reserve price does not preserve its original set of equilibria.

To see this, consider a GSP mechanism with a fixed reserve price c. Bidder i is affected by the reserve price if either: (I) $v_i > c > b_i$, in which case bidder i has an incentive to raise her bid, as otherwise she will lose the slot; or (II) $v_i < c < b_i$, in which case she has an incentive to lower

---

[1]The proof in fact shows a stronger result: truth-telling is a SSE in *dominant strategies*. Thus VCG^* is *group-strategyproof*.

her bid, as otherwise she will pay more than the slot's worth to her. In both cases it follows that the modified GSP mechanism no longer preserves the SNE properties characterized by Varian (even with respect to unilateral deviations). The reason for the difference between VCG and GSP is that VCG induces truthful revelation in equilibrium; hence cases (I) and (II) suggested above cannot be realized.

Appendix E

Proofs for Chapter 7

E.1 Proofs for Section 7.3

Lemma 7.3. *Every SP mechanism is monotone.*

Proof. Suppose that f is SP, and assume toward a contradiction that f is not monotone. Thus there are $\mathbf{a} \in V^n$, $j \in N$, $b_j > a_j$ such that $x' = f(a_{-j}, b_j) < f(\mathbf{a}) = x$. We have that $|x' - a_j| \geq |x - a_j|$, since otherwise j can benefit by reporting b_j in the profile a. Since $x' < x$, this implies $x' < a_j < b_j$. Thus $|x - b_j| < |x' - b_j|$, and thus j can benefit by reporting a_j instead of b_j. $\square$

Lemma 7.4. *A monotone mechanism f is Pareto iff it is unanimous.*

Proof. Pareto clearly entails unanimity. It remains to show that unanimity implies Pareto. Note that the notion of Pareto on a line is equivalent to $f(\mathbf{a}) \in [\min_{j \in N} a_j, \max_{j \in N} a_j]$. Let $\mathbf{a} \in L^n$, $a' = \min_{j \in N} a_j$ and $a'' = \max_{j \in N} a_j$. Also let $\mathbf{a}' = (a', \ldots, a')$ and $\mathbf{a}'' = (a'', \ldots, a'')$. By unanimity, $f(\mathbf{a}') = a'$ and $f(\mathbf{a}'') = a''$. By monotonicity,

$$\min_{j \in N} a_j = a' = f(\mathbf{a}') \leq f(\mathbf{a}) \leq f(\mathbf{a}'') = a'' = \max_{j \in N} a_j,$$

as required. $\square$

Lemma 7.5. *Every SP, unanimous mechanism for the line is 1-SI.*

Proof. Since f is SP and unanimous, it is MON (by Lemma 7.3) and thus also Pareto (by Lemma 7.4). Suppose by way of contradiction that f is not 1-SI. Then, there exists at least one pair of profiles that violates the 1-SI property. Assume w.l.o.g. that the two profiles differ only in agent 1's report, and also that $a_1' = a_1 + 1$. By the violation of the 1-SI property, it holds that $f(a_1, a_{-1}) = x \neq x' = f(a_1', a_{-1})$, while $d([a, a'], f(\mathbf{a}')) > 1$.[1] Among these pairs, let $\mathbf{a}, \mathbf{a}'$ be the two profiles that maximize $\sum_{j \in N} a_j$.

---

[1] This is w.l.o.g a violation of part (b) of Definition 7.8. The other, symmetric, case is when $d([a, a'], f(\mathbf{a})) > 1$.

Since $a_1' > a_1$, MON implies that $x' > x$. Let $I_a = [a_1, a_1']$ and $I_x = [x, x']$. We distinguish between the following cases:

case a: The intervals I_a, I_x intersect on at most one point. It follows that either $a_1 \geq x'$ or $a_1' \leq x$. In the former case, agent 1 can benefit by reporting a_1' instead of a_1 in **a**, and similarly, in the latter case, agent 1 can benefit by reporting a_1 instead of a_1' in **a**'. Thus, a contradiction is reached.

case b: One of the intervals I_a, I_x strictly contains the other. Since $a_1' = a_1+1$ and $f(a_1, a_{-1}) \neq f(a_1', a_{-1})$, the inclusion must be $I_a \subsetneq I_x$. Further, since $d(a_1', x') \geq 2$, it must hold that $x \leq a_1'-2$ (i.e. that $x < a_1$), as otherwise $a_1' \to a_1$ is a manipulation for agent 1.

Since f is Pareto, and $x < a_1$, then there must be some other agent (w.l.o.g. agent 2) s.t. $a_2 \leq x$.

We define two new profiles, **b**, **b**', that differ from **a**, **a**' only by relocating agent 2 so that $b_2 = b_2' = x + 1$. Denote the new output locations by $y = f(\mathbf{b})$ and $y' = f(\mathbf{b}')$. One can easily verify that $b_2 > a_2$ (and clearly $b_2' > a_2'$). It, therefore, follows from MON that $y \geq x$, $y' \geq x'$, and also $y' \geq y$. We further distinguish between two sub-cases.

If $y' > y$, then $y' \geq x' \geq a_1' + 2$. Then **b**, **b**' is still a violating pair. However, since $b_2 > a_2$ and all other agents in **a**, **b** are the same, $\sum_{i \in N} b_i > \sum_{i \in N} a_i$ in contradiction to maximality of the pair **a**, **a**'.

If $y = y'$, then consider the pair of profiles **a**, **b** and their outcomes $x = f(\mathbf{a})$, $y = f(\mathbf{b})$. Note that $y = y' \geq x' > a_1 \geq x + 1 = b_2$, and thus $d(y, b_2) > 1 = d(x, b_2)$. Therefore $b_2 \to a_2$ is a manipulation for agent 2 under profile **b**, which is a contradiction to SP. $\qquad\square$

Lemma E.1. *Every 0-SI, MON mechanism f for the line is SP.*

Proof. Let **a** be a profile, j an agent, and a_j' a deviation of j and assume that $f(a_j, a_{-j}) \neq f(a_j', a_{-j})$. W.l.o.g., assume $a_j < a_j'$. From monotonicity we get that $f(a_j, a_{-j}) < f(a_j', a_{-j})$ and from f being 0-SI $a_j \leq f(a_j, a_{-j}) < f(a_j', a_{-j}) \leq a_j'$. Therefore, we get that j prefers $f(a_j, a_{-j})$ in **a** and hence this is not a manipulation. $\qquad\square$

Theorem 7.2. *An onto mechanism f on the line is SP if and only if it is MON and 1-SSI.*

Proof. Suppose f is an onto SP mechanism; then, by Lemmas 7.1 and 7.3, it is also monotone and unanimous, and therefore, by Lemma 7.5, it is 1-SI. Suppose that f does not satisfy 1-SSI; then, there is an agent i that violates DI (i.e., caused the violation).

Therefore, there is a profile (a_i, a_{-i}) and deviation a_i' s.t. $f(a_i, a_{-i}) = x \neq x' = f(a_i', a_{-i})$ but $|A \cap X| \in \{0, 1\}$ (A and X are the segments as used in Def. 7.9). W.l.o.g. assume $a_i < a_i'$. f satisfies 1-SI and hence $d([a_i, a_i']) < 2$. This means (by MON and 1-SI) that either the facility moved from $x = a_i - 1$ to a_i (which is a manipulation for i), or the facility moved from $x = a_i'$ to $x' = a_i' + 1$. In the latter case the movement $a_1' \to a_i$ is manipulation for i.

We now prove the other direction. Suppose f is an onto, monotone and 1-SSI mechanism. We will show that f is also SP. Suppose some agent j moves from a_j to $a_j' > a_j$ and by that causes the facility to move from $x = f(\mathbf{a})$ to $x' = f(a_j', a_{-j})$(the proof for movement to the left is symmetric). By monotonicity, $x' \geq x$. If $x \geq a_j$, then agent j does not benefit from the deviation. Otherwise, $x < a_j$; then, by 1-SI it holds that $x = a_j - 1$ (otherwise the facility will not move). By DI, it must hold that $|[a_j, a_j'] \cap [x, x']| \geq 2$, which means that $x' \geq a_j + 1$. Here again, agent j does not benefit from the deviation. $\qquad\square$

E.2 Proofs for Section 7.4

Let $\mathbf{a}, \mathbf{a}'$ be two profiles that differ only by the location of one agent (w.l.o.g. agent 1), and denote $x = f(\mathbf{a}), x' = f(\mathbf{a}')$.

Lemma 7.6. *If agent 1 moves* closer *to x along the shorter arc between them, then $x' = x$. I.e., if* $|(a, x]| \leq \lfloor k/2 \rfloor$ *and $a' \in (a, x]$ then $x' = x$.*

Proof. W.l.o.g. we assume that a moves clockwise, and prove by induction on the number of steps toward x. Let $a' = a + 1$. Assume, toward a contradiction, that $y = f(a', a_{-1}) \neq x$. Then either $y \in [a, x)$ (in which case $a \to a'$ is a manipulation), or $y \in (x, a)$. If $|[a, y]| \leq \lfloor k/2 \rfloor$, then since $x \in (a', y)$ it is closer to $a' = a + 1$ than y, meaning that $a' \to a$ is a manipulation.

Therefore, the shorter arc between a, y is $[y, a]$, of length $\leq \lfloor k/2 \rfloor$. Of course, $d(y, a) \geq d(x, a)$ (otherwise $a \to a'$) is a manipulation. However, this means that

$$d(a', x) = d(a, x) - 1 \leq d(a, y) - 1 = (d(a', y) - 1) - 1 < d(a', y),$$

i.e.,that $a' \to a$ is a manipulation. $\square$

Lemma 7.7. *Suppose that agent 1 moves one step* away *from x (along the longer arc between x and x'). Let y be the point on the longer arc s.t. $d(a', y) = d(a, x)$. Then either $x' = x$ (no change); or $d(x', y) \leq 1$.*
(If x is antipodal to a, then trivially a cannot move it.)

Proof. W.l.o.g. $a' = a + 1$. Denote $x' = f(a', b)$. If $x' \in (x, y - 2]$ then $a \to a'$ is a manipulation. If $x' \in [y + 2, x)$ then $d(a', x') > d(a', x)$, and thus $a \to a'$ is a manipulation. $\square$

Definition E.1. *Let $a_1, \ldots, a_n$, s.t. the minimal arc (consecutive part of the cycle) that includes all the points is of size $< k/2$.[2] A point $x \in R_k$ is cycle-Pareto (w.r.t. the profile a_i), in either of the following cases:*

- *x lies on the arc.*

- *k is odd, the arc size is $\lfloor k/2 \rfloor$, and there is an agent i next to x, i.e., $d(a_i, x) = 1$.*

If there is no such arc, every point $x \in R_k$ is cycle-Pareto.
A mechanism f is cycle-Pareto, if for any profile $x = f(a_1, a_2, \ldots, a_n)$ is a cycle-Pareto outcome.

Lemma E.2. *For an odd cycle, a profile $(a_1, \ldots, a_n)$, and a point x:*

  i *If x is a cycle-Pareto outcome, then there is no point y s.t. $d(a_i, y) < d(a_i, x)$ for every agent i.[3]*

  ii *If x is not a cycle-Pareto outcome, then there exists a point y s.t. $d(a_i, y) \leq d(a_i, x)$ for every agent i and $d(a_{i'}, y) < d(a_{i'}, x)$ for some agent i'.[4]*

Proof.

---

[2] Notice that the minimal arc is uniquely defined in such case.
[3] In the literature this criterion is usually referred to as 'Strong Pareto Dominance' and is equivalent to definition 7.3.
[4] In the literature this criterion is usually referred to as 'Weak Pareto Dominance'.

i Clearly, if x is a cycle-Pareto outcome due to the first condition (lies on the arc), it is also Pareto.

Otherwise, x does not lie on the arc, the arc size is exactly $\lfloor k/2 \rfloor$, and there is an agent s.t. $d(a_i, x) = 1$. W.l.o.g, the agents are ordered clockwise $a_1, a_2, \ldots, a_n$ s.t. $d(a_1, a_n) = \frac{k-1}{2}$, $d(x, a_1) = 1$, $d(x, a_n) = \frac{k-1}{2}$. The only point that is closer to a_1 than x is a_1 itself and it is not closer to a_n than x.

ii If x is not cycle-Pareto then the minimal arc is of size $\leq (k-1)/2$ and x does not lie on this arc. W.l.o.g, the agents are ordered clockwise $a_1, a_2, \ldots, a_n$ and a_1 is the closest to x. I.e., $d(a_1, x) \leq d(a_i, x)$ for all i. Denote by $t = d(x, a_1) > 0$.

If $t + d(a_1, a_n) \leq (k-1)/2$ (x and all the points lie on a semi-cycle), then for all agents $d(a_1, a_i) \leq d(x, a_i)$ and $d(a_1, a_1) = 0 < d(x, a_1)$ so $y = a_1$ satisfies the conditions.

If $t > d(a_1, a_n)$, then for all agents $d(a_i, a_n) \leq d(a_1, a_n) < d(a_1, x)$ so $d(x, a_i) = \min\left(d\left(a_i, a_1\right) + d\left(a_1, x\right), d\left(a_i, a_n\right) + d\left(a_n, x\right)\right) \geq \min\left(d\left(a_1, x\right), d\left(a_i, a_n\right)\right) = d\left(a_i, a_n\right)$ and $d(a_n, a_n) = 0 < d(x, a_n)$ so $y = a_n$ satisfies the conditions.

Otherwise, the point y is defined as the point on the arc $[a_1, a_n]$ s.t. $d(a_1, y) = t - 1$. For any agent: If $d\left(a_i, a_1\right) + d\left(a_1, x\right) < k/2$ then $d\left(a_i, y\right) < d\left(a_i, x\right)$. Otherwise, $d\left(a_i, y\right) - d\left(a_i, x\right) = \left(d\left(a_i, a_1\right) - d\left(a_1, x\right) + 1\right) - \left(k - d\left(a_i, a_1\right) - d\left(a_1, x\right)\right) = 2d\left(a_i, a_1\right) - k + 1 \leq 0$ so y satisfies the conditions.

$\square$

Lemma E.3. *If f is an SP mechanism for R_k for $n > 2$ agents that does not satisfy cycle-Pareto then there exists an SP mechanism g for R_k for 2 agents that does not satisfy cycle-Pareto.*

Proof. Let $(a_1, \ldots, a_n)$ be a profile s.t. $x = f(a_1, \ldots, a_n)$ is not a cycle-Pareto outcome. So we know that all the points lie on an arc smaller than $k/2$. W.l.o.g, assume a_1, a_2 are the extreme points of this arc. We define g by $g(u, v) = f(u, v, a_3, \ldots, a_n)$.

Since f is SP, so is g and clearly $x = g(a_1, a_2)$ is not a cycle-Pareto outcome. $\square$

E.2.1 Two agents

Lemma E.4. *Let f be onto and SP rule on R_k ($k \geq 13$). Suppose that $x = f(a, b)$ is violating cycle-Pareto. Then x is at distance (exactly) 2 from some agent, and agents are almost antipodal, i.e. $k/2 > d(a, b) \geq k/2 - 1$.*

Proof. As our proof will show, this will be true for *any* number of agents. However we consider the case of two agents first. Let $f(a, b) = x$ such that x is not cycle-Pareto. Moreover, let a, b be the profile minimizing $d(a, b)$ under this condition. W.l.o.g. $[a, b]$ is the shorter arc (we denote $a < b$), thus $x \in (b, a)$. By unanimity, $d(a, b) \geq 5$, as otherwise there is a manipulation $a \to b$ or vice versa (as either $d(a, x) > 4$ or $d(b, x) > 4$). We denote $u = f(a+1, b)$ and $w = f(a, b-1)$. By minimality of $d(a, b)$, $u, w \neq x$ and both u, w are cycle-Pareto (w.r.t. their respective profiles). See Figure E.1 for an illustration. We prove the following series of claims.

- $u \neq w$ (W.l.o.g. that $u = b$)

  Indeed, suppose that they are equal, then $u = w \in [a, b]$, and thus $d(a, u) + d(b, u) = d(a, b)$. Also, from SP we have that $d(a, x) \leq d(a, u)$ and $d(b, x) \leq d(b, u)$. By joining the inequalities,

  $$d(a, b) = d(a, u) + d(b, u) \geq d(a, x) + d(b, x) = k - d(a, b).$$

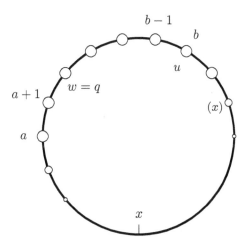

Figure E.1: An illustration of the original violating profile, where $x = f(a, b)$. Agents' locations $(a, b,$ etc.) appear outside the cycle, and facility locations $(x, x',$ etc.) appear inside. The conclusion of this part of the proof is that the facility must be close to one of the agents (appears in brackets).

This entails that $[a, b]$ is the long arc, which is a contradiction.

- Either $w = a$ or $u = b$.
  Consider $q = f(a + 1, b - 1)$. If $u \neq b$, then $q = f(a + 1, b - 1) = f(a + 1, b) = u$ by Lemma 7.6. Similarly, if $w \neq a$, then $q = f(a + 1, b - 1) = f(a, b - 1) = w$. Therefore if neither of the two equalities holds then $u = q = w$ in contradiction to the previous claim.

- $d(q, b - 1) \leq 1$
  Otherwise $b - 1 \to b$ is a manipulation for agent 2 (under $a + 1$).

- $d(q, b) = d(q, b - 1) + 1 \leq 2$.

- $a \neq w$
  If $a = w$, then $d(q, a + 1) \leq 1$, i.e. $q = a + 1$ or $q = a + 2$, and thus (since $k \geq 13$) $d(q, b) = d(a, b) - d(q, a) \geq 5 - 2 = 3$, in contradiction to the previous result.

- $1 \leq d(x, b) \leq 2$
  Deviation of agent 1 $a \to a + 1$ is not beneficial (under b) and hence $d(x, b) \leq d(w, b) = d(q, b) \leq 2$

- $d(x, b) = 2$
  If k is even, then $d(a, b) < k$, as otherwise every outcome is Pareto. It then follows by Lemma 7.8 that $d(x, b) > 1$ (i.e. $d(x, b) = 2$). Similarly, if k is odd, then $d(a, b) \leq \lfloor k/2 \rfloor$ (otherwise $a \to b$ is a manipulation). Then $d(b, x) = 2$ as well, since $d(a, x) = 1$ would not violate cycle-Pareto by definition. Thus we get the first part of the lemma.

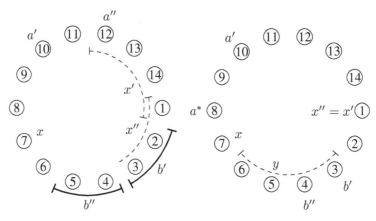

(a) The ranges of the critical locations of agent 2 b', b'' are shown, as well as the ranges of the outcomes $x' = f(a', b'), x'' = f(a'', b'')$.

(b) An illustration of case (ii).

Figure E.2: Illustrations of profiles defined in the second part of the proof.

- $d(a, b) \geq k/2 - 1$. Suppose otherwise, i.e. that $d(a, b) < k/2 - 1$. Since $d(x, b) = 2$, then $d(a, x) > d(a, b)$, and $a \to b$ is a manipulation for agent 1.

Finally, due to Lemma E.3, SP mechanisms on R_k, $k \geq 13$ must be cycle-Pareto, for every n. □

Lemma 7.9. *Let $k \geq 13$, $n = 2$. If f is SP and onto on R_k, then f is cycle-Pareto.*

Proof. Recall that by Lemma E.4 cycle-Pareto can only be violated when the facility is at distance (exactly) 2 from some agent, and agents are almost antipodal.

- For any location of agent 1 on $[x, a] = \{b + 2, b + 3, \ldots, a\}$, the location of the facility does not change (by Lemma 7.6). In particular, this includes the locations $a' = x + 3 = b + 5$ and $a'' = x + 5 = b + 7$ (since $k \geq 13$ it holds that $a', a'' \in [x, a]$).

  We claim that the existence of profiles (a', b) and (a'', b) leads to a contradiction. This claim completes our proof, and will also be used in the proof of Lemma 7.10.

  For each of the profiles a', b and a'', b, we move agent 2 counterclockwise (away from x), and denote by b' [respectively, b''] the first step s.t. $f(a', b') \neq x$ [resp., $f(a'', b'') \neq x$]. See Figure E.2(a) for an illustration.

- $b'' > b'$
  Indeed, the facility cannot move before agent 2 crosses the point antipodal to a'' (i.e. while $|[b - t, a'']| < |[a'', b - t]|$), as otherwise we would have a profile violating cycle-Pareto, where $d(x, a''), d(x, b - t) \neq 2$. Similarly, the facility *must* move after the crossing (i.e. when $|[b - t, a'']| > |[a'', b - t]|$). Thus for odd k we get that $b'' = a'' - \lceil k/2 \rceil$. For even k, the location of the facility can be anywhere when a'', b'' are exactly antipodal, thus $b'' \in [a'' - k/2 - 1, a'' - k/2]$.

- We can summarize both cases with the following constraint:

$$d(b'', x) = |(b'', x]| = |(b'', a'']| - 5 = \left(\frac{k}{2} + \frac{1}{2} \pm \frac{1}{2}\right) - 5 \leq \frac{k}{2} - 4. \qquad \text{(E.1)}$$

A similar analysis for a', b' shows the following:

$$d(b', x) = |(b', x]| = |(b', a']| - 3 = \left(\frac{k}{2} + \frac{1}{2} \pm \frac{1}{2}\right) - 3 \geq \frac{k}{2} - 3. \qquad \text{(E.2)}$$

- We denote $x' = f(a', b'), x'' = f(a'', b'')$. By Lemma 7.7, x' is roughly the same distance from b' as x is, i.e.

$$d(b'', x'') = d(b'' - 1, x) \pm 1 \leq d(b'', x) \leq k/2 - 4 \qquad \text{(By Eq. (E.1))}$$
$$d(b', x') = d(b' - 1, x) \pm 1 \geq d(b', x) - 2 \geq k/2 - 5 \qquad \text{(By Eq. (E.2))}$$

We get that either (i) x'' is strictly closer that x' to b' (i.e. $x'' < x'$), or (ii) $x'' = x', b'' = b' + 1$. Also note that by Lemma 7.7 $d(b', x') \leq d(b' - 1, x)$, which entails (for $k \geq 13$) that $x' \geq a''$. See Figure E.2(a) for an illustration.

(i) Suppose that $x'' > x'$. This case leads to a simple contradiction. Denote $z = f(a'', b')$. By Lemma 7.6, $z = f(a'', b'') = x''$. Similarly, since $x' \geq a'$, $z = f(a', b') = x'$, in contradiction to the assumption.

(ii) Suppose that $x' = x''$, $b' = b'' - 1$ (see Figure E.2(b)). In particular it must hold that k is even and $d(a', b') = k/2$, i.e. $k \geq 14$. We move agent 1 two steps from x' counter clockwise, to $x + 1$. We denote this location of agent 1 by a^*. Since $b'' > b'$, $f(a', b'') = x$ and thus by Lemma 7.6 $f(a^*, b'') = x$ as well.

We argue that $y = f(a^*, b') \neq x'$. Suppose otherwise, then $y = x'$ is violating cycle-Pareto. Moreover, $d(a^*, b') < k/2 - 1 \leq d(a, b)$ in contradiction to minimality. It thus follows that $y \in [b', a^*]$. We further argue that $y \in [b', x)$. Indeed, if $y \in [x, a^*]$, then $d(a', y) \leq 3$. On the other hand,

$$d(a', x') = d(a', b') - d(b', x') = k/2 - (k/2 - 5) = 5,$$

thus $a' \to a^*$ is a manipulation for agent 1 under b'.

- Finally, it follows that agent 2 has a manipulation by moving from b'' to b' under a^*. This is since the facility moves from $x = f(a^*, b'')$ (where $d(x, b'') \geq 2$) to $y = f(a^*, b')$, where $y \in (x, b']$ and thus $d(y, b'') < d(x, b'')$.

$\square$

E.2.2 Three agents

Lemma 7.12. *Assume $k \geq 13$, $n = 3$. Let f be a unanimous SP mechanism on R_k. Then either f has a 1-dictator, or any pair is a 1-dictator. That is if there are two agents j, j' s.t. $a_j = a_{j'}$, then $d(f(\mathbf{a}), a_j) \leq 1$.*

Proof. Let f be an SP unanimous rule for $n = 3$ agents. We define a two agent mechanism for every pair $j, j' \in N$ by letting j be a duplicate of j' (For ease of notation we'll refer to the agents of $g^{j,j'}$ by agent I and agent II, the third agent by j'', and the original agents by agent 1, agent 2, and agent 3),

$$g^{12}(a,b) = f(a,a,b)$$
$$g^{23}(a,b) = f(b,a,a)$$
$$g^{31}(a,b) = f(a,b,a).$$

Clearly, the mechanism $g^{j,j'}$ is unanimous, since $g^{j,j'}(a,a) = f(a,a,a) = a$ for all j, j'.

We argue that $g^{j,j'}$ is SP. Indeed, otherwise there is a manipulation either for agent II (which is also a manipulation in f, which is a contradiction to SP) or for agent I (say, $a \to a'$). In the latter case we can construct a manipulation in f by iteratively switching agents j, j' from a to a'. Either j or j' strictly gains by this move and thus has a manipulation.

Since $g^{j,j'}$ is a unanimous and SP, by Theorem 7.11 it has a 1-dictator. If the dictator is agent II then j'' is also a 1-dictator of f. Otherwise, suppose that $f(a_j, a_{j'}, a_{j''}) = x$, and $d(x, a_{j''}) > 1$. However It the follows by Lemma 7.6 that $f(x, x, a_{j''}) = x$ as well, which is a contradiction.

If agent I is a 1-dictator of g, then whenever $a_j = a_{j'}$, $d(f(\mathbf{a}), a_j) \leq 1$. $\qquad\square$

Lemma 7.13. *Let f be an SP, unanimous rule for 3 agents on R_k for $k \geq 13$. For all $a, b, c \in R_k$, $x = f(a,b,c)$, $d(a,x) \leq 1$ or $d(b,x) \leq 1$ or $d(c,x) \leq 1$.*

Proof. By Lemma 7.12, either there is a 1-dictator (in which case we are done), or every pair of agents standing together serve as a 1-dictator.

Let $u_1, u_2, u_3, x = f(u_1, u_2, u_3)$ s.t. x is at least 2 steps from all agents. We have that there is a semi-cycle in which x and two other points are consequent, and thus x must be between them (otherwise the more distant agent of the two has a manipulation, similarly to Lemma 7.8). W.l.o.g. $u_1 + 1 < x < u_2 - 1$ (i.e., ordered that way on an arc). Now suppose that agent 3 moves to u_1 or u_2, whichever closer to her (assume u_1). Then $y = f(u_1, u_2, u_1)$ is close to u_1. We thus have

$$d(u_3, y) \leq d(u_3, u_1) + d(u_1, y) \leq (d(u_3, x) - 2) + 1 < d(u_3, x),$$

i.e.,there is a manipulation for agent 3. $\qquad\square$

Theorem 7.14. *Assume $k \geq 22$, $n = 3$. Let f be an onto SP mechanism on R_k, then f is a 1-dictator.*

Proof. Assume, toward a contradiction, that there is no 1-dictator.

We begin from a profile where $a = 0$, $b'' = 5$. Let $x = f(a, b'', a)$. By Lemma 7.12, $d(x, a) \leq 1$. Moreover, we can assume w.l.o.g. that $x = a = 0$, since otherwise we can move all agents toward x.

We also define an alternative profile, where $b' = b'' + 3 = 8$. See Figure E.3 for an illustration.

We now move agent 3 counterclockwise from a to b' (i.e., along the long arc). Suppose $c_0 = a - 3$. Then the facility is either near a or near c_0. If it is near c_0, then it must follow agent 3 all the way to b' (otherwise he will have a manipulation). In particular, the facility must visit one of the points $b' + 2, b' + 3, b' + 4$. However since $k \geq 22$, then all three points are at distance of at least 10 from a. This means that agent 1 can manipulate $a \to b'$, bringing the facility (by Lemma 7.12) to $b' \pm 1$.

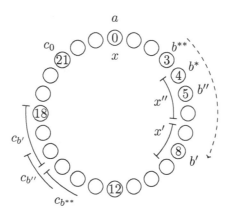

Figure E.3: An illustration of the profiles on R_{24}. Note that $c_{b'}$ must be roughly half way between b' and a (along the long arc), and likewise for $c_{b''}$ w.r.t. $[b'', a]$. Moving along the dashed arrow, agent 2 must change the critical point c_b. Thus there is at least one step along this path that is a manipulation for agent 2.

Therefore, $f(a, b', c)$ is either near a or near b' for all $c \in [b', a]$. Moreover, when it is near a we can still assume it equals $x = a$ (since otherwise we again move agents 1 and 2 toward the facility).

We can now apply exactly the same argument on the initial profile (a, b'', c_0), thus $f(a, b'', c)$ is either near a or near b'' for all $c \in [b'', a]$.

Next, let c_b' denote the last point on the long arc s.t. $f(a, b', c_{b'}) = x$, meaning that $d(x', b') \leq 1$, where $x' = f(a, b', c)$ for all $c \in (b, c_{b'+1}]$. Similarly, $c_{b''}$ will denote the critical switching point when agent 2 is at b'', and $x'' = b'' \pm 1$ is the new location of the facility after the switch.

Our plan is as follows: First to show that $c_{b'}, c_{b''}$ are roughly on the middle of the long arc $[b', a]$ and $[b'', a]$, respectively. It will then follow that $c_{b'} > c_{b''}$, which will lead to a manipulation of agent 2.

Let us study the constraints on c_b (for any location b of agent 2). For convenience, we denote $r_b = k - c_b = d(c_b, a)$. The location of the facility after the switch is denoted by z. Indeed, $r_b = d(x, c_b) \leq d(z, c_b)$, otherwise there is a manipulation $c_b \to c_b + 1$ for agent 3. Thus,

$$r_b = d(x, c_b) \leq d(z, c_b) = d(b, c_b) + d(b, z) \leq d(b, c_b) + 1 = k - b - r_b + 1,$$

i.e., $r_b \leq \frac{k-b+1}{2}$.

Similarly, $d(c_b + 1, z) \leq d(c_b + 1, x) = r_b + 1$ (otherwise $c_b + 1 \to c_b$ is a manipulation), thus

$$r_b \geq d(c_b + 1, z) - 1 = d(c_b, z) - 2 \geq k - b - r_b - 1 - 2 = k - b - r_b - 3,$$

i.e., $r_b \geq \frac{k-b-3}{2}$.

Substituting b for the actual values b', b'', we get that

$$c_{b'} = k - r_{b'} \geq k - \frac{k - b' + 1}{2} = k - \frac{k - 8}{2} = \frac{k}{2} + 4,$$

whereas

$$c_{b''} = k - r_{b''} \leq k - \frac{k - b'' - 3}{2} = k - \frac{k - 9}{2} = \frac{k}{2} + 4\frac{1}{2}.$$

Thus either $c_{b'} > c_{b''}$, or both are equal to $\lceil \frac{k}{2} + 4 \rceil$. In the first case, agent 2 can manipulate in profile $(a, b'', c_{b'})$ by reporting b'. This will move the facility from x (where $d(x, b'') = 5$) to $b' \pm 1$, which is at most 4 steps from b''.

In the latter case, consider $b^* = 4$ and $b^{**} = 3$. Computing the critical point for b^{**},

$$c_{b^{**}} = k - r_{b^{**}} \leq k - \frac{k - b^{**} - 3}{2} = k - \frac{k-7}{2} < c_{b''}.$$

Thus either $c_{b^*} < c_{b''}$, in which case agent 2 has a manipulation $(a, b^*, c_{b''}) \to b''$, or $c_{b^{**}} < c_{b^*} = b_{b''}$, in which case agent 2 has a manipulation $(a, b^{**}, c_{b^*}) \to b^*$. □

Theorem 7.15. *Let f be an onto and SP mechanism on R_k, where $k \geq 22$, then f is 1-dictatorial.*

Proof. We assume by induction for every $m < n$ (we know it holds for $n \leq 3$). Let f be an SP unanimous rule for $n \geq 4$ agents. We define two mechanisms for $n - 1$ agents:

$$g(a_{-1}) = f(a_1 = a_2, a_{-1}) \quad ; \quad h(a_{-3}) = f(a_3 = a_4, a_{-3}).$$

Now, similarly to the proof of Lemma 7.12, both g, h are unanimous and SP and therefore both are 1-dictator mechanisms.

Let $i^* \in N \setminus \{1\}, j^* \in N \setminus \{3\}$ be the dictators of g and h, respectively. Suppose first that $i^* \neq j^*$. Take any profile where $d(a_{i^*}, a_{j^*}) > 2$ (this is always possible for $k > 4$). Also, if $i^* = 2$ then set $a_1 = a_2$, and if $j^* = 3$ then set $a_4 = a_3$. We then have that $x = f(\mathbf{a})$ holds both $d(x, a_{i^*}) \leq 1$ and $d(x, a_{j^*}) \leq 1$, i.e., $d(a_{i^*}, a_{j^*}) \leq 2$ in contradiction to the way we defined the profile.

Thus $i^* = j^*$. This means that i^* acts as a 1-dictator of f whenever $a_1 = a_2$ or $a_3 = a_4$. W.l.o.g. $i^* \notin \{1, 2\}$ (in the symmetric case $i^* \notin \{3, 4\}$). For any profile $\mathbf{b} = b_{-\{1,2,i^*\}}$, consider the mechanism

$$q_{\mathbf{b}}(a_1, a_2, a_{i^*}) = f(a_1, a_2, a_{i^*}, \mathbf{b}).$$

Note that is is onto and SP, and thus has a 1-dictator. If i^* is the dictator for any $\mathbf{b}$ then we are done. Otherwise, w.l.o.g. agent 1 is the 1-dictator for some $q_{\mathbf{b}}$. Then, consider some profile where $a_1 = a_2$, and $d(a_1, a_{i^*}) > 2$ to reach a contradiction. □

E.2.3   Small cycles

Proposition 7.16. *There are onto and anonymous SP mechanisms on R_k:*

(a) for $n = 2$, and all $k \leq 12$.

(b) for $n = 3$, and all $k \leq 14$ or $k = 16$.

For $n = 2, k \leq 9$, we can use the same "median-like" mechanism described next, adding a third dummy agent at an arbitrary location. Tie-breaking is made in favor of the dummy agent, and then clockwise. For $k \in \{10, 11, 12\}$ we provide a tabular description of the mechanisms online.[5]

---

[5]http://tinyurl.com/mrqjcbt

Proof for $n = 3, k \le 7$. We define a "median-like" mechanism as follows: let $(a_3, a_1]$ be the longest clockwise arc between agents, then $f(\mathbf{a}) = a_2$. Break ties clockwise, if needed. An agent (say a_1) can try to manipulate. The current dictator (say a_2) must be the one closer a_1, as otherwise $|(a_1, a_2]| > |(a_3, a_1]|$. Thus changing the identity of the dictator from 2 to 3 cannot benefit agent 1. The only way to gain is to become the dictator, by moving away from a_2, making the arc $[a_3, a_1']$ smaller. For agent 1 to become the dictator, the size of $(a_2, a_3]$ must be at least 3, otherwise there is a longer arc (as the sum is $k = 7$). We have that $|(a_3, a_1]| \ge |(a_2, a_3]| \ge 3$, since agent 2 is the dictator for $\mathbf{a}$. As a result, $|(a_1, a_2]| \le 7 - 3 - 3 = 1$, i.e. either $a_1 = a_2 = f(\mathbf{a})$ (in which case clearly there is no manipulation), or $a_1 = a_2 - 1$. In the latter case, we will have that $f(\mathbf{a}') = a_1' \ne a_1$, so it is still not an improvement for agent 1.

It is easy to verify that the mechanism also works for smaller cycles. $\qquad\square$

For $k \in \{8 - 14, 16\}$ we provide mechanisms as three-dimensional arrays in Matlab format.

Corollary 7.18. *Every SP mechanism on R_k for $k \ge 22$ has an approximation ratio of at least $\frac{9}{10}n - 1$. The ratio converges to $n - 1$ as k tends to infinity.*

Proof. If the mechanism is not unanimous, it has an infinite approximation ratio. Otherwise it is a 1-dictator, w.l.o.g. agent n is the 1-dictator. Let $a_1 = a_2 = \ldots = a_{n-1} = k$, and $a_n = \lfloor \frac{k}{2} \rfloor$. Clearly, the optimal location is $\mathbf{opt} = a_1$, and the optimal total distance from all agents is $\lfloor \frac{k}{2} \rfloor$. However, $f(\mathbf{a}) = \lfloor \frac{k}{2} \rfloor \pm 1$, and the total distance from the agents is at least $(n-1)\left(\lfloor \frac{k}{2} \rfloor - 1\right)$ (in fact $\min\{(n-1)\lfloor \frac{k}{2} \rfloor, n\left(\lfloor \frac{k}{2} \rfloor - 1\right)\}$). Thus the approximation ratio for $k \ge 22$ is

$$\frac{SC(f(\mathbf{a}))}{SC(\mathbf{opt}(\mathbf{a}))} \ge (n-1)\frac{\lfloor \frac{k}{2} \rfloor - 1}{\lfloor \frac{k}{2} \rfloor} \ge \frac{9}{10}(n-1) \ge\ge \frac{9}{10}n - 1,$$

thereby proving the assertion. $\qquad\square$

Corollary 7.19. *Let $G = (V, E)$ be a graph that contains some minimal cycle $R \subseteq V$ that is sufficiently large (according to Table 7.1). Then any SP onto mechanism on G has a "cycle 1-dictator" $i \in N$. That is, if all agents lie on R then $d(f(\mathbf{a}), a_i) \le 1$.*

Proof. Let f be an onto SP mechanism on G. We argue that whenever $\mathbf{a} \in (R)^n$ (i.e. all agents are on the cycle R), then $f(\mathbf{a}) \in R$ as well.

Assume otherwise, i.e. $f(\mathbf{a}) \notin R$. Let $y^* \in \operatorname{argmin}_{y \in R} d(y, x)$ and $r = d(x, y^*)$. Let $S \subseteq N$ be the agents s.t. $|(a_i, y^*]| < |(y^*, a_i]|$, and T be the agents s.t. $|(a_i, y^*]| \ge |(y^*, a_i]|$.[6]

If either S or T contains all agents then there is a manipulation by moving all agents to the location of the agent closest to y^*.

We now iteratively move all S agents toward y^* one step at a time. At each step we will move the farthest agent from y^* toward y^*.

In each step an agent takes, the facility can keep its location, move to a different location not on R of the same distance from y^* as $f(\mathbf{a})$, or move to $y_S \in R$, where $y_S = y^* + r$ (otherwise this is a manipulation to the moving agent in one of the directions).

At some step the location of the facility must change to a location on the cycle (i.e. the third alternative occurs), otherwise there is a manipulation by unanimity: when all agents of S reach y^* and all the agents of T join them one by one (for each T agent joining, the facility cannot jump to the arc since it will be a manipulation). Similarly, if we hold S and move all agents from T towards y^* then the facility must move to y_T, where $y_T = y^* - r$.

---

[6] a_i and y^* all are on a cycle and the notation $[a, b)$ notates the segments as we used for the cycle graphs.

W.l.o.g. the facility jumps to y_S when agent $1 \in S$ moves from a_1 to $a_1 + 1$, and with agent $2 \in T$ when she moves from a_2 to $a_2 - 1$ and they are the farthest agents (counter-clockwise and clockwise respectively).

We freeze all other agents s.t. if either agent 1 or agent 2 moves the facility jumps, and consider the three profiles $f(a_1, a_2, a_{-12}) = f(\mathbf{a})$, $f(a_1 + 1, a_2, a_{-12}) = y_S$ and $f(a_1, a_2 - 1, a_{-12}) = y_T$. Clearly y_S cannot be farther from y^* than a_2 (and similarly for y_T and a_1) otherwise there is a manipulation by unanimity when all agents join a_2 one by one (for each agent joining, the facility cannot jump to the arc since it will be a manipulation).

Then we get a contradiction as $f(a_1 + 1, a_2 - 1, a_{-12}) = f(a_1 + 1, a_2, a_{-12}) = y_S$ but also $f(a_1 + 1, a_2 - 1, a_{-12}) = f(a_1, a_2 - 1, a_{-12}) = y_T \neq y_S$ otherwise there is a manipulation. $\square$

E.3   Proofs for Section 7.5

Proposition E.5. *The approximation ratio of the* **SRD** *mechanism is at least* 2.4 *on some instances with three agents (i.e., strictly higher than* $\left(3 - \frac{2}{n}\right) = 2\frac{1}{3}$).

Example . Consider the line graph L_2 (i.e., $V = \{0, 1, 2\}$), with the constraint $V' = \{0, 2\}$. Assume w.l.o.g. that an agent placed in $a = 1$ (and is thus indifferent between the allowed locations) reports her prefered location as 0.

We define three agents, where $a_1 = a_2 = 2$, and $a_3 = 1$. We set agents' weights as follows: $w_1 = w_2 = 0.29$, and $w_3 = 0.42$.

Observe first that $SC(0, \mathbf{a}) = 0.79$, whereas $d^* = SC(2, \mathbf{a}) = 0.21$. However, the **SRD** mechanism selects agent 3 (and thus the location 0) with probability of $\frac{0.42^2}{0.29^2 + 0.29^2 + 0.42^2} \cong 0.511$. Therefore,

$$SC(\mathbf{SRD}(\mathbf{a}), \mathbf{a}) > 0.51 \cdot 0.79 + 0.49 \cdot 0.21 = 0.5058 > 2.4 \cdot 0.21 = 2.4 \cdot d^*,$$

which proves the lower bound. $\Diamond$

Proposition E.6. *The approximation ratio of the* **SRD** *mechanism is at least* 1.39 *on some* uncon-strained *instances with three agents (i.e., strictly higher than* $\left(2 - \frac{2}{n}\right) = 1\frac{1}{3}$).

Example . We use L_1, i.e. $V' = V = \{0, 1\}$, and three agents, where $a_1 = a_2 = 1$, and $a_3 = 0$. We set agents' weights as follows: $w_1 = w_2 = 0.363$, and $w_3 = 0.274$.

We have that $SC(0, \mathbf{a}) = 0.763$, and $d^* = SC(1, \mathbf{a}) = 0.274$. The **SRD** mechanism selects agent 3 with probability of $\frac{0.274^2}{0.363^2 + 0.363^2 + 0.274^2} \cong 0.222$. Therefore,

$$SC(\mathbf{SRD}(\mathbf{a}), \mathbf{a}) > 0.222 \cdot 0.763 + 0.778 \cdot 0.274 > 0.382 > 1.39 \cdot 0.274 = 1.39 \cdot d^*,$$

which proves the lower bound for the unconstrained case. $\Diamond$

Theorem 7.20. *The following hold for Mechanism 2, w.r.t. any profile* $\mathbf{a}$:

(a) $\alpha_{\mathbf{w}} \leq 2 - \frac{2}{n}$.

(b) **CRD** *has an approximation ratio of* $1 + \alpha_{\mathbf{w}}$, *i.e., at most* $3 - \frac{2}{n}$.

(c) *for unconstrained instances, the approximation ratio is* $\frac{\alpha_{\mathbf{w}}}{2} + 1$, *i.e., at most* $2 - \frac{1}{n}$.

Proof. We first prove that $\alpha_{\mathbf{w}} \leq 2 - \frac{2}{n}$.

Let $g(x) = \frac{1}{2-2x}$. Note that g is convex. Also, since $\sum_{i \in N} w_i = 1$, we have that

$$\frac{1}{n} \leq \sum_{i \in N} w_i^2 \leq 1. \tag{E.3}$$

$$
\begin{aligned}
(\alpha_{\mathbf{w}})^{-1} = \sum_{i \in N} p_i' = \sum_{i \in N} w_i \frac{1}{2 - 2w_i} &= \sum_{i \in N} w_i g(w_i) \\
&\geq g\left(\sum_{i \in N} w_i \cdot w_i\right) = \frac{1}{2 - 2\sum_{i \in N} w_i^2} \qquad \text{(from Jensen's inequality)} \\
&\geq \frac{1}{2 - 2(1/n)}, \qquad \text{(from (E.3))}
\end{aligned}
$$

thus $\alpha_{\mathbf{w}} \leq 2 - \frac{2}{n}$, which proves (a).

Denote $c_i = \mathbf{opt}(a_i)$; $c^* = \mathbf{opt}(\mathbf{a})$. Note that for all i, $d(c_i, c^*) \leq 2d(a_i, c^*)$, since otherwise c^* is closer to a_i than c_i.

$$
\begin{aligned}
SC(\mathbf{CRD}(\mathbf{a}), \mathbf{a}) = \sum_{i \in N} p_i SC(c_i, \mathbf{a}) &= \sum_{i \in N} p_i \sum_{j \in N} w_j d(c_i, a_j) \\
&= \sum_{i \in N} \left(p_i w_i d(c_i, a_i) + \sum_{j \neq i} p_i w_j d(c_i, a_j) \right) \\
&\leq \sum_{i \in N} \left(p_i w_i d(c^*, a_i) + \sum_{j \neq i} p_i w_j (d(c_i, c^*) + d(c^*, a_j)) \right) \quad \text{(by triangle ineq.)} \\
&= \sum_{i \in N} p_i d(c_i, c^*) \sum_{j \neq i} w_j + \sum_{i \in N} \sum_{j \in N} p_i w_j d(c^*, a_j) \\
&= \alpha_{\mathbf{w}} \sum_{i \in N} \frac{w_i}{2(1 - w_i)} d(c_i, c^*)(1 - w_i) + \sum_{j \in N} w_j d(c^*, a_j) \sum_{i \in N} p_i \\
&\leq \alpha_{\mathbf{w}} \sum_{i \in N} \frac{w_i}{2} 2d(a_i, c^*) + \sum_{j \in N} w_j d(c^*, a_j) \\
&= (\alpha_{\mathbf{w}} + 1) \sum_{j \in N} w_j d(c^*, a_j) = (\alpha_{\mathbf{w}} + 1) SC(c^*, \mathbf{a}) \leq \left(3 - \frac{2}{n} \right) d^* \\
&\qquad \text{(from (a))}
\end{aligned}
$$

Now, in the unconstrained case, $a_i = c_i$ for all i.

$$
\begin{aligned}
SC(\mathbf{CRD}(\mathbf{a}), \mathbf{a}) &= \sum_{i \in N} p_i SC(c_i, \mathbf{a}) = \sum_{i \in N} p_i \sum_{j \in N} w_j d(a_i, a_j) = \sum_{i \in N} p_i \sum_{j \neq i} w_j d(a_i, a_j) \\
&\leq \sum_{i \in N} \sum_{j \neq i} p_i w_j (d(a_i, c^*) + d(a_j, c^*)) \qquad\qquad\qquad\qquad\text{(T.I.)} \\
&= \sum_{i \in N} p_i d(a_i, c^*) \sum_{j \neq i} w_j + \sum_{i \in N} p_i \sum_{j \neq i} w_j d(a_j, c^*) \\
&= \sum_{i \in N} p_i d(a_i, c^*)(1 - w_i) + \sum_{i \in N} p_i (r^*(F) - w_i d(a_i, c^*)) \\
&= \alpha_{\mathbf{w}} \sum_{i \in N} \frac{w_i}{2(1 - w_i)} d(a_i, c^*)(1 - w_i) + r^*(F) - \sum_{i \in N} p_i w_i d(a_i, c^*) \\
&= \frac{\alpha_{\mathbf{w}}}{2} \sum_{i \in N} w_i d(a_i, c^*) + r^*(F) - \sum_{i \in N} p_i w_i d(a_i, c^*) \\
&= \frac{\alpha_{\mathbf{w}}}{2} r^*(F) + r^*(F) - \sum_{i \in N} p_i w_i d(a_i, c^*) \\
&\leq \left(\frac{\alpha_{\mathbf{w}}}{2} + 1 \right) r^*(F) \leq \left(2 - \frac{1}{n} \right) r^*(F),
\end{aligned}
$$

which completes the proof. □

Theorem 7.21. *The following hold for Mechanism 3:*

o $\beta_{\mathbf{w}} \leq 1 - \frac{2}{n}$.

o *RRD has an approximation ratio of at most 4, and at least 3 (in the worst case).*

o *for unconstrained instances, the approximation ratio is $1 + \beta_{\mathbf{w}}$, i.e., at most $2 - \frac{2}{n}$.*

Proof. Let $q(x) = \frac{1}{1-2x}$. Note that q is convex.

$$
\begin{aligned}
(\beta_{\mathbf{w}})^{-1} = \sum_{i \in N} p_i' &= \sum_{i \in N} w_i \frac{1}{1 - 2w_i} = \sum_{i \in N} w_i q(w_i) \\
&\geq q \left(\sum_{i \in N} w_i \cdot w_i \right) = \frac{1}{1 - 2\sum_{i \in N} w_i^2} \qquad \text{(from Jensen's inequality)} \\
&\geq \frac{1}{1 - 2(1/n)}, \qquad\qquad\qquad\qquad\qquad \text{(from (E.3))}
\end{aligned}
$$

thus $\beta_{\mathbf{w}} \leq 1 - \frac{2}{n}$.

For the upper bound, we will need the following.

Lemma E.7. *For all $i \in N$, $p_i \leq 2w_i$.*

Proof. Let $h(x) = \frac{x}{1-2x}$. Note that h is convex. Thus by Jensen's inequality

$$\frac{1}{n-1}\sum_{j\neq i} h(w_j) \geq h\left(\frac{1}{n-1}\sum_{j\neq i} w_j\right) = h\left(\frac{1-w_i}{n-1}\right). \tag{E.4}$$

Next,

$$\sum_{j\in N}\frac{w_j}{1-2w_j} = \frac{w_i}{1-2w_i} + \sum_{j\neq i}\frac{w_j}{1-2w_j} = \frac{w_i}{1-2w_i} + \sum_{j\neq i} h(w_j)$$

$$\geq \frac{w_i}{1-2w_i} + (n-1)h\left(\frac{1-w_i}{n-1}\right) \qquad \text{(by Eq. (E.4))}$$

$$= \frac{w_i}{1-2w_i} + (n-1)\frac{\frac{1-w_i}{n-1}}{1-2\frac{1-w_i}{n-1}} = \frac{w_i}{1-2w_i} + \frac{1-w_i}{1-2\frac{1-w_i}{n-1}}$$

$$\geq \frac{w_i}{1-2w_i} + \frac{1/2}{1-2\frac{1/2}{n-1}} = \frac{w_i}{1-2w_i} + \frac{1}{2\frac{n-2}{n-1}} > \frac{w_i}{1-2w_i} + \frac{1}{2}.$$

Therefore,

$$p_i = \beta_{\mathbf{w}}p_i' = \left(\sum_{j\in N}\frac{w_j}{1-2w_j}\right)^{-1}\frac{w_i}{1-2w_i} < \frac{1}{\frac{w_i}{1-2w_i}+\frac{1}{2}}\cdot\frac{w_i}{1-2w_i}$$

$$= \frac{w_i}{w_i + \frac{1-2w_i}{2}} = \frac{w_i}{w_i - w_i + \frac{1}{2}} = 2w_i. \qquad \square$$

We now bound the social cost of **RRD**. We skip some steps that are detailed in the upper bound proof of the **CRD** mechanism.

$$SC(\mathbf{RRD}(\mathbf{a}),\mathbf{a}) = \sum_{i\in N} p_i SC(c_i,\mathbf{a}) = \sum_{i\in N} p_i d(c_i,c^*)\sum_{j\neq i} w_j + \sum_{i\in N}\sum_{j\in N} p_i w_j d(c^*,a_j)$$

$$= \beta_{\mathbf{w}}\sum_{i\in N}\frac{w_i}{1-2w_i}d(c_i,c^*)(1-w_i) + \sum_{j\in N} w_j d(c^*,a_j)\sum_{i\in N} p_i$$

$$\leq \beta_{\mathbf{w}}\sum_{i\in N}\frac{2w_i(1-w_i)}{1-2w_i}d(a_i,c^*) + r^*(S)$$

$$= \beta_{\mathbf{w}}\sum_{i\in N}\left(\frac{w_i(1-2w_i)}{1-2w_i}d(a_i,c^*) + \frac{w_i}{1-2w_i}d(a_i,c^*)\right) + r^*(S)$$

$$= \beta_{\mathbf{w}}\sum_{i\in N} w_i d(a_i,c^*) + \beta_{\mathbf{w}}\sum_{i\in N}\frac{w_i}{1-2w_i}d(a_i,c^*) + r^*(S)$$

$$= \beta_{\mathbf{w}}r^*(S) + \beta_{\mathbf{w}}\sum_{i\in N}\frac{w_i}{1-2w_i}d(a_i,c^*) + r^*(S) \leq \sum_{i\in N} p_i d(a_i,c^*) + 2r^*(S)$$

$$\leq 2\sum_{i\in N} w_i d(a_i,c^*) + 2r^*(S) = 2r^*(S) + 2r^*(S) = 4r^*(S).$$

In the unconstrained case, recall that $a_i = c_i$ for all i.

$$SC(\mathbf{RRD}(\mathbf{a}), \mathbf{a}) = \sum_{i \in N} p_i SC(c_i, \mathbf{a}) = \sum_{i \in N} p_i \sum_{j \in N} w_j d(a_i, a_j) = \sum_{i \in N} p_i \sum_{j \neq i} w_j d(a_i, a_j)$$

$$\leq \sum_{i \in N} \sum_{j \neq i} p_i w_j (d(a_i, c^*) + d(a_j, c^*)) \tag{T.I.}$$

$$= \sum_{i \in N} p_i d(a_i, c^*) \sum_{j \neq i} w_j + \sum_{i \in N} p_i \sum_{j \neq i} w_j d(a_j, c^*)$$

$$= \sum_{i \in N} p_i d(a_i, c^*)(1 - w_i) + \sum_{i \in N} p_i (r^*(S) - w_i d(a_i, c^*))$$

$$= \beta_{\mathbf{w}} \sum_{i \in N} \frac{w_i}{1 - 2w_i} d(a_i, c^*)(1 - w_i) - \beta_{\mathbf{w}} \sum_{i \in N} \frac{w_i}{1 - 2w_i} w_i d(a_i, c^*) + r^*(S)$$

$$= \beta_{\mathbf{w}} \sum_{i \in N} \frac{w_i(1 - 2w_i)}{1 - 2w_i} d(a_i, c^*) + r^*(S)$$

$$= \beta_{\mathbf{w}} \sum_{i \in N} w_i d(a_i, c^*) + r^*(S) = \beta_{\mathbf{w}} r^*(S) + r^*(S)$$

$$= (1 + \beta_{\mathbf{w}}) r^*(S) \leq \left(2 - \frac{2}{n}\right) r^*(S),$$

which proves the upper bound. $\qquad \square$

Appendix F

Proofs for Chapter 8

Theorem 8.3. *Let* $2k \geq 18$ *(or* $2k \geq 12$ *for* $n = 2$*). An onto mechanism on the cycle* R_{2k} *is SP if and only if it is 1-dictatorial, Cube-monotone (CMON), and IDA.*

Proof. For the first direction, we must prove that every onto SP mechanism must be IDA and CMON (in addition to being 1-dictatorial). Suppose that some agent violates CMON on coordinate i. This is either by crossing the location of the facility (i.e. $x \in [a_j, a'_j]$), or the antipodal point (i.e. $x + k \in [a_j, a'_j]$). In the first case, this is clearly a manipulation, as shown in Lemma 7.3. In the latter case, assume w.l.o.g. that $x = 0$ and j moved clockwise. By Lemma 7.6, the agent moved along the longer arc $[a_j, x)$, thus $|[x, a_j)| \leq k$. By violation of CMON, the facility also moved clockwise, thus getting closer to a_j, which is a manipulation.

Now suppose IDA is violated by agent j (moving w.l.o.g. clockwise). This means that $[a_j, a'_j]$ does not contain neither x nor $k + x$. If j is the dictator, then this is clearly a violation (again, as in Theorem 7.2). Otherwise, the facility can only move one or two steps. If the facility moves clockwise, then $a_j \to a'_j$ is a manipulation. Otherwise, $a'_j \to a_j$ is a manipulation.

In the other direction, we show that if f is 1-dictatorial (where agent 1 is the dictator), IDA and CMON, then it must be SP. Indeed, suppose that agent j moves from a_j to a'_j, thereby moving the facility from x to x', where w.l.o.g. $x = 0$. If $j = 1$, then the only way to gain is by moving one step, bringing the facility to a_1. However this would contradict IDA. Therefore assume that j is not the dictator. By Lemma 7.6, j must move along the longer arc $[a_j, x]$. Consider first $a_1 = x = 0$. Note that the facility can only move to $x' = 2k - 1$ (if $x'(k) \neq x(k)$) or $x' = 1$ (if $x(1) \neq x'(1)$).

(I) If j is not crossing neither $x = 0 = 0^k$, nor $k = 1^k$. Then by IDA coordinates 1 and k of the facility cannot change. Since changing any other coordinate puts x' at distance at least 2 from the dictator, the facility cannot move.

(II) If $a_j = x$, then j cannot gain.

(III) $k \in [a_j, a'_j]$ (w.l.o.g. j is moving clockwise, from $a_j \in [1, k]$ to $a'_j \in [k, 2k - 1]$). We part the movement to $a_j \to k$, and $k \to a'_j$, and denote $f(a_{-j}, k) = y$. In the first part, only coordinates between 2 and k of a_j change (from 0 to 1). Then by IDA $y(1) = x(1) = 0$, and the facility can only move to $y = 2k - 1$. However this means that $d(y, a_j) > d(x, a_j)$, i.e. that j does not gain.

Now, if $y = 2k - 1$, then by IDA $x' = 2k - 1$ as well. Therefore suppose that $y = x = 0$. Since only coordinates $< k$ change between k and a'_j, $x'(k) = y(k)$. On the other hand, $a'_j(1) = 0 < k(1)$, thus by CMON $x'(1) \leq x(1) = 0$ as well. Therefore, $x' = x$.

It is left to handle the case where $a_1 \neq x$. Since agent 1 is a 1-dictator $d(a_1, x) = 1$, and $d(a_1, x') \leq 1$. The only difference is that in case (III) it is possible that $y = 2k - 2$ (if $a_1 = 2k - 1$). However this is still not a manipulation, as $d(y, a_j) \geq d(x, a_j)$ (rather than strictly larger). $\qquad \square$

Theorem 8.6. *There exist concept classes for which any deterministic SP mechanism has an approximation ratio of at least $\Omega(n)$, even if all the weights are equal.*

Proof sketch. We explain how the results of [Meir et al., 2010] can be slightly altered to prove Theorem 8.6.

The proof of Theorem 3.1 in [Meir et al., 2010] is using a scenario with two input point $\mathcal{X} = \{a, b\}$, and three classifiers $\mathcal{C} = \{c_a, c_b, c_{ab}\}$, where each classifier classifies as positive its corresponding point (or points). The proof then continued, showing that this scenario is equivalent to voting over the set of candidates $\mathcal{C}$, then applying the Gibbard-Satterthwaite theorem to show that any SP mechanism must use a dictator. The reason we cannot apply the proof from [Meir et al., 2010] directly, is that it used a scenario without shared inputs (i.e., the agents controlled different set of samples). To complete the proof, it is required to show that each agent can express all possible 6 preference orders over the set of candidates $\mathcal{C}$, even with shared inputs (this corresponds to Table 1 in [Meir et al., 2010]).

To that end, we define $\mathbf{S}$ with $k = 9$ examples as follows. 4 examples on a, divided to the sets $|A_1| = 1, |A_2| = 3$, and 5 examples on b, divided so that $|B_1| = 1, |B_2| = 4$ on b.[1] For all agents $X_i = X = A_1 \cup A_2 \cup B_1 \cup B_2$, thus we have shared inputs.

The following table can be used to easily verify that i can express any possible preference order on $\mathcal{C}$ using labels.

Preference order	Label given by agent i				Number of errors on S_i		
	$Y_i(A_1)$	$Y_i(A_2)$	$Y_i(B_1)$	$Y_i(B_2)$	c_a	c_b	c_{ab}
$c_a \succ_i c_{ab} \succ_i c_b$	+	+	+	-	1	8	4
$c_a \succ_i c_b \succ_i c_{ab}$	-	-	-	-	4	5	9
$c_{ab} \succ_i c_b \succ_i c_a$	+	+	+	+	5	4	0
$c_{ab} \succ_i c_a \succ_i c_b$	+	+	-	+	4	5	1
$c_b \succ_i c_a \succ_i c_{ab}$	-	-	+	-	6	3	7
$c_b \succ_i c_{ab} \succ_i c_a$	+	-	+	+	8	1	3

Finally, once we know that our mechanism must select a dictator, we can assume w.l.o.g. that it always picks agent 1 (since all agents have equal weights). We define $Y_1(A_2) = $ "-", and all other labels of all agents as "+". Thus our dictator selects c_b (with $n/2$ errors), while the optimal classifier c_{ab} makes only 3 errors. $\qquad \square$

---

[1] The odd number is in order to avoid tie-breaking issues.

Appendix G

Proofs for Chapter 9

G.1   Proofs for Section 9.4

Proposition 9.11. Every *online algorithm under Assumption UV has a worst-case approximation ratio of at most $\frac{3}{4}$, even on an interval. If we relax Assumption UV, then the bound is at most $\frac{1}{2}$.*

Proof. Consider the following two sequences of n agents, where $n = m$. The first $n/2$ agents (denoted N') are of type (g_1, n), with goal g_1 and maximum distance to walk n. They can be allocated any slot. Our two instances differ in the next $n/2$ agents (denoted N''). In H_1, we have $n/2$ agents of type $(g_2, \frac{1}{2}n)$. In H_2, we have $n/2$ agents of type $(g_1, \frac{1}{2}n)$. Note that $\mu(H_1) = \mu(H_2) = n$.

Let r_1, r_2 be the expected number of agents from N' that are allocated slots by the mechanism in half of the interval that is closer to g_1 and g_2, respectively. Since $r_1 + r_2 \leq |N'| = n/2$, at least one of them is at most $n/4$. We divide into two cases: (a) if $r_1 \leq n/4$, then on instance H_1 all of N'' are placed closer to g_2; (b) if $r_2 \leq n/4$, then on instance H_2 all of N'' are placed closer to g_1.

In both cases, the total number of allocated slots is at most $\frac{1}{2}n + n/4 = \frac{3}{4}n$. Thus for any mechanism M either $SW(M, H_1) \leq \frac{3}{4}n = \frac{3}{4}\mathbf{opt}(H_1)$, or $SW(M, H_2) \leq \frac{3}{4}n = \frac{3}{4}\mathbf{opt}(H_2)$.

Next, suppose that we drop Assumption UV, and set $\phi_1 \gg \phi_2$. Let N' contain n agents of type (g_2, n), and N'' contain n agents of type (g_1, n). Once again we define two instances H_1, H_2. In H_1, only N' arrive. In H_2, N' arrive and then N''.

Denote by r the expected number of agents from N' placed by the mechanism. If $r \leq n/2$ we are done since $SW(M, H_1) \leq \frac{1}{2}|N'| = \frac{1}{2}\mathbf{opt}$. Otherwise, consider the performance of M on H_2. Note that since $\phi_1 \gg \phi_2$, we can practically ignore the type 2 agents in the welfare computation. However strictly less than $n - r \leq \frac{1}{2}n$ of the type 1 agents are placed in expectation, so the approximation is at most $\frac{1}{2}$. $\qquad\square$

Proposition 9.13. *The THRESHOLD mechanism with the threshold $\hat{t} = m/2$ provides us with a $\frac{1}{2}$-approximation for two goals on the interval.*

Proof. We will prove that running the THRESHOLD mechanism for the threshold $\hat{t} = m/2$ provides us with a $\frac{1}{2}$-approximation. Let t^* be the minimal true optimal threshold. Let N_1, N_2 be the sets of agents from each goal that are allocated in the optimal allocation. By the Lemma 9.8, $|N_1| = t^*$. We divide in two cases. Note that $\mu = \alpha|N_1| + |N_2|$.

If $t^* < \hat{t}$, then our mechanism will allocate to all of N_1, as none of them is restricted by $\hat{t}$. Also, all of N_2 will be allocated unless all top $m/2$ slots are full. Thus the total utility in our mechanism is

$$\alpha|N_1| + \min\{|N_2|, m/2\} \geq \alpha|N_1| + |N_2|/2 \geq \mathbf{opt}/2.$$

If $t^* \geq \hat{t}$, then $|N_1| \geq m/2$, and thus our mechanism allocates all of the bottom $m/2 \geq |N_1|/2$ lower slots to g_1. Also, all of N_2 are allocated. Thus the total utility is at least

$$\alpha|N_1|/2 + |N_2| \geq \frac{\alpha|N_1| + |N_2|}{2} = \mathbf{opt}/2.$$

$\square$

Proposition 9.14. *No online algorithm can guarantee an approximation ratio better than $1/\alpha$.*

Proof. We start with a single goal g' with a low value ϕ', and for every slot $s \in S$ add another goal g_s with a high value $\phi_s = \alpha\phi'$. For every subset of slots $T \subseteq S$ (including $T = \emptyset$), we define an instance H_T as follows. First, m agents of type (g', ∞) arrive (i.e. they can be placed anywhere). Then for every $s \in T$, arrives an agent of type $(g_s, 0)$, where $g_s = s$.

Suppose that after the first sequence of agents, some slots $T^* \neq \emptyset$ are allocated. Then on instance H_{T^*}, we have $SW = |T^*|\phi'$ and $\mu = |T^*|\alpha\phi' + (m - |T^*|)\phi' \geq \alpha SW$. On the other hand, if $T^* = \emptyset$, then on instance $H_\emptyset$ we have $SW = 0 < \mu/\alpha$. $\square$

Proposition 9.15. *Setting fixed prices at 0 guarantees a $1/2\alpha$ approximation.*

Proof. By setting all prices to 0, we get a *maximal* cardinality matching of size t, whose welfare is at least $t \cdot \min_j \phi_j$. By Observation 9.5, the *maximum* cardinality matching is of size at most $2t$. Thus the approximation is at least $\frac{t \cdot \min_j \phi_j}{2t \cdot \max_i \phi_i} = \frac{1}{2\alpha}$. $\square$

Proposition 9.16. *Under Assumption KG, for any number of goals k, RANDOM-PARTITION is a $\frac{1}{k}$-approximation mechanism. Moreover, it can be derandomized.*

Proof. Let $P = (N_1, \ldots, N_k)$ be the allocated agents in some optimal partition σ^*, where $N_{id} \subseteq N_i$ is the set of agents s.t. $m_j \leq d$. Denote by $S_i' \subseteq S_i$ the set of slots allocated by the mechanism to agents following goal g_i. We argue that in expectation at least $|S_i'| \geq |N_i|/k$.

Let $R_{i,d}$ be the set of slots of distance at most d from g_i. Consider some goal g_i and let m' be the smallest distance s.t. $(S_i \setminus S_i') \cap R_{i,m'} \neq \emptyset$. That is, the smallest distance of an available slot in our allocation. All agents of type (g_i, m_j) with $m_j \geq m'$ are allocated, as otherwise we would assign j to an available slot. For every $d < m'$ (and in particular $d = m' - 1$), we have $S_i \cap R_{i,d} = S_i' \cap R_{i,d}$. By our random assignment, $|S_i' \cap R_{i,d}| = |S_i \cap R_{i,d}| = |R_{i,d}|/k$ in expectation. Clearly $|N_{i,d}| \leq |R_{i,d}|$. Finally,

$$|S_i'| = |S_i' \cap R_{i,d}| + |S_i' \setminus R_{i,d}| \geq |N_{i,d}|/k + |N_i \setminus N_{i,d}| \geq |N_i|/k.$$

The total welfare at out allocation is thus

$$\sum_{i \leq k} \phi_i |S_i'| \geq \sum_{i \leq k} \phi_i |N_i|/k = \frac{1}{k} \sum_{i \leq k} \phi_i |N_i| = \frac{\mu}{k}.$$

If we want to de-randomize the allocation of S_i and thus the mechanism, this is not too hard. We sort the slots by their distance from each of the k goals. Thus we have k priority queues, each containing all of the slots. We iteratively traverse all slots in a round-robin over goals, when in each iteration t we take the next slot in queue $i = t \mod k + 1$ and assign in to S_i. We then remove the assigned slot from all queues. Using the same notations as in the randomized algorithm, it now holds that $|S_i' \cap R_{i,d}| = |S_i \cap R_{i,d}| \geq |R_{i,d}|/k - k$, since all slots of distance at most d from g_i have been divided either equally (up to a rounding factor of k), or in favor of goal i. Thus it still holds that

$$|S_i'| = |S_i' \cap R_{i,d}| + |S_i' \setminus R_{i,d}| \geq |N_{i,d}|/k - k + |N_i \setminus N_{i,d}| \geq |N_i|/k - k,$$

and thus

$$\sum_{i \leq k} \phi_i |S_i'| \geq \sum_{i \leq k} \phi_i (|N_i|/k - k) = \frac{1}{k} \sum_{i \leq k} \phi_i |N_i| - k^2 = \frac{\mu}{k} - k^2.$$

As the number of agents increases as k remains constant, the additive factor is negligible. $\qquad \square$

Proposition 9.17. *For the case of two goals on a line, under Assumption KP, there exists no optimal SP mechanism.*

Proof. We set $\phi_1 = 2, \phi_2 = 1$. Our proof shows that an adaptive adversary can force an approximation ratio of at least $\frac{5}{6}$. It follows that the approximation of any *deterministic* mechanism against a static adversary is also at least $\frac{5}{6}$. While some randomized mechanisms might do better, clearly none can guarantee a perfect performance (e.g. against an adversary that plays a random sequence).

Consider a line with 8 slots, $\{s_1, \ldots, s_8\}$, where $g_1 = s_4, g_2 = s_7$. The vacant slots are $a = s_1, b = s_5, c = s_6$, and $d = s_8$. All other slots are blocked. The population has five agents: $(g_1, 1); (g_1, 8); (g_2, 1); (g_2, 1); (g_2, 8)$. Note that in the optimal solution σ^* we can place both type 1 agents and two other agents, thus $\mu = 2\phi_1 + 2\phi_2 = 6$.

We can model the arrival process as a zero-sum game in extensive form between the mechanism (which is setting prices), and an adversary (which is setting the order of arrival). The goal of the mechanism is to maximize the welfare. We will show that the adversary can coerce a situation such that either not all slots are full, or only one high value agent is placed.

While the adversary has full information, the mechanism only observes its own actions and the currently occupied slots. That is, if at a given pricing there are several agents that would pick s_1, then all states where one of these agents arrived and occupied s_1 belong to the same information set of the mechanism player. Crucially, the mechanism cannot condition the pricing in the next step based on the identity of the agent occupying s_1.

Therefore, for every sequence of prices, the adversary can choose (part of) the order in retrospect, as long as selections are consistent with the information sets. We denote by p_x^i the price of slot $x \in \{a, b, c, d\}$ in step i. Note that agent $(g_1, 1)$ can only be placed in b. Thus if b is being occupied by any other agent, the adversary wins. Thus we can assume that $p_a < p_b$ as long as there is at least one active agent with range m (and in particular in the first step).

Consider the first step. Case A: p_a^1 is strictly lower than all other prices. Then the adversary sends either $(g_1, 8)$ or $(g_2, 8)$, which occupy slot a. Note that both states are in the same information set, thus the next action of the mechanism must be the same for both.

Case A-A: Suppose p_b^2 is the cheapest price. Then the adversary places $(g_1, 8)$ in a (i.e. chooses from the information set of case A), and sends $(g_2, 8)$, which occupies slot b (and thus wins).

Case A-B: Either $p_c^2 \geq p_b^2$, or $p_d^2 \geq p_b^2$. Then the adversary sends a $(g_2, 1)$ agent, which occupies one of $\{c, d\}$. Note that the adversary does not select an option from the information set yet.

In the 3rd step, then once again if b is cheapest, we are in case A-A. Otherwise, b remains the only empty slot.

Case A-B-A: $p_b^4 \leq \phi_2$. As in case A-A, the adversary sets $(g_1, 8)$ in a, and $(g_2, 8)$ in b.

Case A-B-B: $p_b^4 > \phi_2$. The adversary selects $(g_2, 8)$ from the information set, and sends $(g_1, 8)$, which occupies b. In all cases b is occupied by an agent other than $(g_1, 1)$.

Case B: $p_x^1 \leq p_a^1$, for $x \in \{c, d\}$. Then the adversary sends either $(g_1, 8)$ or $(g_2, 1)$, which occupy slot x. As in Case A, both states belong to the same information set. Denote by y the slot from $\{c, d\}$ that is not x.

Case B-A: $p_a^2 < p_y^2$. The adversary selects $(g_2, 1)$ from the information set (which occupies x), and continue as if we are in Case A (only with one less available slot). We saw that in Case A the adversary wins.

Case B-B: $p_a^2 \geq p_y^2$. The adversary selects $(g_1, 8)$ from the information set (which occupies x), and sends $(g_2, 8)$, which will occupy y. However, now there is no agent that can occupy slot a, and thus the adversary wins again.

We saw that the adversary can always enforce a suboptimal outcome. We next compute the attained approximation. In Case B-B, the welfare is at most $2\phi_1 + \phi_2 = 5$. In all other cases, the welfare is at most $\phi_1 + 3\phi_2 = 5$ as well. Thus any pricing mechanism has an approximation ratio of at most $\frac{5}{6}$. $\qquad \square$

Proposition 9.18. *Under Assumption KP, there is a $\frac{1}{2}$-approximation mechanism.*

Proof. We enumerate the distinct values of goals s.t. $\phi_1 > \phi_2 > \cdots > \phi_{k'}$. It is possible that $k' < |G|$ if some goals have the same value. We compute an optimal partition σ^* offline. Denote by $S_i = \bigcup_{j:\phi_j = \phi_i} \{\sigma^*(j)\}$ the set of all slots allocated to goals with value ϕ_i. We set the price of all slots in each S_i to $\frac{\phi_i + \phi_{i+1}}{2}$ (thus no agent wants a slot that is allocated to higher types in σ^*).

Let N_j be all agents whose value is equal to ϕ_j (i.e. we merge groups with the same value). Consider the set of allocated agents $A \subseteq N$, and denote by $T \subseteq N$ the agents participating in the original optimal (offline) allocation. Suppose we want to allocates slots to all of T. For every $j \in T \setminus A$, j's original slot is occupied by an agent with same or higher value. Denote $A_i = \bigcup_{j \leq i} (A \cap N_j)$, and $O_i = \bigcup_{j \leq i} (T \cap N_j)$.

Thus $\sum_{j \leq i} |A \cap N_j| \geq \sum_{j \leq i} |(T \setminus A) \cap N_j|$ for all i, which means

$$|A_i| = \sum_{j \leq i} |A \cap N_j| \geq \frac{1}{2} \sum_{j \leq i} |T \cap N_j| = \frac{1}{2} |O_i|.$$

Finally, let $a_j = |A \cap N_j|$. Note that $\phi_j - \phi_{j+1} > 0$.

$$
\begin{aligned}
SW(A) = \sum_{i \leq k'} a_i \phi_i &= \sum_{i \leq k'} (|A_i| - |A_{i-1}|) \phi_i \\
&= \sum_{i \leq k'} |A_i| \phi_i - \sum_{i \leq k'} |A_{i-1}| \phi_i = \sum_{i < k'} |A_i| (\phi_i - \phi_{i+1}) + |A_{k'}| \\
&\geq \sum_{i < k'} \frac{1}{2} |O_i| (\phi_i - \phi_{i+1}) + \frac{1}{2} |O_{k'}| \frac{1}{2} \sum_{i \leq k'} (|O_i| - |O_{i-1}|) \phi_i = \frac{1}{2} \mathbf{opt}.
\end{aligned}
$$

To see that the analysis of this mechanism is tight, consider an instance with two goals on the edges of an internal, $\phi_1 = \phi_2 + \epsilon$. There are $m/2$ agents of type (g_1, m) (arriving first), and $m/2$ of type $(g_2, m/2)$. While clearly $\mu = m(1 + \frac{\epsilon}{2})$, in this mechanism the first $m/2$ agents will occupy all cheap slots of goal 2, and thus $SW(A) = \frac{m}{2}(1 + \epsilon)$. $\qquad\square$

G.2 Proofs for Section 9.5

Suppose we optimally assign the m' closest slots (ordered by non-decreasing distance) to the m' lowest-cost agents (ordered by non-increasing cost), that is $\sigma(i) = i$. Let $\mathbf{p} = (p_1, \ldots, p_{m'})$ be a vector of SNE prices for the first m' slots, based on the first m' agents (in the translated GSP instance).

Lemma 9.19. *By setting $p(s) = p_s x_s$ for all $s \leq m'$, the agents' utility is non-decreasing in the distance from g. That is, $u_j(j) \leq u_i(i)$ for all $j < i \leq m'$.*

Proof. Suppose that slots are ordered by increasing distance $d_s = d(g, s)$, and the m' agents are sorted by decreasing cost c_i. Then in the optimal allocation $\sigma(i) = s_i$.

In every SNE (see Equations (6.2) and (6.3), and [Varian, 2007]), we have $p_{m'} = 0$, and for any $i < m'$,

$$
\begin{aligned}
p(i) = p_i x_i = b_{i+1} x_i &\in [b_{i+1}^L x_i, b_{i+1}^U x_i] \\
&= b_{i+2} x_{i+1} + [v_{i+1}(x_i - x_{i+1}), v_i(x_i - x_{i+1})] \\
&= p(i+1) + [c_{i+1}(d_{i+1} - d_i), c_i(d_{i+1} - d_i)].
\end{aligned}
$$

Since $x_i > x_{i+1}$, this range is non-singleton whenever $c_i > c_{i+1}$. The utility of agent i is

$$
\begin{aligned}
u_i(s_i) = \phi - d_i c_i - p(i) &\leq \phi - d_i c_i - (p(i+1) + (d_{i+1} - d_i)c_i) \\
&= \phi - d_{i+1} c_i - p(i+1) \leq \phi - d_{i+1} c_{i+1} - p(i+1) = u_{i+1}(s_{i+1}).
\end{aligned}
$$

$\qquad\square$

Theorem 9.20. *Under Assumption KP, GSP-PARK is optimal for a single goal.*

Proof. Let $\sigma = \sigma_{m^*}$. We should show that on arrival of each agent $j \leq m$, she will indeed select $\sigma(j)$ (or $\sigma(j')$ is $c_{j'} = c_j$). Note that $\sigma(j) = j$ for all $j \leq m^*$.

Due to envy-freeness, we know that each agent $j \leq m^*$ prefers the slot allocated to her over any other slot at these prices. Indifference between slots might pose a problem in principle, since j may select any slot maximizing her utility. Specifically: if we set $p(j)$ equal to $p_j^L x_j$, then agent $j+1$ might be indifferent between slots $j, j+1$; if we set $p(j)$ equal to $p_j^U x_j$, then agent j might be indifferent between slots $j-1, j$.

Suppose that $x_j > x_{j+1}$ and $c_j < c_{j+1}$. Then $v_j < v_{j+1}$ and by Equations (6.2) and (6.3),

$$p_j^U x_j = b_{j+1}^U x_j = v_j(x_j - x_{j+1}) + b_{j+2}^U x_j$$
$$\geq v_j(x_j - x_{j+1}) + b_{j+2}^L x_j > v_{j+1}(x_j - x_{j+1}) + b_{j+2}^L x_{j+1} = p_j^L x_j$$

Thus we can set $p(j)$ strictly between $p_j^L x_j$ and $p_j^U x_j$ (for all $j \leq m^*$) in order to avoid indifference.

If $x_j = x_{j+1}$ or $c_j = c_{j+1}$, then agent j can take any of these slots without hurting efficiency. Thus we known that any $j \leq m^*$ prefers her own slot over all others (whenever it matters).

Suppose that all agents above m^* (that should not be allocated, if exist) are sorted by non-decreasing cost, so that

$$c_n \geq \cdots \geq c_{m^*+2} \geq c_{m^*+1} \geq c_1 \geq c_2 \geq \cdots c_{m^*}.$$

The translation γ is required to prevent high-cost agents $j > m^*$. from selecting a slot on arrival. Indeed, for every j s.t. $c_j > c_{m^*}$,

$$u_j(s_1, p'(1)) = u_j(s_1, p(1)) - \gamma = u_j(s_1, p(1)) - u_1(s_1, p(1)) + \epsilon < 0.$$

Thus no such agent will be interested in the first slot. Moreover, since agent 1 prefers the first slot to any other, this must apply for any agent whose cost c_j is higher. Thus at prices $\mathbf{p}'$, any agent with $c_j > c_1$ will avoid all slots. A slight complication is when $c_j = c_1$ for some $j > m^*$. It can be similarly shown that these agents will forgo any slot assigned to agents of lower-cost types.

It remains to prove that the new mechanism is individually rational, i.e. all agents $j \leq m^*$ want their slot at the modified price p'. Indeed, since $c_{m^*+1} > c_1$ (and the distance of every slot is non-zero), $u_1(s_1, p'(1)) = u_1(s_1, p(1)) - \gamma = \epsilon > 0$. By Lemma 9.19, $u_j(s_j, p'(j)) \geq u_1(s_1, p'(1)) > 0$ for all $j \leq m^*$. $\qquad \square$

Bibliography

Aadithya, K. V., T. P. Michalak, and N. R. Jennings (2011). Representation of coalitional games with algebraic decision diagrams. In *Proceedings of the 10th International Joint Conference on Autonomous Agents and Multi-Agent Systems (AAMAS)*, pp. 1121–1122. 31

Abdulkadiroğlu, A., P. A. Pathak, A. E. Roth, and T. Sönmez (2005). The Boston public school match. *American Economic Review*, 368–371. 111

Aggarwal, G., G. Goel, C. Karande, and A. Mehta (2011). Online vertex-weighted bipartite matching and single-bid budgeted allocations. In *Proceedings of the 22nd Annual ACM-SIAM Symposium on Discrete Algorithms (SODA)*, pp. 1253–1264. 97

Airiau, S. and U. Endriss (2009). Iterated majority voting. In *Proceedings of the 1st International Conference on Algorithmic Decision Theory (ADT)*, pp. 38–49. Springer Verlag. 54

Alon, N., D. Falik, R. Meir, and M. Tennenholtz (2013). Bundling attacks in judgment aggregation. In *Proceedings of the 27th AAAI Conference on Artificial Intelligence (AAAI)*, pp. 39–45. 7

Alon, N., M. Feldman, A. D. Procaccia, and M. Tennenholtz (2010). Strategyproof approximation of the minimax on networks. *Mathematics of Operations Research 35*(3), 513–526. 74

Alon, N., F. Fischer, A. Procaccia, and M. Tennenholtz (2011). Sum of us: Strategyproof selection from the selectors. In *Proceedings of the 13th Conference on Theoretical Aspects of Rationality and Knowledge*, pp. 101–110. ACM. 4

Alon, N., R. Meir, and M. Tennenholtz (2013). The value of ignorance about the number of players (short paper). In *Proceedings of the 27th AAAI Conference on Artificial Intelligence (AAAI)*. 7

Andelman, N., M. Feldman, and Y. Mansour (2007). Strong price of anarchy. In *Proceedings of the 18th Annual ACM-SIAM Symposium on Discrete Algorithms (SODA)*, pp. 189–198. 57

Arthur, W. B. (1994). Inductive reasoning and bounded rationality. *The American Economic Review 84*(2), 406–411. 53

Ashlagi, I., F. Fischer, I. Kash, and A. D. Procaccia (2010). Mix and match. In *Proceedings of the 11th ACM Conference on Electronic Commerce (ACM-EC)*, pp. 305–314. 4

Aumann, R. (1959). Acceptable points in general cooperative n-person games. In A. Tucker and R. Luce (Eds.), *Contribution to the Theory of Games, Vol. IV, Annals of Mathematical Studies*, Number 40, pp. 287–324. Princeton University Press. 57

Aumann, R. and J. Dréze (1974). Cooperative games with coalition structures. *International Journal of Game Theory 3*(4), 217–237. 13, 29, 30, 35

Aumann, R. J. (1961). The core of a cooperative game without side payments. *Transactions of the American Mathematical Society 98*(3), 539–552. 109

Aziz, H., F. Brandt, and P. Harrenstein (2010). Monotone cooperative games and their threshold versions. In *Proceedings of the 10th International Joint Conference on Autonomous Agents and Multi-Agent Systems (AAMAS)*, pp. 1017–1024. 31

Aziz, H., O. Lachish, M. Paterson, and R. Savani (2009). Power indices in spanning connectivity games. In *Algorithmic Aspects in Information and Management*, pp. 55–67. Springer. 34

Bachrach, Y. (2010). Honor among thieves: collusion in multi-unit auctions. In *Proceedings of the 9th International Joint Conference on Autonomous Agents and Multi-Agent Systems (AAMAS)*, pp. 617–624. 59

Bachrach, Y., E. Elkind, R. Meir, D. Pasechnik, M. Zuckerman, J. Rothe, and J. S. Rosenschein (2009a). The cost of stability in coalitional games. In *Proceedings of the 2nd International Symposium on Algorithmic Game Theory (SAGT)*, pp. 122–134. 19, 20, 21, 22, 23, 30, 31, 32, 33, 42

Bachrach, Y., E. Elkind, R. Meir, D. Pasechnik, M. Zuckerman, J. Rothe, and J. S. Rosenschein (2009b). The cost of stability in coalitional games. Technical report, arXiv:0907.4385 [cs.GT], ACM Comp. Research Repository. 115

Bachrach, Y., O. Lev, S. Lovett, J. S. Rosenschein, and M. Zadimoghaddam (2013). Cooperative weakest link games. In *The 4th Workshop on Cooperative Games in Multiagent Systems (CoopMAS @ AAMAS'13)*. 31

Bachrach, Y., R. Meir, M. Feldman, and M. Tennenholtz (2011). Solving cooperative reliability games. In *Proceedings of the 27th Annual Conference on Uncertainty in Artificial Intelligence (UAI)*, pp. 27–34. 7

Bachrach, Y., R. Meir, K. Jung, and P. Kohli (2010). Coalitional structure generation in skill games. In *Proceedings of the 25th AAAI Conference on Artificial Intelligence (AAAI)*, pp. 703–708. 34

Bachrach, Y., R. Meir, M. Zuckerman, J. Rothe, and J. S. Rosenschein (2009). The cost of stability in weighted voting games (extended abstract). In *Proceedings of the 8th International Joint Conference on Autonomous Agents and Multi-Agent Systems (AAMAS)*, pp. 1289–1290. 31

Bachrach, Y. and N. Shah (2013). Max games and agent failures. Manuscript. 31

Bajaj, C. (1986). Proving geometric algorithm non-solvability: An application of factoring polynomials. *Journal of Symbolic Computation 2*(1), 99 – 102. 73

Barberà, S. and B. Peleg (1990). Strategy-proof voting schemes with continuous preferences. *Social Choice and Welfare 7*, 31–38. 76

Barthèlemy, J.-P., B. Leclerc, and B. Monjardet (1986). On the use of ordered sets in problems of comparison and consensus of classifications. *Journal of Classification 3*, 187–224. 88

Bejan, C. and J. Gómez (2009). Core extensions for non-balanced TU-games. *International Journal of Game Theory 38*(1), 3–16. 26, 29, 31

Bernheim, B. D., B. Peleg, and M. D. Whinston (1987). Coalition-proof Nash equilibria I. Concepts. *Journal of Economic Theory 42*(1), 1–12. 58

Bhawalkar, K. and T. Roughgarden (2011). Welfare guarantees for combinatorial auctions with item bidding. In *Proceedings of the Twenty-Second Annual ACM-SIAM Symposium on Discrete Algorithms*, pp. 700–709. SIAM. 3

Bilbao, J. M. (2000). *Cooperative Games on Combinatorial Structures*. Kluwer Publishers. 33, 41

Bodlaender, H. L. and T. Kloks (1996). Efficient and constructive algorithms for the pathwidth and treewidth of graphs. *Journal of Algorithms 21*(2), 358–402. 35

Bodlaender, H. L. and B. van Antwerpen-de Fluiter (2001). Parallel algorithms for series parallel graphs and graphs with treewidth two 1. *Algorithmica 29*(4), 534–559. 35

Border, K. and J. Jordan (1983). Straightforward elections, unanimity and phantom voters. *Review of Economic Studies 50*, 153–170. 79

Borgers, T. (1993). Pure strategy dominance. *Econometrica 61*(2), 423–430. 47

Brandt, F., V. Conitzer, and U. Endriss (2012). Computational social choice. In G. Weiss (Ed.), *Multiagent Systems*. Available from http://dare.uva.nl/document/354859. 3

Brânzei, S., I. Caragiannis, J. Morgenstern, and A. D. Procaccia (2013). How bad is selfish voting? In *Twenty-Seventh AAAI Conference on Artificial Intelligence*. 54, 55

Brânzei, S. and K. Larson (2011). Social distance games. In *Proceedings of the 22nd International Joint Conference on Artificial Intelligence (IJCAI)*, pp. 91–96. 41

Breton, M., G. Owen, and S. Weber (1992). Strongly balanced cooperative games. *International Journal of Game Theory 20*, 419–427. 34

Brooks, N. (2004). The Atlas rank report: How search engine rank impacts traffic. Atlas Institute. PDF available from http://tinyurl.com/d9ueco9. 69

Budish, E. (2012). Matching "versus" mechanism design. *SIGecom Excehanges 11*(2), 4–15. 110

Camerer, C. F. (2003). *Behavioral Game Theory: Experiments in Strategic Interaction*. Princeton university press. 111

Chalkiadakis, G., E. Markakis, and N. R. Jennings (2012). Coalitional stability in structured environments. In *Proceedings of the 11th International Joint Conference on Autonomous Agents and Multi-Agent Systems (AAMAS)*, pp. 779–786. 34

Chandrasekaran, R. and A. Tamir (1990). Algebraic optimization: the Fermat-Weber location problem. *Mathematical Programming 46*(1-3), 219–224. 73

Chawla, S., J. D. Hartline, D. L. Malec, and B. Sivan (2010). Multi-parameter mechanism design and sequential posted pricing. In *Proceedings of the 42nd Annual ACM Symposium on the Theory of Computing (STOC)*, pp. 311–320. 97

Cheng, Y., W. Yu, and G. Zhang (2011). Strategy-proof approximation mechanisms for an obnoxious facility game on networks. *Theoretical Computer Science.* 74

Chopra, S., E. Pacuit, and R. Parikh (2004). Knowledge-theoretic properties of strategic voting. In *Logics in Artificial Intelligence*, pp. 18–30. Springer. 53

Chvatal, V. (1979). A greedy heuristic for the set-covering problem. *Mathematics of Operations Research 4*(3), 233–235. 25

Claus, A. and D. Kleitman (1973). Cost allocation for a spanning tree. *Networks 3*, 289–304. 31

Cohen, R. F., P. Eades, T. Lin, and F. Ruskey (1997). Three-dimensional graph drawing. *Algorithmica 17*(2), 199–208. 123

Conitzer, V. and T. Sandholm (2006). Complexity of constructing solutions in the core based on synergies among coalitions. *Artificial Intelligence 170*(6–7), 607–619. 25, 41, 59

Courcelle, B. (1990). Graph rewriting: An algebraic and logic approach. In J. van Leeuwen (Ed.), *Handbook of Theoretical Computer Science, Volume B: Formal Models and Semantics*, pp. 193–242. Elsevier and MIT Press. 34

Dash, R. K., N. R. Jennings, and D. C. Parkes (2003). Computational-mechanism design: A call to arms. *Intelligent Systems, IEEE 18*(6), 40–47. 2

de Borda, J.-C. (1781). Memoires sur les elections au scrutin. *Paris: Histoire de l'Academie Royale des Sciences. Translation in Alfred de Grazia, 1953, "Mathematical Derivation of an Election System". Isis 44:42-51.* 3

de Condorcet, M. (1785). Essai sur l'application de l'analyse à la probabilité de décisions rendues à la pluralité de voix. Imprimerie Royal. Facsimile published in 1972 by Chelsea Publishing Company, New York. 3

Dekel, O., F. Fischer, and A. D. Procaccia (2008). Incentive compatible regression learning. In *Proceedings of the 19th Annual ACM-SIAM Symposium on Discrete Algorithms (SODA)*, pp. 277–286. 4

Demange, G. (2004). On group stability in hierarchies and networks. *Journal of Political Economy 112*(4), 754–778. 34, 37, 41, 42

Deng, X., T. Ibaraki, and H. Nagamochi (1999). Algorithmic aspects of the core of combinatorial optimization games. *Mathematics of Operations Research 24*(3), 751–766. 25, 31, 41

Deng, X. and C. H. Papadimitriou (1994). On the complexity of cooperative solution concepts. *Mathematics of Operations Research 19*(2), 257–266. 41

Desmedt, Y. and E. Elkind (2010). Equilibria of plurality voting with abstentions. In *Proceedings of the 11th ACM Conference on Electronic Commerce (ACM-EC)*, pp. 347–356. 53

Devanur, N., M. Mihail, and V. Vazirani (2005). Strategyproof cost-sharing mechanisms for set cover and facility location games. *Decision Support Systems 39*, 11–22. 24

Devroye, L., L. Györfi, and G. Lugosi (1997). *A Probabilistic Theory of Pattern Recognition.* Springer-Verlag New York, Inc. 87

Dhillon, A. and B. Lockwood (2004). When are plurality rule voting games dominance-solvable? *Games and Economic Behavior 46*, 55–75. 53

Dietrich, F. (2007). Aggregation and the relevance of some issues for others. Research Memoranda 002, Maastricht : METEOR, Maastricht Research School of Economics of Technology and Organization. 90

Dietrich, F. and C. List (2007). Arrow's theorem in judgment aggregation. *Social Choice and Welfare 29*(1), 19–33. 90

Dokow, E., M. Feldman, R. Meir, and I. Nehama (2012). Mechanism design on discrete lines and cycles. In *Proceedings of the 13th ACM Conference on Electronic Commerce (ACM-EC)*, pp. 423–440. 6

Dokow, E. and R. Holzman (2010). Aggregation of binary evaluations. *Journal of Economic Theory 145*, 495–511. 88

Eckhardt, U. (1980). Weber's problem and Weiszfeld's algorithm in general spaces. *Mathematical Programming 18*(1), 186–196. 73

Edelman, B., M. Ostrovsky, and M. Schwarz (2007). Internet advertising and the generalized second price auction: Selling billions of dollars worth of keywords. *American Economic Review 97*(1), 242–259. 3, 59

Edelman, B. and M. Schwarz (2010). Optimal auction design and equilibrium selection in sponsored search auctions. *American Economic Review 100*, 597–602. 59

Elliott, M. and B. Golub (2013). A network approach to public goods. In *Proceedings of the fourteenth ACM conference on Electronic commerce*, pp. 377–378. ACM. 34

Falik, D., R. Meir, and M. Tennenholtz (2012). On coalitions and stable winners in plurality. In *Proceedings of the 8th International Workshop on Internet and Network Economics (WINE)*, pp. 256–269. Springer. 58, 68

Farquharson, R. (1969). *Theory of Voting*. Yale University Press. 53

Feldman, J., A. Mehta, V. Mirrokni, and S. Muthukrishnan (2009). Online stochastic matching: Beating 1-1/e. In *Proceedings of the 50th Symposium on Foundations of Computer Science (FOCS)*, pp. 117–126. 96

Feldman, M., R. Meir, and M. Tennenholtz (2011). Revenue enhancement in ad auctions. In *Proceedings of the 7th International Workshop on Internet and Network Economics (WINE)*, pp. 391–398. 7

Feldman, M., R. Meir, and M. Tennenholtz (2012). Stability scores: Measuring coalitional stability. In *Proceedings of the 11th International Joint Conference on Autonomous Agents and Multi-Agent Systems (AAMAS)*, pp. 771–778. 6

Feldman, M., R. Meir, and M. Tennenholtz (2013). Competition in the presence of social networks: How many service providers maximize welfare? In *Web and Internet Economics*, pp. 174–187. Springer Berlin Heidelberg. 7

Feldman, M. and M. Tennenholtz (2009). Partition equilibrium. In *Proceedings of the 2nd International Symposium on Algorithmic Game Theory (SAGT)*, pp. 48–59. 57

Fishburn, P. and A. Rubinstein (1986). Aggregation of equivalence relations. *Journal of Classification 3*, 61–65. 88

Forsythe, R., T. Rietz, R. Myerson, and R. Weber (1996). An experimental study of voting rules and polls in three-candidate elections. *International Journal of Game Theory 25(3)*, 355–83. 45

Freixas, J. and S. Kurz (2011). On α-roughly weighted games. *arXiv preprint arXiv:1112.2861*. 31

Friedgut, E., G. Kalai, and N. Nisan (2008). Elections can be manipulated often. In *Proceedings of the 49th Symposium on Foundations of Computer Science (FOCS)*, pp. 243–249. 45

Friedman, E. and D. Parkes (2003). Pricing wifi at starbucks: issues in online mechanism design. In *Proceedings of the 4th ACM Conference on Electronic Commerce (ACM-EC)*, pp. 240–241. 96

Garey, M. R. and D. S. Johnson (1979). *Computers and Intractibility*. W.H. Freeman and Company. 42, 127

Geng, Y. and C. G. Cassandras (2011). A new ÃŠsmart parkingÃŞ system based on optimal resource allocation and reservations. In *Proc. of 14th IEEE Intelligent Transportation Systems Conf.*, pp. 979–984. 96

Gerding, E., V. Robu, S. Stein, D. Parkes, A. Rogers, and N. Jennings (2011). Online mechanism design for electric vehicle charging. In *Proceedings of the 10th International Joint Conference on Autonomous Agents and Multi-Agent Systems (AAMAS)*. 95, 96

Gibbard, A. (1973). Manipulation of voting schemes. *Econometrica 41*, 587–602. 3, 12

Gibbard, A. (1977). Manipulation of schemes that mix voting with chance. *Econometrica 45*, 665–681. 93

Goemans, M. X. and M. Skutella (2004). Cooperative facility location games. *Journal of Algorithms 50(2)*, 194–214. 31

Gohar, N. (2012). *Manipulative Voting Dynamics*. Ph. D. thesis, University of Liverpool. 54, 110

Gottlob, G., N. Leone, and F. Scarcello (2001). Hypertree decompositions: A survey. In *Proceedings of the 26th International Symposium on Mathematical Foundations of Computer Science (MFCS)*, pp. 37–57. 41, 42

Gottlob, G., N. Leone, and F. Scarcello (2003). Robbers, marshals, and guards: game theoretic and logical characterizations of hypertree width. *Journal of computer and system sciences 66(4)*, 775–808. 42

Grabisch, M. (2009). The core of games on ordered structures and graphs. *4OR: A Quarterly Journal of Operations Research 7*, 207–238. 34

Graham, D. A. and R. C. Marshall (1987). Collusive bidder behavior at single-object second-price and english auctions. *Journal of Political Economy 95*, 579–599. 59

Grandi, U., A. Loreggia, F. Rossi, K. B. Venable, and T. Walsh (2013). Restricted manipulation in iterative voting: Condorcet efficiency and borda score. In *Algorithmic Decision Theory*, pp. 181–192. Springer. 54, 110

Granot, D. and G. Huberman (1981). Minimum cost spanning tree games. *Mathematical Programming 21*, 1–18. 31

Greco, G., E. Malizia, L. Palopoli, and F. Scarcello (2011a). On the complexity of core, kernel, and bargaining set. *Artificial Intelligence 175*(12–13), 1877–1910. 34

Greco, G., E. Malizia, L. Palopoli, and F. Scarcello (2011b). On the complexity of the core over coalition structures. In *Proceedings of the 22nd International Joint Conference on Artificial Intelligence (IJCAI)*, pp. 216–221. 31, 34, 42

Greco, G., E. Malizia, L. Palopoli, and F. Scarcello (2011c). On the complexity of the core over coalition structures. In *Proceedings of the 22nd International Joint Conference on Artificial Intelligence (IJCAI)*, pp. 216–221. 31

Guo, M., V. Conitzer, and D. Reeves (2009). Competitive repeated allocation without payments. In *Proceedings of the 5th International Workshop on Internet and Network Economics (WINE)*, pp. 244–255. 4

Hansen, P., D. Peeters, and J.-F. Thisse (1982). An algorithm for a constrained Weber problem. *Management Science*, 1285–1295. 73

Harrenstein, B. P., M. M. de Weerdt, and V. Conitzer (2009). A qualitative vickrey auction. In *Proceedings of the 10th ACM Conference on Electronic Commerce (ACM-EC)*, pp. 197–206. 4

Hart, S. and N. Nisan (2012). Approximate revenue maximization with multiple items. *arXiv preprint arXiv:1204.1846.* 3

Hartline, J. D. (2011). Approximation in economic design. *Lecture Notes,* `http://www.isid.ac.in/~dmishra/reading2013/amd.pdf.` 2, 4

Holzman, R. and N. Law-Yone (1997). Strong equilibrium in congestion games. *Games and Economic Behavior 21*, 85–101. 57, 60

Ieong, S. and Y. Shoham (2005). Marginal contribution nets: a compact representation scheme for coalitional games. In *Proceedings of the 6th ACM Conference on Electronic Commerce (ACM-EC)*, pp. 193–202. 34, 41

Immorlica, N., M. Mahdian, and V. Mirrokni (2005). Limitations of cross-monotonic cost sharing schemes. In *Proceedings of the 16th Annual ACM-SIAM Symposium on Discrete Algorithms (SODA)*, pp. 602–611. 32

Jain, K. and M. Mahdian (2007). Cost sharing. In N. Nisan, T. Roughgarden, E. Tardos, and V. V. Vazirani (Eds.), *Algorithmic Game Theory*, pp. 385–410. Cambridge University Press. 24, 25, 32

Jain, K. and V. Vazirani (2001). Applications of approximation algorithms to cooperative games. In *Proceedings of the 33rd Annual ACM Symposium on the Theory of Computing (STOC)*, pp. 364–372. 32

Kahneman, D. and A. Tversky (1979). Prospect theory: An analysis of decision under risk. *Econometrica XLVII*, 263–291. 111

Kalai, E. and E. Muller (1977). Characterization of domains admitting nondictatorial social welfare functions and nonmanipulable voting procedures. *Journal of Economic Theory 16*, 457–469. 80

Kalyanasundaram, B. and K. Pruhs (1991). On-line weighted matching. In *Proceedings of the 2nd Annual ACM-SIAM Symposium on Discrete Algorithms (SODA)*, pp. 234–240. 97

Kalyanasundaram, B. and K. R. Pruhs (2000). An optimal deterministic algorithm for online b-matching. *Theoretical Computer Science 233*(1), 319–325. 97

Karande, C., A. Mehta, and P. Tripathi (2011). Online bipartite matching with unknown distributions. In *Proceedings of the 43rd Annual ACM Symposium on the Theory of Computing (STOC)*, pp. 587–596. 96

Karp, R. M., U. V. Vazirani, and V. V. Vazirani (1990). An optimal algorithm for on-line bipartite matching. In *Proceedings of the 22nd Annual ACM Symposium on the Theory of Computing (STOC)*, pp. 352–358. 96, 97, 99, 103, 105

Khmelnitskaya, A. B. (2010). Values for rooted-tree and sink-tree digraph games and sharing a river. *Theory and Decision 69*(4), 657–669. 34

Koutsoupias, E. (2011). Scheduling without payments. In *Proceedings of the 4th International Symposium on Algorithmic Game Theory (SAGT)*, pp. 143–153. 4

Koutsoupias, E. and A. Nanavati (2004). The online matching problem on a line. In *Approximation and online algorithms*, pp. 179–191. Springer. 96

Kuhn, H. W. (1973). A note on Fermat's problem. *Mathematical Programming 4*(1), 98–107. 73

Kukushkin, N. S. (2011). Acyclicity of improvements in finite game forms. *International Journal of Game Theory 40*(1), 147–177. 53

Kuminov, D. and M. Tennenholtz (2009). User modeling in position auctions: re-considering the GSP and VCG mechanisms. In *Proceedings of the 8th International Joint Conference on Autonomous Agents and Multi-Agent Systems (AAMAS)*, pp. 273–280. 59

Leclerc, B. (1984). Efficient and binary consensus functions on transitively valued relations. *Mathematical Social Sciences 8*, 45–61. 88

Lev, O. and J. S. Rosenschein (2012). Convergence of iterative voting. In *Proceedings of the 11th International Joint Conference on Autonomous Agents and Multi-Agent Systems (AAMAS)*, pp. 611–618. 54

Lewis, P. R., P. Marrow, and X. Yao (2010). Resource allocation in decentralised computational systems: an evolutionary market-based approach. *Autonomous Agents and Multi-agent Systems 21*, 143–171. 95

Li, L. and X. Li (2011). The covering values for acyclic digraph games. *International Journal of Game Theory 40*(4), 697–718. 34

Likhodedov, A. and T. Sandholm (2005). Approximating revenue-maximizing combinatorial auctions. In *Proceedings of the 20th AAAI Conference on Artificial Intelligence (AAAI)*, Volume 20, pp. 267–275. 3

Lu, P., X. Sun, Y. Wang, and Z. A. Zhu (2010). Asymptotically optimal strategy-proof mechanisms for two-facility games. In *Proceedings of the 11th ACM Conference on Electronic Commerce (ACM-EC)*, pp. 315–324. 74

Lu, P., Y. Wang, and Y. Zhou (2009). Tighter bounds for facility games. In *Proceedings of the 5th International Workshop on Internet and Network Economics (WINE)*, pp. 137–148. 74

Lucier, B., R. Paes Leme, and É. Tardos (2012). On revenue in the generalized second price auction. In *Proceedings of the 21st International Conference on World Wide Web (WWW)*, pp. 361–370. 3, 59, 66

Maschler, M., B. Peleg, and L. S. Shapley (1979). Geometric properties of the kernel, nucleolus, and related solution concepts. *Mathematics of Operations Research 4*(4), 303–338. 26, 28

Maschler, M., E. Solan, and S. Zamir (2013). *Game Theory*. Cambridge University Press. 9

Maskin, E. S. (2008). Mechanism design: How to implement social goals. *The American Economic Review 98*(3), 567–576. 2

McAfee, R. P. and J. McMillan (1987). Auctions and bidding. *Journal of Economic Literature 25*, 699–738. 59

McKelvey, R. D. and R. Niemi (1978). A multistage representation of sophisticated voting for binary procedures. *Journal of Economic Theory 18*, 1–22. 53

McLean, I. and A. B. Urken (1995). *Classics of social choice*. University of Michigan Press. 3

Megiddo, N. (1978). Cost allocation for Steiner trees. *Networks 8*, 1–6. 32

Mehta, A., A. Saberi, U. Vazirani, and V. Vazirani (2007). Adwords and generalized online matching. *Journal of the ACM 54*(5). 96

Meir, R. (2008). Strategy proof classification. Master's thesis, The Hebrew University of Jerusalem. Available from: http://tinyurl.com/cpqlram. 6, 74, 75, 87, 88, 89

Meir, R., S. Almagor, A. Michaely, and J. S. Rosenschein (2011). Tight bounds for strategyproof classification. In *Proceedings of the 10th International Joint Conference on Autonomous Agents and Multi-Agent Systems (AAMAS)*, pp. 319–326. 84, 93, 94

Meir, R., Y. Bachrach, and J. S. Rosenschein (2010). Minimal subsidies in expense sharing games. In *Proceedings of the 3rd International Symposium on Algorithmic Game Theory (SAGT)*, pp. 347–358. 6, 31

Meir, R., Y. Chen, and M. Feldman (2013). Efficient parking allocation as online bipartite matching. In *Proceedings of the 12th International Joint Conference on Autonomous Agents and Multi-Agent Systems (AAMAS)*, pp. 303–310. 6, 97

Meir, R., T. Lu, M. Tennenholtz, and C. Boutilier (2013). On the value of using group discounts under price competition. In *Proceedings of the 27th AAAI Conference on Artificial Intelligence (AAAI)*, pp. 683–689. 7

Meir, R., M. Polukarov, J. S. Rosenschein, and N. Jennings (2010). Convergence to equilibria of plurality voting. In *Proceedings of the 24th AAAI Conference on Artificial Intelligence (AAAI)*, pp. 823–828. 6, 54

Meir, R., A. D. Procaccia, and J. S. Rosenschein (2008). Strategyproof classification under constant hypotheses: A tale of two functions. In *Proceedings of the 23rd AAAI Conference on Artificial Intelligence (AAAI)*, pp. 126–131. 4, 88

Meir, R., A. D. Procaccia, and J. S. Rosenschein (2009). Strategyproof classification with shared inputs. In *Proceedings of the 21st International Joint Conference on Artificial Intelligence (IJCAI)*, pp. 220–225. 74, 84, 87, 88, 89, 94

Meir, R., A. D. Procaccia, and J. S. Rosenschein (2010). On the limits of dictatorial classification. In *Proceedings of the 9th International Joint Conference on Autonomous Agents and Multi-Agent Systems (AAMAS)*, pp. 609–616. 88, 89, 93, 162

Meir, R., A. D. Procaccia, and J. S. Rosenschein (2012). Algorithms for strategyproof classification. *Artificial Intelligence 186*, 123–156. 6, 74, 93

Meir, R. and J. S. Rosenschein (2013). Avoid fixed pricing: Consume less, earn more, make clients happy. In *Proceedings of the 12th International Joint Conference on Autonomous Agents and Multi-Agent Systems (AAMAS)*, pp. 239–246. 7

Meir, R., J. S. Rosenschein, and E. Malizia (2011). Subsidies, stability, and restricted cooperation in coalitional games. In *Proceedings of the 22th International Joint Conference on Artificial Intelligence (IJCAI)*, pp. 301–306. 6, 126

Meir, R. and M. Tennenholtz (2013). Equilibrium in labor markets with few firms. *arXiv preprint arXiv:1306.5855.* 7

Meir, R., M. Tennenholtz, Y. Bachrach, and P. Key (2012). Congestion games with agent failures. In *Proceedings of the 26th AAAI Conference on Artificial Intelligence (AAAI)*, pp. 1401–1407. 7

Meir, R., Y. Zick, E. Elkind, and J. S. Rosenschein (2013). Bounding the cost of stability in games over interaction networks. In *Proceedings of the 27th AAAI Conference on Artificial Intelligence (AAAI)*, pp. 690–696. 6

Meir, R., Y. Zick, and J. S. Rosenschein (2012). Optimization and stability in games with restricted interactions. In *The 3rd Workshop on Cooperative Games in Multiagent Systems (CoopMAS @ AAMAS'12).* 6, 41

Messner, M. and M. K. Polborn (2002). Robust political equilibria under plurality and runoff rule. Mimeo, Bocconi University. 53

Mirkin, B. (1975). On the problem of reconciling partitions. In H. Blalock (Ed.), *Quantitative sociology: international perspectives on mathematical and statistical modeling*. New York: Academic Press. 88

Mirrokni, V., M. Schapira, and J. Vondrák (2008). Tight information-theoretic lower bounds for welfare maximization in combinatorial auctions. In *Proceedings of the 9th ACM conference on Electronic commerce*, pp. 70–77. ACM. 3

Monderer, D. and L. S. Shapley (1996). Potential games. *Games and Economic Behavior 14*(1), 124–143. 53

Monderer, D. and M. Tennenholtz (2004). K-implementation. *Journal of Artificial Intelligence Research 21*, 37–62. 4

Moulin, H. and S. Shenker (2001). Strategyproof sharing of submodular costs: Budget balance versus efficiency. *Economic Theory 18*(3), 511–533. 32

Mullainathan, S. and R. H. Thaler (2000). Behavioral economics. Technical report, National Bureau of Economic Research. 111

Myerson, R. B. (1977). Graphs and cooperation in games. *Mathematics of Operations Research 2*(3), 225–229. 5, 33, 58

Myerson, R. B. (1981). Optimal auction design. *Mathematics of Operations Research 6*, 58–73. 3, 11

Myerson, R. B. and R. J. Weber (1993). A theory of voting equilibria. *The American Political Science Review 87*(1), 102–114. 53, 55

Nash, J. F. (1950). Equilibrium points in N-person games. *Proceedings of the National Academy of Sciences of the United States of America 36*, 48–49. 10

Nehama, I. (2011). Approximate judgement aggregation. In *Proceedings of the 7th International Workshop on Internet and Network Economics (WINE)*, pp. 302–313. 88

Nehring, K. and C. Puppe (2007). The structure of strategy-proof social choice – part I: General characterization and possibility results on median spaces. *Journal of Economic Theory 135*(1), 269 – 305. 78

Nisan, N. (2007). Introduction to mechanism design (for computer scientists). In N. Nisan, T. Roughgarden, E. Tardos, and V. Vazirani (Eds.), *Algorithmic Game Theory*, Chapter 9. Cambridge University Press. 2, 3

Nisan, N., T. Roughgarden, E. Tardos, and V. Vazirani (Eds.) (2007). *Algorithmic Game Theory*. Cambridge University Press. 3, 58

Obraztsova, S., E. Markakis, and D. R. Thompson (2013). Plurality voting with truth-biased agents. In *Algorithmic Game Theory*, pp. 26–37. Springer. 54

Pál, M. and É. Tardos (2003). Group strategyproof mechanisms via primal-dual algorithms. In *Proceedings of the 44th Symposium on Foundations of Computer Science (FOCS)*, pp. 584–593. 32

Papadimitriou, C. (2001). Algorithms, games, and the internet. In *Proceedings of the 33rd Annual ACM Symposium on the Theory of Computing (STOC)*, pp. 749–753. 2

Papadimitriou, C. H. (2005). The interaction between algorithms and game theory. In *Experimental and Efficient Algorithms*, pp. 1–3. Springer. 2

Peleg, B. and P. Sudhölter (2003). *Introduction to the Theory of Cooperative Games*. Kluwer Publishers. 9, 22

Potters, J. and H. Reijnierse (1995). γ-component additive games. *International Journal of Game Theory 24*(1), 49–56. 41

Povich, E. S. (2012). Mobile apps revolutionaize municipal parking. AolGovernment (Innovation), `http://tinyurl.com/dylyp3p`. 95

Procaccia, A. D. and M. Tennenholtz (2009). Approximate mechanism design without money. In *Proceedings of the 10th ACM Conference on Electronic Commerce (ACM-EC)*, pp. 177–186. 4, 74

Rahwan, I. and K. Larson (2009). Argumentation and game theory. In *Argumentation in Artificial Intelligence*, pp. 321–339. Springer. 2

Reijngoud, A. and U. Endriss (2012). Voter response to iterated poll information. In *Proceedings of the 11th International Joint Conference on Autonomous Agents and Multi-Agent Systems (AAMAS)*, pp. 635–644. 51, 54, 55, 110

Resnick, E., Y. Bachrach, R. Meir, and J. S. Rosenschein (2009). The cost of stability in network flow games. In *Proceedings of the 34th International Symposium on Mathematical Foundations of Computer Science (MFCS)*, pp. 636–650. 31

Reyhani, R., M. C. Wilson, and J. Khazaei (2012). Coordination via polling in plurality voting games under inertia. In *Proceedings of the 20th European Conference on Artificial Intelligence (ECAI)*. 54

Richtel, M. (2011). Now, to find a parking spot, drivers look on their phones. The New York Times (Technology), `http://tinyurl.com/d9nvcew`. 95

Riley, J. G. (1989). Expected revenue from open and sealed bid auctions. *The Journal of Economic Perspectives 3*(3), 41–50. 3

Roozbehani, M., M. A. Dahleh, and S. K. Mitter (2011). Volatility of power grids under real-time pricing. *CoRR abs/1106.1401*. 95

Rosenschein, J. S. and G. Zlotkin (1994). *Rules of Encounter: Designing Conventions for Automated Negotiation among Computers*. the MIT Press. 2

Rosenthal, R. (1973). A class of games possessing pure-strategy nash equilibria. *International Journal of Game Theory 2*, 65–67. 60

Roth, A. E. (2002). The economist as engineer: Game theory, experimentation, and computation as tools for design economics. *Econometrica 70*(4), 1341–1378. 2

Roth, A. E., T. Sönmez, and M. U. Ünver (2004). Kidney exchange. *The Quarterly Journal of Economics 119*(2), 457–488. 111

Rubinstein, A. (1991). Comments on the interpretation of game theory. *Econometrica: Journal of the Econometric Society*, 909–924. 110

Saari, D. G. (1990). Susceptibility to manipulation. *Public Choice 64*, 21–41. 45

Satterthwaite, M. (1975). Strategy-proofness and Arrow's conditions: Existence and correspondence theorems for voting procedures and social welfare functions. *Journal of Economic Theory 10*, 187–217. 3, 12

Schmeidler, D. (1969). The nucleolus of a characteristic function game. *SIAM Journal on Applied Mathematics 17*(6), 1163–1170. 26

Schummer, J. and R. V. Vohra (2004). Strategy-proof location on a network. *Journal of Economic Theory 104*(2), 405–428. 74, 75, 79, 80, 82, 83, 84

Schummer, J. and R. V. Vohra (2007). Mechanism design without money. In N. Nisan, T. Roughgarden, E. Tardos, and V. Vazirani (Eds.), *Algorithmic Game Theory*, Chapter 10. Cambridge University Press. 4

Sertel, M. R. and M. R. Sanver (2004). Strong equilibrium outcomes of voting games are the generalized Condorcet winners. *Social Choice and Welfare 22*, 331–347. 53, 68

Simon, H. (1957). A behavioral model of rational choice. In *Models of Man, Social and Rational: Mathematical Essays on Rational Human Behavior in a Social Setting*. New York: Wiley. 111

Skorin-Kapov, D. (1995). On the core of the minimum cost Steiner tree game in networks. *Annals of Operations Research 57*, 233–249. 32

Slavík, P. (1996). A tight analysis of the greedy algorithm for set cover. In *Proceedings of the 28th Annual ACM Symposium on the Theory of Computing (STOC)*, pp. 435–441. 25

Smith, A. (1776). *An Inquiry into the Nature and Causes of the Wealth of Nations*. W. Strahan and T. Cadell, London. 1

Stein, S., E. Gerding, V. Robu, and N. Jennings (2012). A model-based online mechanism with pre-commitment and its application to electric vehicle charging. In *Proceedings of the 11th International Joint Conference on Autonomous Agents and Multi-Agent Systems (AAMAS)*. 95, 96

Svensson, L.-G. (1999). The proof of the Gibbard-Satterthwaite theorem revisited. Working Paper No. 1999:1, Department of Economics, Lund University. Available from: http://www.nek.lu.se/NEKlgs/vote09.pdf. 80

Thang, N. K. (2010). On randomized strategy-proof mechanisms without payment for facility location games. In *Proceedings of the 6th International Workshop on Internet and Network Economics (WINE)*, pp. 13–16. 74, 75

Thompson, D. R. M., O. Lev, K. Leyton-Brown, and J. S. Rosenschein (2013). Empirical analysis of plurality election equilibria. In *Proceedings of the 12th International Joint Conference on Autonomous Agents and Multi-Agent Systems (AAMAS)*, pp. 391–398. 54

Thompson, D. R. M. and K. Leyton-Brown (2009). Computational analysis of perfect-information position auctions. In *Proceedings of the 10th ACM Conference on Electronic Commerce (ACM-EC)*, pp. 51–60. 59

Varian, H. R. (1995). Economic mechanism design for computerized agents. In *First USENIX Workshop on Electronic Commerce*, pp. 13–21. 2

Varian, H. R. (2007). Position auctions. *International Journal of Industrial Organization* 25(6), 1163–1178. 3, 59, 62, 63, 105, 142, 167

Vickrey, W. (1961). Counter speculation, auctions, and competitive sealed tenders. *Journal of Finance* 16(1), 8–37. 11

Voice, T., M. Polukarov, and N. R. Jennings (2012). Coalition structure generation over graphs. *Journal of Artificial Intelligence Research* 45, 165–196. 34

von Neumann, J. and O. Morgenstern (1944). *Theory of Games and Economic Behavior*. Princeton University Press. 2

Weber, A. (1929). *Alfred Weber's Theory of the Location of Industries*. The University of Chicago Press. 73

Wilson, R. (1975). On the theory of aggregation. *Journal of Economic Theory* 10, 89–99. 88

Wooldridge, M., U. Endriss, S. Kraus, and J. Lang (2012). Incentive engineering for Boolean games. *Artificial Intelligence*, 418–439. 5

Xia, L. and V. Conitzer (2010). Stackelberg voting games: Computational aspects and paradoxes. In *Proceedings of the 24th AAAI Conference on Artificial Intelligence (AAAI)*, pp. 921–926. 53

Xia, L., J. Lang, and M. Ying (2007). Sequential voting rules and multiple elections paradoxes. In *Proceedings of the 11th Conference on Theoretical Aspects of Rationality and Knowledge (TARK)*, pp. 279–288. 109

Xu, D. and D. Du (2006). The k-level facility location game. *Operation Research Letters* 34(4), 421–426. 21

Yildirim, M. B. (2001). Congestion toll pricing models and methods for variable demand networks. Ph.D. thesis, University of Florida. 95

Zick, Y., M. Polukarov, and N. R. Jennings (2013). Taxation and stability in cooperative games. In *Proceedings of the 12th International Joint Conference on Autonomous Agents and Multi-Agent Systems (AAMAS)*, pp. 523–530. 31

www.ingramcontent.com/pod-product-compliance
Lightning Source LLC
Chambersburg PA
CBHW080411060326
40689CB00019B/4209